LIVING
IN
AN
ALIBI
SOCIETY

Cover. Epicurus, Greek Philosopher 342-270 B.C. *Hulton Picture Library*

By the same author

English Accountancy 1800-1954 - A Study in Social and Economic History, London, 1954.

Industrial Market Research - Management and Technic. London, 1963.

Mergers in Modern Business. London, 1966. Revised 1970.

The Changing Patterns of Distribution. London, 1958. Revised and enlarged 1965.

LIVING IN AN ALIBI SOCIETY

A Catalogue of Pretensions

NICHOLAS A.H. STACEY

The Rubicon Press

The Rubicon Press Limited
57 Cornwall Gardens
London SW7 4BE

British Library Cataloguing in Publication Data

Stacey, Nicholas A. H. (Nicholas Anthony
  Howard), *1920-*
  Living in an alibi society : a catalogue of
  pretensions.
  1. Social values. Effects of social.change
  I. Title
  303.3'72
  ISBN 0-948695-10-2

Printed and bound in England

CONTENTS

To my mother Lily and to the
memory of my father Maurusz Szecsi

PREFACE

Because alibis are evergreen and omnipresent in everyone's life, including my own, they have long hovered on the margins of my consciousness. What brought them to the fore, to a more graphic appreciation of their importance, was the decision to start my own business some years ago. A well-nigh uniform reaction by friends and others to my new venture made a durable impression on me. On being asked, in varying degrees of familiarity, friendliness and concern, how my new venture was progressing, I reported with enthusiasm modest progress. Their reactions were sometimes prefaced by exclaiming 'My God, you did start at the right time', or 'How lucky you were spotting the trend'—comments offering a hint of defensiveness; their anodyne remarks unconsciously deflated my modestly successful efforts at risk-taking, judgement, desire for freedom, even free will or a self-generated determination to start something new, by attributing it to favourable external circumstances. By invoking a *deus ex machina*, they absolved themselves from feeling at a disadvantage. That was their alibi, and mine a reassuring one in return that anyone can start up a business and anyway, in 'getting my act together', I was merely lucky. I am sure I was.

My careerings in journalism, in professional administration, in the universities, in the visual arts and music, in finance and industry, brought me in touch with a great number of people at many different social, occupational and educational levels; this variegated experience conspired to sharpen my perception of the diverse application of alibi syndromes, both in my personal and in professional and business relationships. My reading of history and literature, such as it is, prepared me for a better understanding of their psychological hinterland. The need for alibis of all kinds—many innocent, some destructive, others useful—is the explanation for writing this book.

Few moral lessons are to be mined from these essays: rather, I was hoping to convey a cautionary tale. Alibis abound today, perhaps just a little more than they did yesterday, but my reading of the signs is that they will probably not continue to wax freely. The need for alibis and the chance to use them have grown with the rising complexity of all activities, including everyday living. However, should the use of alibis continue to proliferate unchecked, this is likely to confer a degree of frailty upon us as a people—leading us towards heightened unrealities and more escapism; for it cannot be gainsaid that in England the sense of unreality has never been greater than it has been until relatively recently, with passionate adherence to redundant folk-memories. These reveal a struggle between form and content, good and bad, substance and shadow, restriction and competition—struggles influencing our judgement. Not all alibis are debilitating, but many of them are, and some can invite disaster.

NICHOLAS A H STACEY

Chelsea London
Aghios Stephanos Corfu
August 1988

ACKNOWLEDGEMENTS

I have written these essays during the mid-1980s; they reflect the accumulated prejudices and enthusiasms of a varied career. They comprise a *mélange* of philosophical verities, history of ideas and social critique encompassing comments on manners, class, cowardice, the market-place, the bourgeoisie, the intellectual, and the professions. Everybody I know or have known has contributed to the making of this work by my absorbing their wisdoms and unwisdoms; they mirror the human condition in the subjective way I have perceived it.

My wife Marianne Ehrhardt has aided, abetted and encouraged my writing about the eccentric world of alibis; she has also corrected the proofs with consummate skill. I wish to thank her for her loving support. My personal secretary for many years, Pamela Trotman, typed the manuscript and collated the pages with enthusiasm and unstinting energy; I remain in her debt.

INTRODUCTION

Alibis offer powerful and convenient justifications for rejecting or carrying out actions—for acts of commision or omission—and they have a long and respectable history. Alibis are social devices offering cover for acts discharged or for measures that need to be taken or prevented from being carried out. In certain recognized circumstances, alibis are fashioned deliberately to exonerate decision makers from direct responsibility, as exercised in the machinery of justice where juries decide and judges administer.

Alibis are neither good nor bad—though they are certainly not neutral—but take the colouring of the purposes and motives to which they are assigned; always, they serve a specific purpose. Some alibis are valid, many are ephemeral or mere sophistries, and many more are inventions. Sometimes they endeavour to conceal motives of which even their inventor, perhaps, remains unaware, so deep have some alibis eaten into the subconscious mind. Losing a war can perpetuate alibis for failure for several generations; winning one can supply an alibi for unwarranted feelings of superiority. Alibis, if long enough sustained, are converted into folk-memories which long endure! Wishing to understand the evergreen function of alibis and their impact on society is reason enough to scrutinize their *raison d'être*. Their rise in significance and growth in application during the twentieth century is largely a matter of record; it must be apparent even to the moderately perceptive that in England we have embarked on the long march which has now led to many of us 'living in an alibi society'. The increasing receptivity to the use of alibis may be attributed, partially, to the wider absorption of the spirit as well as the letter of the teachings of the social sciences, which have analysed and assessed the role and conduct of people and of groups anew and have given them a fresh awareness of themselves and their milieu. Once unleashed upon the world, the strictures of the social sciences—and of some disciplines within them more than others—have also led to a better appreciation of the actions and reactions of men and women, of their motives and causes, concealed or concrete; while this, in turn, has led to a better grasp of their springs of action, it has certainly not diminished the need for alibis, indeed appetite for them has probably sharpened.

The growing tendency for societies and individuals to explain more freely their ideas or actions, has not led invariably to a heightened awareness of issues, old and new; and as the twentieth century has dragged on, it is difficult to avoid the impression that issues of all kinds have multiplied in number and in variety and many have become more clearly delineated. A better understanding of the need to explain has led to a more informed society, learning more of the complexities involved and the difficulties in appreciating and finally in reconciling divergent views. As a result, informed judgement has become more compassionate, and hence more tolerant, about enforcing rights and chastising wrongs, about responsibilities and irresponsibilities and about deserts and punishments; often, compassion has led to the invention of alibis, just as a better appreciation of psychological influences has led to the same ends. It needs to be emphasized that the more frequent recourse to alibis also tends to bring with it more readily eroding lines of demarcation. Whether in public affairs or in private pursuits, lines of demarcation are certainly less clear nowadays than they appear to have been, even in recent memory. The ground has shifted, judgements on all manner of things have become softer and less simplistic while, simultaneously, the decision making machinery grows more complex, perhaps more informed—but also certainly more cumbersome. In the end, the wider acceptance of alibis has resulted in more people 'getting off the hook'. Perhaps this is not altogether unsatisfactory as long as we are aware of our actions.

Two important consequences follow from such changes of attitudes and opinions. First, it will be revealed that in general more alibis are likely to be fabricated or invented with more enthusiasm to exonerate, to soften, or to predispose judgement. Predictably, this has already led to some moral contortions with the effect that individuals and particularly institutions, even agencies of State are less willing to admit to having blundered. Second, since society is tending to become more lenient, lame alibis are being marshalled less reluctantly, and almost equally often accepted, resulting in limited punishment, a mere cautioning, or no chastisement of any kind. Thus, with judgement becoming more elastic, punishment is meted out less ferociously and the incidence of mitigation is more recurrent. This state of affairs could imply that when one of the plethora of acceptable alibis has been invoked, the community, or society, will tend to treat its members more leniently, with more tolerance, greater compassion, and not unimportant, more decorum. If punishment is to follow a misdeed or an error, as is the rule, it is often applied less strenuously nowadays than before, due to the acceptance of well, or less well, constructed alibis as mitigating circumstances.

Perhaps such ameliorative judgement of tasks incompetently performed, battalions badly commanded, laws infringed, companies poorly managed, trade unions ill led, or legislation cumbersomely framed—to mention but a few—has become inevitable in more recent times in the changed pattern of life and social organization. Judgements are often passed on leadership or performance in their thousand different forms and varieties. An increasing number of functions in modern society call for judging on how well or how badly individual responsibilities have been discharged. The history of industrial society—one of the major themes in these essays—will show that modern industry constantly needs men with ever greater skills and their exercise calls for responsible judgement; that is, it needs more and more decision takers. This example from industry is equally relevant to the civil service, and of course to the professions. At the same time, the impression strengthens that, nowadays, responsibilities, particularly at work, are less eagerly being sought; a tranquil life has become the objective of many—a signal perhaps of the hedonistic process of the pursuit of happiness—a viewpoint at variance with risk bearing or decision taking. Thus, to encourage the supply of decision takers—those prepared to stick their necks out—the collective wisdom of society not always judges the results of their performance against the more rigorous standards of yesterday. Perhaps the instinctive wisdom of society displayed by this change is all for the good! If responsibility for taking decisions were to be judged nowadays on the understanding and standards of the past, society may well be discouraging its potential decision takers from emerging in the increasing numbers needed to operate a complex, modern society.

In previous incarnations, the assumption of more responsibility resulted in expecting and often receiving higher rewards. But it could be argued that advancement is status and rises in pay are less pressing today as living standards have risen to acceptable levels for most people. Why then assume more responsibility when the additional rewards to be earned by assuming greater responsibilities, as well as greater exposure to criticism, are only marginally more attractive? Morality and exposure to censure (and not the marginal rate of income tax) are intertwined in this dilemma once again. In this context I am constrained to suggest that in western industrial societies the good old days are now! The Reverend Malthus is further accelerating his exit!

The use of alibis then has accelerated, noticeably since the end of the nineteenth century. This has been a world-wide phenomenon, in which Britain and some other countries have claimed a notable lead. I attribute this development in some measure to the decline in individualism and the rise of collectivism—a trend in which progressive political and social ideologies have played a vanguard role. The allures of socialization as an *avant-garde* doctrine in Britain and elsewhere have given credence to notions which encouraged the development of giantism, i.e. large scale social, political and industrial organization. In this march towards the collective, politics enjoyed the blessings of science and technology as its allies and alibis. The confluence of such powerful forces, in turn, led to the emergence of very large industrial and social monoliths—in political organization, in commercial and industrial companies, in trade unions, even in style of dwellings; Victorian optimism and faith in progress have pushed in the direction of large scale enterprise and expressed it in many different forms, so noticeable in architecture. What have been the effects on the individual?

The larger the organization, the fewer share the burdens and pleasures of responsibility; the many are shielded from decision making. Such and similar developments for nearly a century have, I suspect, led to individuals experiencing reduced opportunities for exercising responsibilities; if such a tendency were allowed to continue, in the end decision making and a sense of responsibility may atrophy in the citizen. This could bring with it an even greater flowering of alibis. Because politics plays a central role in determining the disposition of government, its colouring offers the choice of fostering either individualism or collectivism. It should be constantly remembered that the attitude of government as well as the laws it enacts exert a profound influence in shaping social organization and, ultimately, the disposition of individuals.

Significant shifts in political direction during the 1980s have nurtured in Britain the emergence of changed values, largely antipathetic to alibis; the ethos of the decade has proved to be increasingly resistant to finding too many excuses for failures to often. The national disposition has shifted with some speed, marching towards the minimal state, the liberalization of the markets and greater opportunities for individual success, as well as failure; all of this, in turn, helps to free the human spirit from the long popular ideology of collectivism; of merging in the crowd. Attitudes in Britain have perceptibly changed in the direction of self-help, self-reliance and renewed self-confidence. But one must be vigilant against the recidivists of collectivism whose hallmark is a fear of freedom. If this fashion for greater freedom and its concomitant, greater accountability endures, the burdens of responsibility by individuals will be more consciously assumed. This then is the recipe for pushing back the frontiers of the 'Alibi Society' and liberating the spirit of individual responsibility! As Thomas Paine exhorted: 'Those who expect to reap the blessings of freedom must, like a man, undergo the fatigue of supporting it'!

ON CLASS

Introduction

Class has been a reality and more often than not a divisive issue of greater or lesser magnitude throughout recorded history. The Greeks and Romans had a precisely defined class structure and the early Christian Church took over a similar hierarchy of gradations, its organization adopting the example of differentiated classes then extant in the secular state of fourth-century Byzantium. This differentiation then extended both to its theological rankings as well as to its ecclesiastical grades. Self-assurance was certainly not lacking in the patristic fathers when they determined the hierarchical order in the world above with the same aplomb as they did in the world below and, indeed, in the world in between—where they spent their years of unremitting toil. The Middle Ages continued the practice of class divisions and though it was difficult to rise from humble stock, exceptional talent was rewarded and its owner upgraded. This state of affairs, the virtual absence of class mobility, was only alleviated, albeit partially, by the Renaissance and the arrival of the Reformation. Early in its career, at the beginning of the sixteenth century, Protestantism tacitly proclaimed the novelty that the salvation of man can lie through good works as well as through faith—a revolutionary notion and very different from traditional belief in such matters since the days of St Augustine 1,100 years previously. In essence, this innovation in salvation ushered in modern capitalism, in the wake of good works. Men consciously endeavoured to better themselves because success was rewarded and acknowledged as the new orthodoxy. Thus, the arrival of Protestantism heralded and indeed its sucess realized, a measure of social osmosis; until this idea of greater perfectability through work was introduced, virtually no class mobility could exist. Rising social mobility at the end of the Middle Ages also caused a decline in the importance of kinship which, in turn, contributed to, as well as partly caused, the rise of the powers of the centralized state: the result was a gradual disintegration of tribalism and the evolution of the patriarchal family. Though, for another three centuries, class rigidities changed very slowly—except for the co-mingling of the upper and the lower but monied classes—from about 1600 onwards, family advancement and individual fulfilment were increasingly realizable, both in the eyes of God as well as under the more immediate scrutiny of one's fellow men. The portraiture of the well-to-do and newly important by Rembrandt and the younger Teniers and the rise of a new upper crust under the Tudors, though a hundred years apart, are appropriate illustrations. Art certainly reflected the rise of a class called the new rich.

These early advances in social mobility—initiated, one may assume not always deliberately, by the reformed church and enhanced by prosperous economic activities especially in Northern Europe (implying greater freedom and added opportunities for transferring from one class to another, higher, class)—were greatly reinforced in the secular state of England by the seventeenth-century Puritan revolution. Despite subsequent retrograde legislation at the time of the Restoration, such as the Clarendon Code, which had significant repercussions for endeavouring to keep Nonconformists in their place for 200 years, social mobility was reinforced by the civil war in England. Similarly, in France the Fronde perhaps eased social emancipation just a little, but the most powerful event of social change—occurring well over a century after the Fronde—was undoubtedly the French Revolution whose tremors were felt throughout the world, but most immediately in Europe. The reason why the French Revolution was so significant in class terms was not solely on account of offering and granting greater freedoms to everyone—after all, that notion was not altogether new and was heralded earlier by the Enlightenment whose writers and thinkers had wide influence before the Revolution. The central importance of the French Revolution in terms of class was two-fold—but as history has revealed, its implications transcended the mere question of class. First, here was a revolution started and carried through by the working class and, second, this working class revolution was the first of its kind to succeed. Thus, the French Revolution and its consequences held up an example to working classes throughout the world; the success of the Revolution also conferred on the working class an importance and power which could no longer be disregarded by other classes or by the state.

In the history of class since the French Revolution, the important twin issues have been, and remain, the mobility of classes and the conflict between them. What influences have helped shape these forces of mobility and conflict which have significantly changed the world in the course of the last (nearly) two hundred years? During this time social emancipation has gathered speed and constituency, resulting in a vastly enlarged 'lumpen middle class' in all the 'developed' countries of today, where the French Revolution had most impact. Thus, two centuries of social progress—not without conflict—have borne fruit. None the less, in different ways, with different implications and in different degrees, class and class consciousness remain indelibly stamped upon the social—and economic—structure everywhere. Class is not eliminated by declaring it redundant; it would pose so many difficult and well-nigh intractable questions if it could be. Some of these interesting, if disturbing, manifestations of social conflict have been graphically revealed in contemporary Britain, a country which traditionally has shown greater and more durable social cohesion since the late seventeenth century than perhaps any other.

Perhaps, too, it has been the absence of class-caused explosion—when fashion in Europe favoured many such outbursts between the end of the eighteenth and the halcyon days of the twentieth century—from which Britain is now suffering. The time for such revolutionary upheavals in the West has now largely passed, and the British are, perforce, required to sort out their class imbroglio by means other than open class warfare.

Why is a concept of class—the nature of which is ever-changing—more strongly held, by comparison, in some countries than in others? How is this manifest, and what are the motive forces? Could over-dimensioned class consciousness cause an internalized conflict between people in a country, just as sharp nationalism can lead to an externalized tussle? Has class become more monolithic or more fragmented now than in the past? Are there fewer manifest class divisions and differences today compared to yesterday? And it may well be asked, are there traditional or natural class enemies in a modern nation state? Not all these questions can be answered clearly even if some casuists find it easy to reply with bland assurances. But, irrespective of attitudes to class, the differences have retained their importance even after their gradual and significant amelioration since 1792, i.e despite the French Revolution and its consequences, which a little later unfolded into another monarchy.

It could be argued that while the French Revolution set out to confer liberty, equality and fraternity, it simultaneously fuelled class animosities; it accomplished this involuntarily, by shattering the importance previously enjoyed by the socially cohesive nature of religion and the centuries-old stability of the church by abolishing God. Such a significant demolishing operation, inevitably, constrained man to concentrate his thoughts for the future more towards his immediate milieu on earth and rather less towards the heavens. Life on earth gained a new, richer, more immediate and different meaning—it was no longer a dress rehearsal but the real performance, a succession of first nights. The less time and devotion were afforded to organized or official religion, the more man's thoughts turned away from the skies (long-term hopes) towards his terrestrial surroundings (short-term opportunities). This involved increasing preoccupation with himself as well as more and more involvement with his fellow men—and as we know, greater familiarity begets not only children but also contempt. Class differences have an element of assumed contempt—since if the differences were not running deep they would prove ephemeral. And when class differences became partly enervated and class dominance shrank to virtual insignificance, the concept of status was newly elevated to ensure that some class distinction remained. Egalitarianism may be desired by prophets but is not cherished by the people as the results of social upheavals have proved.

There are numerous aspects of class—and equally, of class differences and of class friction—which are rewarding, important and worthwhile subjects of inquiry. None more so perhaps, than as a corollary of the way people earn their living. Feelings of class belonging, perceived differences in conduct, acceptability or rejection of a given class relationship are acquired notions which become precepts. The really interesting phenomenon is how they differ in range and intensity in accordance with occupational compartmentalization. Bellicosity of class consciousness is not a special hallmark of the self-employed, of the university teacher or of members of an orchestra as opportunities for friction in such circumstances hardly exist. Class antagonism has more room to flourish where employees are in hierarchical dependency situations—such as in a warehouse, a factory or a governmental department. But class relationship between employer—in whatever guise—and employee is never static. The changing relationship in recent years between the employees of the state and the state is a good example of such a shift by challenging the occupational immunity of a whole class of civil servants. The same changing relationships, less entrenchment and more fluidity has also been introduced in the universities. However, the vital class relationship which effects everyone is the nexus between the producers of wealth in a community. This includes all the participants in the production and distribution of goods and services. If they produce 'added value' efficiently and with enthusiasm the community is enriched; if not, the community is impoverished. For this reason industry and trade have been the mainstay of mature countries' economies for over three centuries; hence, the relationship between the classes who work in industry becomes all important. This then, is the subject I am trying to bring into focus.

Class differences, enhanced by the Industrial Revolution, have been increasingly focused on the readily distinguishable contestants—the employer and the employee. Of course, differences between other classes have not lessened thereby; the Whig aristocracy and the Tory upper-crust remained partly unreconciled; the differences between the upper classes and the bourgeois remained and the discord between farmer and the agricultural worker stayed evergreen. But, and this is important, after the combined effects of the Industrial Revolution and the French Revolution, the importance of class differences gradually shifted to a new scene—to the relationship of dependency and conflict between the employer and the employed in industry and trade.

Class definition in terms of rich and poor by using wealth as a sole determination of class, was never precisely delineable nor was it exclusive. Class was and, of course, remains related to money; but it is also related to characteristics other than money, and of these nature of occupation, family relationships, life-styles and, particularly in the past, education, play an important part. Money was never the sole arbiter in Britain; for the past two centuries, dominated by manufacturing industry, and today even more than ever before, there have been prosperous industrial workers, poor shopkeepers or ne'er-do-well self-employed artisans, all belonging to different classes, all rubbing shoulders on the socio-economic scene. More widely discernable and, perhaps conspicuously apparent class differences arising from wealth were a by-product of a later Britain, when the country became a mature industrial society a century or more after the start of the Industrial Revolution—I set this stage at, say, about 1850–1860. By that time, large numbers of workers found employment in the factories and workshops owned by a growing number of entrepreneurs—many of them well-to-do, and some very well-to-do. It must have been the spectacle of the rapidly growing riches of a fast multiplying entrepreneurial class that showed up inequalities more starkly. Inequalities have always existed, and will continue to be with us probably for all time; but prior to the rise of the industrial entrepreneurial class in the eighteenth and nineteenth centuries, examples of new rich were neither so obvious nor so numerous.

Industrially created wealth could boast of a growing cadre of recipients, while representatives of the older, land-based wealth were so many fewer, with no accretions in their number, that in any way matched the growth of bourgeois wealth. That is why in the loom of language, 'land riches' and the upper class were and remain associated with 'old money.' Yet 'old money' with all its implications of superior social position, usually attracts less hostility than 'new money' whose representatives are not the inheritors but the creators of wealth. This acquiescence in the legitimacy of permitted inequalities recurs throughout the history of class and class conflict. In Britain, its history is particularly interesting—since working class dislike of wealth creation and 'conspicuous consumption' may well derive its origins from handed down upper-class prejudices of the busy parvenu money makers in the late eighteenth and early nineteenth centuries. The upper classes seem to have invented a better alibi than the middle-classes for their entitlement to wealth.

Social prophets from Shaftesbury to Marx thundered away on

social or economic conditions, but in reality they were discovering and some lamenting the growing gulf between the classes. So were the stirrings of working men, resulting in practical efforts to combine and to improve their position and rewards. All this made the working classes more conscious of their common, exposed position. The rapid absolute growth of national wealth—coupled with a corresponding amelioration of wage earners' income throughout the nineteenth century—did not significantly bridge the gulf between the classes, a chasm which the commentaries and criticisms of social pathfinders aptly described. Many crass inequalities continued in social relationship, in employment opportunities and in religious esteem: no surprise that social reformers were never short of causes or of recipes for action; some calling for revolutionary measures, others for less drastic but urgent steps within the law and the existing social order for improving the lot of the working class. Appeals were made to employers not to exploit their workers, Owenite sentiments established early co-operatives which failed in the end, and appeals were directed increasingly at government to redress the balance between the employer and employee—whether in factory acts or in agitation for abolishing the Corn Laws. The working classes too were organizing—they were on the march. Thus, I put the modern genesis of this more combative and vocal nature of 'conflict' between workers and bosses (capitalists, i.e. the bourgeoisie)—now reassuringly called the 'class war'—from about the middle of the last century, nearly 130 years ago, although protective associations for workers were started soon after the repeal of the Combination Acts in 1824. There were class conflicts before—mostly intermittent, often smouldering, sometimes revolutionary; and just as religious heresies until the seventeenth century, so controversies about basic economics, (i.e. the Corn Laws) in the mid-nineteenth century, often concealed the real nature of these troubles which, in essence, were class or political conflicts. Peasants' revolts throughout the Middle Ages were a common form of seeking material improvement or legal recognition. The modern form of class-war, while certainly aiming to improve the material condition of the worker, also aims at political fulfilment and social repositioning. Class-war based solely on financial rewards and on a reconciliation of income differences now takes a back seat. When most workers earn sufficient for their current needs as is the position nowadays, then the drive solely for money is rarely in top gear. No wonder, therefore, that the modern class discontent of workers is funnelled into inaugurating political change in search of power. Nothing shows this institutionalized approach more clearly than trade union influence in the Labour Party.

Narrowing definition

Class and friction between the classes have many facets, but I am concerned here almost entirely with only two controversial aspects of class attitudes; first, the variegated relationships between the working class and the other classes but especially the boss class and, second, how the impact of these two important classes on each other has shaped the socio-economic life of Britain. I am sympathetic to the notion that a very sizeable portion of Britain's past tardiness in industrial and commercial progress stems from the consequences of class friction, expressed as they commonly are in diverse forms of confrontation. None the less, isolating class as the most important single source of disaffection can be, and is, sometimes over-emphasized.

Minor types of class friction which in Britain might inflame lingering discontent and propel it towards industrial action, would not, axiomatically, cause ripples in other similarly industrialized countries with a discernible historical class structure and without a significant difference in democratic, political outlook. Hence there must be other, perhaps several other, explanations why the effects of class friction in one country are more immediate and more obvious and more damaging than in other similar countries. For this, and other important reasons, a careful scrutiny of class relations in Britain is always in season.

Class is a compartmentalized notion; axiomatically, it is in the nature of any caste system or class structure or systems of differentiation to be divisive. If this divisiveness is gaping, class antagonisms are rife; if they are within recognized, confined limits, class differences can serve as a spring-board for a healthy form of differentiation. As an idea, class offers solace and security to its representatives by their adherence to a common mores and also by offering a sense of belonging—an identifiable commonality of interest as well as shared values. Solidarity between bishops, soldiers, or aristocrats or, say, accountants, doctors, or bureacrats, solidarity between most trade unionists, between professors of economics, sheet metal workers, or deep-sea divers—a kin feeling between practitioners of the same art, craft or profession is natural, even necessary. Mutual recognition by those pursuing the same or similar ends, or using the same or similar means to a particular end, are valuable because they are reassuring to such protagonists. For such bonds offer a sense of togetherness as well as identity and with the underlying similarities in the practice of their skills they claim a type of specialist but communal pride. In some circumstances, but by no means in all, belonging to a certain recognized coterie (a minority perhaps?) brings forth an added sense of personal importance; this may be manifest as an incentive for greater expertise or added professionalism which, in turn, frequently evokes a desire for futher self-improvement which in the end, may result in added esteem of both self and class. In Britain, solidarity of class is simultaneously reinforced, fragmented and sometimes confused by language and accent—and these two variables are often identifiable according to occupation. Some of the so-called class differences have their origins in such slender, yet identifiable linguistic occupational divergences. It is suggested that to recognize nuances which clearly delineate class—in conduct, clothing or manner of speech—requires a particularly well developed sense of sophistication in the observer. Surprisingly, this facility for judgement is the property of all classes in Britain—an indication of the overgrown and overdeveloped social sense of the people: while this reflects a high degree of sophisticated awareness, it also reveals an overdrawn preoccupation with class sensitivity. This might be summed up in the clever comment, 'I want to be insulted and I won't move until I am.' In no other country are language and accent so socially divisive; their reverberations register high on the Richter scale of snobbism.

Entrepreneurs assailed

No wonder that such well developed class sensitivity, coupled with an even more active sense of class solidarity should set up conflicts. Since Marx, class differences have been expressly couched in hostile terms, i.e. as wars. The modern type of class war is expressed, in common parlance, as a 'conflict' between employers and employees.

Just because of the hydra-headed manifestation of divergent class interests throughout modern industrial history, and the propensity to defend those vested interests, we should not make the error of imagining that class antagonisms, as we have come to recognize them, have always been with us in their present form or that they, apparently, represent different and irreconcilable economic interests. The polarization, radicalization and politicization of class in industrial societies is a relatively late development. It is closely connected with but not started until long after the nineteenth-century evolution of socialism, as a suggested alternative economic system to capitalism. One should not forget that capitalism was not always viewed with suspicion and hostility. After all, is not modern capitalism the vehicle which beginning in the mid-eighteenth century has made the world so much richer? And, as a means of economic organization, dedicated to wealth creation, it did fulfil its promise! Was not the entrepreneur, the bourgeois capitalist, the successful key figure in this process of material enrichment for all? Indeed, he was and remains so. The inventors who built the machines, and the capitalists who owned the factories, operated the plant and produced and sold the goods were considered the do-gooders in those early days. Right from the start, capitalism worked—it delivered the goods; perhaps it worked most successfully some two centuries ago, when the industrial world was new, raw materials plentiful and labour eager to leave the villages for the towns for better wages and conditions. For almost a century, from the 1740s, the cornucopia of capitalism was uncritically accepted by a world hungry for goods and grateful for the gradually, less rigorous and less brutal living conditions which, despite many accusations to the contrary, capitalistic enterprise made possible. What is perhaps overlooked is that for a century or more, inventions and the stream of new products which accompanied the development of industrial capitalism have visibly raised living standards and reduced physical toil in Britain and, gradually, over a large part of the globe.

By contrast, in today's Britain high living standards are expected by all—by almost all—as an act of God. Any further addition—conferred by the dominant genre of enterprise, i.e. capitalism—to aid comfort and raise living standards seems marginal, because so much has already been accomplished. It is, therefore, not altogether surprising that capitalism, as a sophisticated venture and as the most efficient engine of production and distribution, of economic wellbeing, is less widely appreciated today than say a hundred or seventy-five years ago. Similarly, the role of the capitalist as innovator and risk-taker receives less approbation. Perhaps it needs emphasizing that such a lachrymose view of capitalistic society is more easily shared by those living under it than by those living in socialist countries.

What are the roots of discontent of those living under capitalism? Attributions are easy to invent but less easy to prove. Is working-class impatience—a fashionable expression—with capitalism significantly inflated by 'unrealizable' rising expectations? Is capitalism not 'delivering' according to the textbooks? Or, perhaps, the expectations in British society have been largely met and a highly competitive society, offering to deliver even more is perhaps no longer particularly desired? If expectations were still as high as those in other capitalist countries with a similar background of working-class strivings, less effort would be devoted to preventing the fuller realization of the nation's industrial and economic potential by fighting the boss (i.e. the manager, also an employee) or the entrepreneur (i.e. the employer); and this applies to the public sector as well as the private. Alternatives to a capitalist economic system, more cumbersome, infinitely more wasteful and not nearly as responsive to consumer needs, are preferred by some—clearly not for economic, industrial or commercial reasons. The reasons for their attraction are diverse, but usually come to rest on social and political grounds. Such alternative systems, usually under socialized banners, claim to be more egalitarian, hence superior. This could be one source of attraction—the seductive lure of egalitarianism. Another source of attraction could be because they are more amenable to control (or better, to use the fashionable word, planning) by central authorities. A further attractive notion is that socialist economies are more amenable to political control. Some are also led to believe that political control of an economic system under socialism confers not only fewer class differences and more equality but also guarantees a better life for the working class. A little knowledge of the economic and political history of socialist countries, however, will not confer such hopes; and a further examination of their class structure—changed, perhaps but even more rigid than before—will offer sobering enlightenment on privilege and inequality. The social, economic and political histories of socialist countries since 1945 offer little solace by way of a successful alibi for their ideologies.

Industrial capitalism has successfully survived, while continuously changing and adopting eventually to a mixed economy in politically and economically sophisticated countries. A testament to its success is the high living standard of its people both in absolute terms and by comparison with non-capitalist lands. But over its two centuries of primacy as a form of economic organization, capitalism has experienced crises which, for a long time, seemed as burdensome and familiar as they were insoluble. The ups-and-downs of early industrial capitalism still bore some resemblance to the chronic economic crises of the old, familiar, agrarian order of the pre-industrial age, bringing with it the recognized evils of poverty, unemployment, and hunger. It was only when capitalism appeared in more mature form in the more intensively industrialized countries, and the effects of the trade cycle became more acute, that the baffling phenomena of booms and slumps took on a menacing aspect. The bewilderment of the working class, faced with alternating cycles of prosperity and depression gave way first to resignation and then to impatience. This was reinforced when economic savants—of which Britain has always had an over-supply—claimed to have analysed the cause of capitalism's imperfections and identified plausible, if contradictory, remedies to counter its debility. Hence, because the disease of booms and slumps appeared diagnosable, the malaise of the trade cycle became, axiomatically, remediable. Thus, to many people and not only to the working class, these contradictions of capitalism became intolerable. Nature's disasters had to be accepted phlegmatically. Acts of God, famines, bad harvests, natural catastrophies, and wars have always been with us; but this novel type of man- and machine-made trade cycle were the handiwork of an identifiable type of economic and industrial organization, combined with management and ownership by a particular class of people. Thus, the responsibility for slumps and depressions, charges of exploitation, payment of low wages, and bad working conditions were pinned—at times justifiably, at times not—on those in command of the industrial, economic and financial mechanism: the entrepreneurs, the capitalists, the money men, a trinity of the new parvenus. It was this type of reasoning, bestowing collective guilt, which made capitalism and the owners of factories, workshops, and banks, as well as the managerial classes growing up within them, the targets of popular and virulent censure; some of this censure was generated by working-class discontent at times of trouble but perhaps even more by its self-appointed non-working class champions, the bourgeois intellectual as social critic. An alibi was invented for the economic ills of the new machine age—and its name was capitalism.

Nineteenth-century friction between employers and employees —caused by a rapidly developing and constantly changing industrial scene and, let it not be forgotten, a vastly increased working population—had also ossified into more rigidly held class attitudes by the end of the last century. In turn, this had led, by the third quarter of the twentieth century, to chronic class conflict. This is comprehensible only in terms of a 180 degree shift between the way that all classes looked upon capitalism in the late eighteenth and early nineteenth centuries, and the way the working and some of the other classes viewed it in the Edwardian age—the high noon of capitalism.

Bruised by revolutions which promised paradise now, resilient capitalism continued successfully in mature industrial lands after the Second World War, particularly in the defeated countries—in Germany and in Japan. By comparison, capitalism was undoubtedly less successful in Britain in the years after 1945. Surprising, in this context, was the failure of British capitalism to take fuller advantage of the 'fall out' on industry brought about by scientific and technological advances during the First and Second World Wars. The crux is to recognize an opportunity, and to seize it. But, at all events, success begets expansion and lack of it breeds pessimism and restriction; the British post-war experience adhered to the latter. As a result, anti-bourgeois and anti-enterprise attitudes have gradually multiplied and hardened in Britain since the end of those few years of post-war boom in the early 1950s. The end of the boom eventually signalled more dirigism, more meddling with capitalism, thus inhibiting the progress and prosperity of the country; shackles on enterprise led to more tampering with economic mechanisms, at the same time business was expected to deliver more and more!

Britain's lack of durable success as an economic powerhouse, or as a cohesive industrial community for the past four decades was certainly induced by a combination of circumstances. First, there has been, since the mid-thirties and more so since the mid-forties a new rise of Utopian socialism (in the thirties organized as a counter-weight to pre-war fascism) which became a skilfully controlled anti-business, anti-capitalist crusade in the post-war years.

The *cri de coeur* of the anti-business, anti-entrepreneur lobby is a disdain of capitalism and money, coupled invariably with a proclamation of entitlement to 'more' and compassionate care for toilers; an idyllically seductive doctrine. Beyond the immediacies of politics and economics, the humanistic aspect of socialism has also had an impact on environmentalism, for instance, though perhaps less from a love of humanity than as just another stick with which to beat business. Second, Britain and its people experienced the trauma of a sudden loss of mission after the dismantling of a 300-year-old empire, in the governance of which the energies of all classes were enlisted and in the benefits of which all classes participated. The dependent people of the former empire regained freedom, the decolonizing operation was successful, and more often than not, the newly liberated countries turned to socialism or communism. The empire having gone, could another 'mission' be mounted this time, perhaps, in Britain? Could it be that just as in the liberated 'old empire' so now in the brave 'old country' more collectivization, more planning, more socialism was needed for the improvement of the human conditions? After all, wasn't the wartime experience of central control and planning so successful? It could work in time of peace as well! Third, many steps were taken during and immediately after the war which had disabling effects on incentives and on risk-taking; nationalizing vast tracts of the economy eliminated large parts of personal responsibility for its performance; retention of too many wartime controls too long, the continuing bureaucratic interference, blunted enterprise; muscular unionization—endorsed by a government owing its existence to labour—enlarged latent cleavages between manager and worker; also, the manifold bounties of the welfare state have taken much of the penalty out of anti-social or economically damaging conduct, both at work and outside it. Fourth, the unchecked—often encouraged—exercise of working-class militancy, culminating in increasingly bitter and more frequent labour disputes, particular since the mid-1960s, have in turn contributed further to the imperfections of capitalist-style economic management in 'modern' Britain's mixed economy. Starry-eyed anticipations of unending income rises unmatched by real higher output, hostility to the boss, lack of concern about the quality of output, overmanning, job sharing and enthusiastic twentieth-century Luddism have led to still further defects in industrial organization. Not even the golden period of world prosperity between 1945 and 1972 seemed to have had an ameliorating effect on the continuing working-class hostility toward the capitalistic system and against the boss class operating the system. In working-class mythology the changing composition of the boss class must be mentioned—as its definition has broadened. Nowadays, it includes not only the perennially maligned entrepreneur—the founder or owner of a business—but also members of the managerial hierarchy at all levels of private, and rather perversely, of public enterprise as well. The socialist worker's dislike of socialized enterprise bosses implies that class relationships and class antagonisms are not invariably guided by political dispositions; but is socialists' disloyalty to socialist institutions all that new?

The need to redefine the traditional target of working-class hostility—now embracing managements of business in public as well as in private ownership—is of the utmost significance. To the working-class, the boss class is omnipresent where negotiations about terms and conditions of employment take place—that is, in all enterprises, private or public, capitalist, or socialized. Thus, working-class dislike towards other classes has been successfully enlarged to embrace those in managerial command, engaged in private money-making businesses as well as those in charge of public services where there is no private gain. Here then is an omnibus concept of some novelty, a native British originality, in terms of the further development of working-class opprobrium—which now spans profit, and non-profit-making organizations alike. Socialism is devouring its public enterprise children by a socialized working class which refuses to make it work properly. Since most industrial disputes in Britain have taken place in socialized enterprises, no wonder that some of them have become increasingly unsuccessful. Equally, no wonder that a radical Tory government in the 1980s should have reversed this trend by denationalizing socialized enterprises.

Permitted inequalities

Working class dislike of 'toffs', then, seems to be based partly on ideological grounds (considering themselves as the exploited class), as well as on social grounds (concerning their own relationship in the organization of industry). This deliberate distancing of the working class from the managerial orders derives some of its roots from historical wrongs perpetuated against the working class, wrongs, partly buried but never quite forgotten and which having been carefully nurtured by folk-memory, surface from time to time. Solely materialistic grounds for such hostility, such as low wages and bad conditions, indifferent living standards, have been eroding now for decades, and some have undoubtedly disappeared. For a long time now, there have been many very well-off among the working class; their income is substantially in excess of the average artisan, of many factory managers and of not a few small businessmen, all of whom usually consider themselves socially as middle class—and what is more, they are so considered by the working class. Thus, the class animosity of a substantial and rising number of the well—or very well—paid, skilled industrial workers, against the boss class cannot now be explained or sustained any longer merely in material terms. The disposition must be different in the case of the unskilled and lower-paid members of the working class. Their class animosity, manifesting itself in more vocal hostility to the boss class, as well as in a more concealed dislike of the well-off working class, has its roots largely in financial envy. It is reassuring that even in social democracies, money has remained the source of evil—what would we do without this easily diabolized symbolism—though its importance has been blunted in many different ways, by its more ready availability, perhaps for the first time since biblical days!

It could be argued that unrealistically high wage demands coupled with perennial requests for shorter hours and improved conditions—without much interest or desire to offer the boss or the company something tangible in return—are largely fuelled by a double misunderstanding. Such demands are fed by a belief that the organization, the company, can pay because it must have the money.

What other explanation can be found for the steel workers' strike in 1980 at a time when the continuing existence of Britain's steel industry could only be ensured by increased tax-payers' subsidy? Or by the coal miners' strike in 1985 which further reduced the importance of as well as the numbers in the National Union of Minerworkers? The class militancy in this type of fantasy thinking is that the boss-class, and its concrete expression, the company, must have money or can get hold of it. It would not occur to too many that a company, especially a large company with large numbers of unionized workers, may not have earned enough added value from the labour of its workers to support a fresh round of wage rises. In smaller companies where the process of how money is earned and spent seems more widely perceived or understood by its workforce, unreasonable demands are rare. There is something in the anatomy of the big corporation—a high degree of unionization explains much—which encourages forms of worker militancy. Nationalized industries are particularly prone to this debility.

Though pay and working conditions are major, surface, causes of industrial unrest, the seductive concept of egalitarianism fans a measure of discontent which finds many conduits for grievances. The drive for egalitarianism has been bequeathed to the working class over several generations by their largely intellectual, bourgeois leaders, many of whom often feel guilty about being well-off, let it be said, often through inherited money. But the notion of airy-fairy egalitarianism coming from guilt-ridden, over-age flower children is unacceptable to any sensible worker. The working class is severely practical; more egalitarianism to them means a way up the socio-occupational ladder rather than down; and the pressure for egalitarianism is for sectional rather than for general realignment. What the social researcher may diagnose as the desire for egalitarianism by the working class may be better revealed by their conscious drive for achieving or maintaining an elitism of their own. Skilled, well-paid workers, understandably, are determined to maintain their pay and other 'differentials'; unskilled workers wish to 'graduate' to such differentials. No compulsory readings in sociology are necessary to realize the superior stance of the craftsman over his less skilled fellow workers. When the determination of the skilled workers' efforts are being gauged by the successful and stubborn maintenance of their differentials in wages negotiations, it is difficult to escape the suspicion that differentials to them imply class—inequality—as well as cash. The growing scarcity of skilled craftsmen in the engineering industries in the 1980s may well be attributed to the erosion of their differentials in the 1970s. After all, differentials, i.e. higher rewards, are a spur to acquire skills. Let there be no misunderstanding about this enthusiasm for differentials: lip-service may well be paid to greater egalitarianism, especially if it can help top up wages. But no class of workers would steadfastly support the logical extension of the principle of egalitarianism by allowing the improvement of the incomes of the less skilled workers below them at their expense.

The rodomontade for greater egalitarianism raises a host of questions, of which one in particular deserves scrutiny; namely, are current working class attitudes towards egalitarianism merely a contemporary form of rejecting suspected latter-day social Darwinism? To find an acceptable answer to the question is difficult: if you are successful (and make a fortune) do you possess certain fairly rare, special, exclusive qualities which make this possible? Hard work, great competence, acquired skills, good timing are all partial answers; and, of course, there is that extra dimension which is a great help—a little luck! Are all these good citizen-like, solid qualities of endeavours stacked up as acceptable explanations for success? Probably not. Only by deliberately rejecting the idea that ceaseless effort and experimentation are recognizable and desirable paths to success, and maybe to riches, is it possible to understand working class dislike of the businessman who has accumulated wealth by taking risks, working and saving hard, investing money and building up a thriving, profitable enterprise: and only in this context can the rejection of the idea of competition be understood, and the idea of effortless gain by dint of good fortune endorsed. Whatever the social position of such a winner, his luck is applauded.

Disdain for the successful, an easily recognizable coterie at all levels of sophistication, has become an 'approved' class reflex, and not among members of the working class alone. I suggest that the dislike of success achieved by hard grind is sufficiently ingrained in contemporary British life for it to transcend—even class barriers. Numerous adherents of the professional classes as well as the upper-middle, and middle-class representatives pretend to find financial success in business of no special merit. Such are contemporary non-working-class reactions to business success, even if the language of dislike is different—i.e. muted. The working class might resent the financial advantages of a successful entrepreneur; the upper strata will resent him for two very different reasons. First, they pretend to dislike conspicuous consumption (in the same way as the aspiring bourgeoisie pretend not to enjoy it) and, second, they hate the historical fact that money can and does pave the way to social acceptability. It has always been like this, with infinite variations. I sometimes wonder whether sympathy for or flirtation with socialism, coupled with genuine or genuinely mistaken ideas of compassion and equality, all the hallmarks of a mature social conscience in twentieth century Britain, have not made the disdain of the entrepreneur and of business, and contracting out of the pursuit of commerce and industry, an almost Pavlovian exercise?

My assumption about the century old popularity of the rejection of the superior effort demanded for above average success, is not a base idiosyncratic slander; it can be tested in a practical way. Dislike of manifest material success in Britain is not confined to any class or part of it. An appropriate illustration of intra-working class hostility towards earned—and not chance—success can be found in the position of the 'moonlighter' who can be described as the illegitimate son of inflation, unemployment, the sluggish performance of existing firms in supplying goods or services, and high taxation. But the most positive characteristic of the moonlighter is his opportunism. The spectre of a working-class chap next door earning mostly tax free twice as much as a worker in regular employment must undoubtedly rankle with his neighbours much more than newspaper reports about an astronomically high income of some obscure company chairman. The 'confrontational', radical ways of demanding more pay, and the unrestrained language of their representatives for many years, may have had their arguments compounded by the wage-earners', and perhaps more so by the union negotiators', envy of the moonlighter's apparent high living standard. Such reactions can only confirm the suspicion that higher financial rewards—i.e. inequalities—born of risk-taking, of thinking to some well defined business purpose and of above-average application, by a fellow worker, seem to rankle, at least with some of the working class. Those workers who feel in this way do not believe for a moment that such riches are undeserved; *au contraire*, they realize that such income or wealth is deservedly earned and this is where the odium lies. If a man has a currently fashionable or even marginally acceptable alibi for being rich—by gambling, or even by inherited wealth—no other men need feel inferior by comparison, because such money has accrued by means of accidental good fortune. As we all know, fortune is kind to some but not to others, a genre of reasoning readily understood and accepted in a country like Britain where gambling has long been a national disease. But, if it were accepted that making a fortune is invariably the result of conscious risk-taking, deliberate hard work and enduring sacrifices in the present for potential—i.e. deferred —rewards at some unspecified, future date, then the good luck alibi as an acceptable form of money-making would appear frayed. Such a primitive notion of detesting successful effort must be as potent a source of working-class dislike of earned wealth—and by implication of its earner the entrepreneur, the moonlighter, the boss—as any economic identikit notion about surplus value or latter-day partisan egalitarianism.

Home and abroad

Discerning visitors to Britain sometimes indicate that they perceive a prevalence of latent class conflict; I suspect this gift of discernment is reinforced in those with a good knowledge of English—but 'foreigners', too, are aware of a degree of social unease. Such and similar intangible notions stem from perception and not knowledge. However, the possible identification of class combat in Britain indicates that native social disequilibrium seems sharper to visitors than to us—inured as we are to the strange multiple class conflicts we have all been acting out for decades. To get Britain's own class differences in perspective, perhaps a relevant inquiry to pursue is an examination of what kind of class wars (are classwars endemic?) are being fought in other countries? Are class animosities elsewhere less or more fierce, are they widely practised and easy to observe by visitors or are they in a minor key? Why is the British variety so optically perfect? Are other countries' records of industrial unrest less bad, as bad or worse than Britain's? In general, neither managers nor men, neither politicians nor social scientists for this reason are too well informed of such matters; in this respect as in so many others, we prefer to remain 'little Englanders' and remain pre-occupied with ourselves. For the greater part, the popular media reflect our preoccupation with such escapism—at a guess and on average—say, twelve column inches to labour relations, fifty-five column inches to foreign news and on good days, some five pages to sport. 'Little Englanderism' is one of the few shared parochialisms cutting across class and income, and too many of us have luxuriated in it for too long. This posture has transmogrified our ingrained class reflexes into a nationally enjoyed defensive stance, while the rest of the world is less concerned merely about what happens within its own frontiers; other lands also seem less disturbed by class differences since they acknowledge their interdependence. Internationalism in Britain, which observes the world, especially among the working class, is probably confined to a fortnight's holiday in foreign parts, watching soccer matches being played abroad and disfigured by imported British hooligans and switching on the ten o'clock news on television. The blinds are half drawn to exclude, if possible, the stimulating lessons of the world outside on class, on social affectation, and yes even on race, excepting South Africa and the Southern States of the USA. In other mature industrial lands the results of recognized interdependence, in which each class has a role to play and each maintains its own dignity, has lead to a higher mutual esteem between them, hence to class co-operation and class tolerance. Compared to the American isolationists who are pilloried from time to time by the British press, too many of us in Britain—particularly the working class and its leadership—are living examples of the strictest compartmentalization, by living in parochial cocoons.

Scrutinizing the social histories of industrialized countries in Western Europe and North America—it will be found that all have experienced working-class militancy at different times, but in the fourth quarter of the twentieth century, protracted militancy has become largely a relic of the past. And here comes the rub—apparently no other country has suffered as much economically and socially as Britain from the debilitating consequences of class conflict. Because, whatever class antagonisms are elsewhere, these appear less intractable and more endurable; peace settlements between capital and labour are dignified by durability and social or political ferment is not constantly bubbling beneath the surface, ready to erupt at the slightest pretext. The turbulent British scene in recent history is unsatisfactory for all parties because there is no beneficiary and in the end all parties to the class war are losers.

Are there ways of betterment? One ingredient must be a better understanding of interdependence and agreement on common goals between industrial classes, as well as a general will for solid improvement, which is only possible by broad co-operation. The net result of class-fuelled intransigence in Britain is that, comparatively, living standards elsewhere have become higher, yet not so many years ago the position was exactly the reverse. The mid-1980s are indicating a reversal, mainly as a result of declining working-class militancy—brought about by sensible trade union legislation. What remains endemic in British industrial class relations is the constant misunderstanding—real or manufactured—of each other's motives; moreover, there also appears to be a deliberate lack of desire to understand the causes of conflicts, their effects and possible remedies. The number and magnitude of misunderstandings between the boss class and the working class is such that, in my view, it cannot just have a single source of bias—i.e. class. Many representatives of the working-class, and their middle-class gurus, continue to live an illusion that lunatic-militant conduct is justified because it has worked in the past. To reverse this belief amiably a scrutiny of illusions is imperative; this is difficult, since illusions are often an indispensable prop to cherished cultural prejudices. How to change folk-memories remains the property of inspired political thinking.

For the greater part the illusions of the working class, and of their middle-class champions operate at three levels; the first is a naive belief that trade unions are still all-powerful, hence government or private employers must find the money to meet wage and other demands forced upon them by the unions; some union officials have been sufficiently vocal in Britain to have given the impression that pay rises are financed by the unions! The second is that endearing truism, which instructs that the rich can pay and all employers, i.e. private firms, nationalized corporations, government departments and agencies are defined as rich—and not by the working-class alone. The inference—or better, the delusion—is that Britain is an increasingly wealthy country, and can afford almost anything it wants to afford. Third, that however shabby the workmanship, many badly made products must sell, not on merit but either

because British is still best or because of the notion that the world
owes Britain a living, both are unhappy sequels to an unrevised folk
memory! The argument runs thus: some British-made products may
fail to perform according to specification, others are delivered late or
have become uncompetitive, but why should all these complaints
matter so much? After all, didn't we fight the Battle of Britain to save
Europe and the world? Didn't we stand up well to the Blitz! Didn't
we suffer, (or perhaps enjoy) rationing! (And, due to our obsession
with fair shares during and after the war rationing endured longer in
Britain than in any other, and poorer, Western European country
involved.) How can such sacrifices be forgotten by all these
foreigners? The belief in the obligation of 'others' to keep Britain and
its people comfortably afloat—as has been the case with American
loans or IMF rescue packages—has been for long an undesirable
article of faith which in their different way other classes have often
shared with the working class. The working class has looked upon
the employer primarily as a milch cow to ensure increasingly better
living conditions; other classes, including the managerial, looked to
external agencies such as the Americans or the World Bank as
underwriting instruments for maintaining British living standards.
After all, is it not in the interest of the Americans to give British
loans, as it was in the interest of the rest of the world for the World
Bank to lend money? National mendicancy on the scale developed in
Britain has deeper roots than some may contemplate. While in the
return to greater prosperity during the 1980s, this notion has
escaped below the surface, it may well return when greater exertions
will be called for with a declining income from the North Sea.

Attitudinizing is rampant in a class society and it tends to aggravate
simple issues. As we are living in a consumer civilization,
wishing to 'keep up with the Jones's' is an accepted criterion in some
quarters as a respectable aspiration. There is, of course, an
anti-bourgeois, intellectually *manqué* 'stream of consciousness' which
rejects materialistic competition with the Jones's; and such an
attitude, of course, is characteristic of the bourgeois intellectual with
money and an enlarged social conscience; no ordinary folk would
tolerate such nonsense! Luckily, the working class does not take such
middle-class posturings too seriously when it comes to raising their
own comfort. Thus, despite such esoteric misgivings by middle- and
upper-middle class intellectuals, who usually, already, possess the

goods they wish the working-class to deny themselves, improved living standards are everywhere warmly welcomed. The British working classes are not stoics, competing in 'conspicuous abstinence' with each other. The realistic question is whether the rise in living standards of the British working class is being considered adequate or not. Because if the working class believe they have been shortchanged, an unending source of class conflict will remain. The heady promise of 'rising expectations' preached by successive governments has never been fully realized but, all the same, much has been accomplished; an unarticulated cause of working-class frustration with the capitalist system today stems from the complaints of the 'casualty class', embracing recruits from all social classes—and from the old and infirm with rather more justification. And there is another illusion, a widely held primitive belief, that come what may, the employer—please note, decreasingly the state in recent years—will have to be forced to offer higher wages at regular intervals to ensure, automatically, a deservedly fuller life for the workers. This is the principle of automatism in the wages rounds which has become almost a birthright. This could be described as the formula compounded of inflation-proof wages and of Buggin's turn.

Why is constructive and consistent co-operation with the boss though decreasingly but still not enthusiastically within the realm of practical working class attitudes in Britain today? Certainly not because the bosses are deemed to have different material objectives from their employees. They both work in the same company, and the success of the enterprise redounds—in the language of logic—to everybody's advantage in factory, company and conmmunity. The indifference to the boss's suggestions for higher output, for instance, is then, in part, the result of an acquired class reflex of 'us' being automatically against 'them'. This particular class reflex remains a cornerstone of all collective working class movements—and it may be said that this class segregation has not been discouraged by the Labour movement or by the trade unions. These expressions, indicating a divergence of interest of people composing the firm, are repeated with such frequency that by now they sound a trifle trite; none the less they remain powerful. In such a polarized vocabulary, 'them' are a suspect term; in the modern folklore of class war the identity of 'them' has become a moveable feast.

In the more radical, early, years of this century, 'them' were unmistakenly the capitalists—the employers, the factory owners. As with many firmly held doctrines, it has gone unnoticed that this formerly clear cut definition has been eroding. Employers are still in the 'them' category—irrespective of whether or not they belong to the 'regular' antipathetic class of 'traditional' entrepreneurs; as the managers of the nationalized corporations or as the superintendants of the health service. This blanket condemnation of 'them', the employer, reinforces the uncomfortable assumption suspected by some foreign observers that at the heart of the class conflict in British society lie social rather than economic beliefs. Happily, social conflict is one of the 'invisibles' Britain has not exported—except perhaps a particularly vicious brand of hooliganism.

Thus, class conflict and class co-operation elsewhere are ordained and resolved differently. Although the British species of class war which most visibly is being fought out in industry, is there for all to see, this variety does not seem to travel well. Class hostility is less apparent among our partners in the Common Market or for that matter in the United States. Yet, many of these countries' class structure is just as vintage and as diverse as that of the United Kingdom. If conclusive proof is needed that others may dispense with the British type of class hostility—which debilitated industry for so long—we have only to look at the excellent industrial performance, high living standards, and absence of any great social animus in these countries. This is definitely not because of a greater or smaller differential in living standards between workers and bosses; or on account of a more immediate comprehension by the different classes of their common, enlightened self-interest or on account of a greater native ability to reconcile their divergent economic interests more easily and more amicably. Nor is it attributable to the superior comprehension of the Frenchman or the American to the dismal science of economics or to the therapeutic nature of long periods without class turmoil; nor to the Continental workers' ethics of not reneging on agreements, nor on account of the incisive, native organizing ability of German, Belgian, Swedish or Japanese capitalists which in turn engender ripples of admiration and studied respect from their working classes. These explanations all have an element of truth but are not the whole story, though they contribute to creating a better milieu in which industry works.

The simple truth is that extreme, antagonistic social posturings have not developed extensively in these other lands and thus have not swamped the workplace; as a result, class feelings and loyalties—which impinge on employment in industry and its performance in Britain—are not such an important issue elsewhere. The classic causes of class warfare such as status, privilege, conspicous consumption, strict group identification, or obstacles in the way of social and occupational advance, appear to be less keenly felt, resented or exploited. Such an array of divisive forces exist to a lesser extent outside manufacturing industry in Britain—but here again experience has been patchy. Perhaps the British working class is more self-consciously aware of these divisive forces—hence their over-rated importance in industrial transigence. In many respects, and certainly concerning incomes, pay differentials in this country between classes, i.e. occupations, are frequently narrower than in comparable, industrially mature lands. At all events, there must be pragmatic reasons accounting for the difference in the generally combative attitude of the British working class towards the British boss class—by definition the bourgeois—and the less calculated, less deeply felt resentments of the working class towards the boss class in other countries with a similar history and development.

Imposed togetherness

One simple explanation may be advanced to partially account for the escalation of working class militancy, and hence of industrial unrest, in Britain over the past forty years. Curiously, the explanation offered has no class connotation, no union bloody mindedness or employer chicanery to account for it. I attribute this social turbulence—partly at least—to the virtual absence of widely felt, sustained hardship and the competitive need for a great effort involving personal scarifice, on the part of the British working class *after* the Second World War to put their country on the road to prosperity. Freedom from worry breeds insolence as an overdose of the welfare state has so aptly mirrored.

Thus the relatively trouble-free post-war experience of the British working class might well account for a large slice of the social-economic troubles after 1945. Their position was radically different from those of her allies or of her enemies—except America.

At the end of the war Europe lay devasted, physically and spiritually exhausted. When looking at the economic-industrial state of either Britain's principal European allies—Belgium, France, Holland, Norway, the USSR—or of her principal enemies—Germany and Italy—all these countries were devastated industrially, reduced agriculturally, and damaged socially and at least two of them destroyed politically. Post-war unemployment, slow industrial recovery, sustained periods of food scarcity during and after the war, and the urgent need to rebuild the basis of civilized life were the Europeans' constant preoccupation for several years after the war. All these vicissitudes and hardships forced a heightened understanding in Britain's friends or foes in the last war of their realistic needlfor all their working classes to co-operate closely and not superficially and not just for a short while but for decades, with all other classes. In this spirit of constructive co-operation, the Europeans have renewed their industries and rebuilt their devastated countries—the German achievement was called a 'miracle' in Britain. Though over the years the German currency has had to be up-valued a number of times to reflect the beneficial results of an ever more efficient industrial culture, German industrialists have not lost out by being priced out of world markets. Workers and employers realized that first to regain and later to safeguard their strenuously fought-for high and rising living standards, innovations and not restrictive practices must be their guiding lights. This is how they mastered international competition. This is the moral of co-operation in industry between the factors of production, born initially of hunger and destruction.

No such traumatic suffering was experienced in Britain, hence no comparable radical solutions were needed or evoked; Britain was in the enviable position of switching her industries for producing from war to peace without dramatic readjustments or large-scale reconstruction on the European model. The consequences of Britain's good fortune allowed the British working class, as well as the boss class, the indulgent luxury of not having to forge a new basis for co-operation and find mutual respect in a double harness in a radically changed world. As the years of peace dragged on so the working and boss classes continued fighting each other with the redundant slogans of the inter-war years. Class animosities, papered over during the war, leapt to life again immediately after it was over.

No readily identifiable, desperate economic or industrial emergency demanded special co-operation from the British industrial classes—working, managerial or entrepreneurial—to work in tandem and build a prosperous, solid future. In fact, circumstances could not have been more deceptively agreeable for British industry and for those working in it. The ease with which British-made goods sold in all the world markets immediately after the war was presumed to be another vindication of the age-old, intrinsic, superiority of British workmanship and not simply attributable to pent-up world demand. Thus, there was little conscious need for greater 'togetherness' to strengthen the economy, to strive for a more competitive industry and to ensure rising comforts for the long term. Success seemed so effortless in the mid and late 1940s.

What remained unappreciated at the time was the temporary nature of Britain's relative success as a leading industrial producer. The working class no doubt believed that such success could continue without any changes which might affect them. The boss class was content to return to producing what they always made best, with minimal innovation; and, despite the growing industrial anarchy, companies made handsome profits. Hence, in the post-war euphoria, despite all the fashionable garbage of planning the economy, neither the unions nor the employers, nor the governments had offered any imaginative, realistic guide lines for the future; and when using the sacred word 'planning' all the government had in mind was applying more controls. The position of planners in a dirigiste economy is straightforward; but the mixed economy of Britain after the war had offered them unrivalled opportunities for industrial and commercial mischief. None of this helped the state of the nation.

One of the post-war victims of the class war in the factories was clearly signalled in the steadily deteriorating value of the pound which continued for four decades with concomitant foreign trading deficits. Had it not been for intensive international support for many years after the war, led by the United States, living standards in post-war Britain, particularly after 1952, would have fallen precipitously, despite the availability of industrial production potential and the skilled labour to produce more competitively. Until the arrival of the oil boom, Britain borrowed her way out of trade deficits. As it turned out, living standards never sufficiently declined to warrant an urgent look at the working-class–boss-class relationship in British industry. Governments' recourse to foreign borrowing to maintain artificially high living standards, instead of earning and deserving them, was the international corollary to the domestic position; to raise artificially or just maintain living standards, without the benefit of competitive industry earning them governments allowed large-scale inflation. Thirty years later, when inflation and unemployment had really got out of hand in the late 1970s, governments endeavoured to grasp the reins more tightly; but until then, the realities of deserts and punishments, rewards or penalties were not on the menu of British governments. But, by that time not only a bad current position had to be remedied but a start also had to be made to put right many weaknesses and self-indulgent errors of three decades. Unthinking economic permissiveness by British governments of all political colourings has only helped to exacerbate class hostilities and divergences.

A scrutiny of different industrial countries' experiences in survival in the post-war world in Europe, for example, may offer another method of understanding the roots of the present social conflict in Britain, and something of the 'impulses' leading to it. Looking at the results of periodical international financial support for Britain since 1945 to safeguard living standards, we cannot congratulate ourselves on having put that help to durable use; now, three decades later, Noth Sea oil is coming to the rescue in a similar support role. Oil income is partly financing bulging imports. Are current, high living standards still being underwritten, this time by oil, once more masking the economic realities from the working and other classes? We are still living above our deserts. But, the urgency for co-operation in industry on a wider front has gained momentum: escape clauses for the failure to co-operate are no longer being invented in profusion. Worker–boss co-operation is more stable, despite high but declining levels of unemployment. What perhaps should also be emphasized is that no democratic government can inculcate a sense of co-operation into anyone by preaching. Government can induce change, if change in the social-economic milieu is desired and those seeking it are ready for it. No-one can impose togetherness, except if desired; people, classes, nations all have to come voluntarily to a realization of its merits. There are signs that the closing decades of the twentieth century may bring new impulses for a more harmonious nexus between man and master, and their institutionalized representatives.

Profile of the boss-class

A contemporary analysis of class, class-conduct and class-conflict must be primarily concerned with the two dominant classes of industrial culture, the employee and the employer—the worker and the capitalist in private enterprise, and the worker and the bureaucrat in socialized enterprise. Although a significant proportion of the labour force is employed by the agencies of the state, directly and indirectly, the majority of working men and women and about half the country's assets are still employed by private, and not public, enterprise. Thus, a better understanding of the characteristics of the working class and the boss class, of the differences between them and of ways to reconcile their divergent interests and encourage greater class harmony remain of seminal importance. All the more so since the nature of capitalism, and the workers' and the bosses' attitudes to it have been changing.

An important feature of keeping alive class conflict in a capitalistic society is the prominence given to the actions and reactions, postures and attitudes of the representatives of workers and their organizations,—the trade unions. Surprisingly there is little corresponding exposure of those of the employer, the manager, the capitalist and their organizations. Yet surely, the disposition, the reactions and the general attitudes of the employer class, as such, deserve study—in just as wide-ranging a manner as those of the working class, about whom, and in whose defence, so much ink has been spilt. A better understanding of the sociology of industry and of its constituent parts is long overdue. And this can be realistically helped along by more and better information about the processes of innovation, more talking and most important of all—a better understanding of attitudes!

Who then are these capitalistic employers and their managers who constitute the industrial capitalist class? Do they exhibit discernible class characteristics, and are they as a class intrinsically hostile to the interests of other classes? In working class folklore, the belief lingers that the employer class is *sui generis*, different from the working-class. In two important respects it is, of course, very different. First, unlike some of the working class most of the time and most of the working class (only) some of the time, the budding or actual capitalist—possibly of working class origins—does not feel victimized or aggrieved about his social or economic position in the scheme of things. One might assume the capitalist does not knowingly go in for much suffering—either on his own or on anyones else's account, and neither directly nor vicariously. He does not feel he has been hard done by or victimized by anyone—a recurring refrain attributed, perhaps too often, to the working class. Second, the capitalist is primarily a risk-taker and assumes responsibility for his actions, as well as for the people he employs and for the obligations he undertakes toward third parties. Unlike his employees, the capitalist—irrespective of social origins—is not overtly conscious of class differences, as such, probably because his mind is fixed on bending economic forces and opportunities to advantage, an absorbing, full-time task. If there is a single, important notion about the disposition of a capitalist, it is that he does not claim active class affinity of any kind—irrespective of his origins—and certainly not at the outset of his career. I am only guessing, but few budding capitalists would consider applying for membership of the Institute of Directors or the Confederation of British Industry when they start making or selling from a back room at home, or even, later, at the time of the incorporation of their companies; they might want to join up in due course, when they have made good in their own estimation. In the pursuit of their goals, entrepreneurs and capitalists are not primarily concerned about affiliations. They do not seek safety by belonging to a coterie; their approach is to get on with their chosen business, take calculated risks, and make a profit. At the onset of their careers they are wholly unprotected from the chill winds of competition.

By comparison, the first step in most workers' careers in the past has been to join a trade union appropriate to their skills; often they have had no choice, as in the case of a closed shop. One of the 'differentiating' characteristics of capitalists is that they do not, instinctively or deliberately, feel defensive and, therefore, inward-looking and protective towards themselves—while their employees appear mostly to be so inclined. The much-voiced disparities in economic muscle—which seems to me not very significant in starting a small firm—between the employer and the employee is considered a good reason for the collective security sought by the latter. It is interesting to reflect that membership of the so-called directors' trade union entitles its members to no protection of any kind. By comparison, membership of an employees' trade union confers entitlement to work, if there is a job,(many jobs cannot be accepted without union membership), to negotiated wages, to bonuses, to holidays, etc. and other advantages will be negotiated on the employee's behalf by collective bargaining. Both the times of work and the times for non-work, i.e. going on strike, or going slow will almost invariably be determined by the union or union representatives. So, it seems—perhaps a trifle perversely—that for the much-vaunted task of job creation, as an employer, one does not need a licence, but for job occupancy one does! There is some sort of reverse class distinction lurking in the shadows here!

The individual capitalist does not often suffer from feeling of social superiority in the pursuit of his working objective—which, to reiterate, is to earn profits and, beyond that, if his talents are durable and his endeavours successful, to build up an organization. Glamour and importance in the social stakes gain desirability for the capitalist only after he has accumulated wealth and is feeling sufficiently confident about his firm's future to divert part of his time and attention away from the proverbial grindstone. Of course, business success frequently brings with it social aspirations. Far from feeling superior on account of his business success, the capitalist is sometimes as insecure as anyone, anywhere, any time. I would go so far as to say that when making representations or pleading some cause face to face with his bank manager or tax inspector, not to mention his civil service mandarins or his political masters, with rare and notable exceptions the capitalist suffers from an in-built inferiority complex. For a full explanatin of this phenomenon see 'Intellectuality in the Market Place' below.

Why does not the British entrepreneur—as opposed to his European or American counterpart— have the confidence to consider himself the equal, perhaps at times the superior, of the politician, the civil servant, or the professional classes generally? The easy answer, and perhaps the most telling, is that the entrepreneur in Britain largely originates from the same class as his employee—that is from the working or artisan classes. There are successful British entrepreneurs with a bourgeois and upper-middle class background and a good education, but their ranks are thin. The successful entrepreneur is thus shown up as an 'unequal' person in relation to his working-class origins—a distinction his working-class cohorts find difficult to forgive; after all, their educational attainment and social origins have been largely the same and their social backgrounds and their working careers, at the outset, have been running on parallel lines.

Looking back a couple or so centuries, it was largely members of the educated middle class who deliberately chose industry and became entrepreneurs—and successful ones at that. The impression more than lingers that no social stigma was attached to business as long as it remained the province of men socially secure in their middle and upper-middle-class backgrounds. Being an entrepreneur in the mid-eighteenth century was undoubtedly a socially and occupationally acceptable pursuit. The Duke of Bridgewater, for example, was not criticized but praised for building an important canal. The upper classes and the entrepreneurs combined in building railways and in pursuit of commerce and manufacture. In this respect, the English upper classes were much in advance of their continental counterparts; they had a healthy appreciation of where money was to be found in the new machine age. How perverse, therefore, the change in sentiment, in 'attitudes' in the middle and upper classes a hundred or so years later, many of whose members have come to genuinely dislike the pursuit of business! Having amassed their fortunes by the 1850s, the educated, entrepreneurial upper classes gradually left industry and trade to the artisan and working classes from whose ranks, most of the entrepreneurs, in any case, have arisen since the mid-seventeenth century. By the mid-nineteenth century the social distance between those members of the working class who had 'made it' and those who watched them make it grew wider and by the end of the last century this gap developed into yet another cause for class friction and division. The aspiring, successful worker, in his role as a capitalist also abandoned business in due course to enhance his social position. Thus, the dignity of business was often disdained by those who benefited from it most. This gentrification did not happen in other countries, and certainly not to the same extent as in Britain.

Educational gambits

Why is it that entrepreneurs who became successful capitalists in Britain rose mainly from the lower-middle, artisan, and working classes, as well as—and this is most important—from among immigrants? The simple answer is that in most educational establishments—and particularly in Britain's schools and universities in the nineteenth century designed for the upper classes—the pursuit of business as a career, and manufacturing in particular, were often stigmatized. Nothing brings home this truth more graphically than asking the question: how many graduates in Britain have started up their own businesses during the past 150 years? The answer is precious few, and those who have will be largely found outside trading or manufacturing industry, and mostly in the provision of professional and other services and finance. The sad truth is that by the time a university student graduates and even if he is drawn to industrial employment, indeed some qualifications make a job in industry axiomatic, few would consider starting their own business . It would be fascinating to know how many of those schooled by say, the top twelve public schools or the two ancient English universities over the past forty years, have become chairmen or managing directors of industrial manufacturing or trading firms established by themselves and not by their fathers or by other umbilical cord relationships. My guess is perhaps a dozen but even this number may be a wild exaggeration!

There is an important, economic (partially class?) element about making a career decision which enters the mind of the working and middle-class student, after graduation, in two discernible ways. First, having enjoyed for a minimum period of three years a reasonable bourgeois standard of living at university, paid for largely by other people's taxes, the graduate would find it impossible to continue in his now accustomed life-style if he were to become self-employed; he would have to accept for a time the prospect of diminution of his standard of living. Starting from nothing, so to speak, existing on borrowed money and having to scrape to get by, perhaps for a longish period, is therefore not an objective a university graduate in Britain will welcome. Second, substantial, prestigious businesses, as well as departments of the State, institutions, the media and other employers are all competing—or have been until recently—for the graduate's services and offer an emolument package which no self-employed graduate could hope to attain for some time. Added to financial blandishments are promises of interesting work, fast track promotion, excellent retirement pension and prospects of working for an institutionalized boss— non-entrepreneurial, therefore less demanding as a rule.

Management in such firms is by committee, hence responsibility is divided (minimum). The advantages of job security which joining a well-established, large organization can confer is a significant added plus. The secondary and trade school educated and trade unionized industrial working classes have been joined by university graduates in believing that jobs are property. In at least this respect there are no differences between the classes today in British society!

A significant aspect of modern education in Britain is its still remaining class connotations , but now with a different twist; I am submitting that all this is perhaps for the better in the end. The important difference to remember is that the class aspect of education has gone into reverse gear: before 1939 education in Britain was largely determined by class, but since 1945 class has become largely determined by education. Is the idea of 'the perfectability of man' with us again, this time through education? The answer is yes, certainly, since Voltaire. More and better education for all has also shifted job opportunities, from the upper classes and the bourgeois to the working classes; this important development has not yet bestowed significantly greater cultural unity on the different social classes—maybe that too will be realized in due course. At all events, in the 1950s it was still possible for a 'well born, but dullish' and badly or little educated pupil at a minor public school to land a reasonable job in the City or industry. Today, it is well-nigh impossible and no amount of nepotism or patronage will afford much help. The result is an educational elite, upon whom new types of privileges have been conferred, different from and more substantial than the elitism and class privileges conferred on individuals by kinship or even wealth in earlier days. However, if the new elite, gaining a good education, cannot bring themselves to start new firms, what is the outlook for industrial and business dynamism in Britain? The entrepreneurial role will have to be carried on: but on the evidence so far, this task will be assumed in the future, as it was in the past, by the less highly but by now somewhat better educated and less job-seduced offspring of whatever class—my guess is probably still mainly from the working class. Such a manner of self-selection has, perhaps, proved reasonably satisfactory in the past, but it carries predictable hazards for the future. The reason is that the relatively less educated and less sophisticated, but aggressive and ambitious young men seeking entrepreneurial outlets for their energies in Britain will, on balance, choose the simpler and not the more sophisticated industrial applications. There have been of course, significant exceptions, as the newly established firms succeeded in the field of computers and other applied sciences. But are they enough? The paradox then emerges that the new, well educated British elite—irrespective of its class origins—will probably continue to be interested in job security, in less strenuous and less risk-taking occupations, than in the rough and tumble of being one's own boss, promising money and success. In their acquired scale of values, money is relegated to rank below certain other considerations. This is interesting when compared with the professed first preference for money by the less well educated but dynamic members of the working class. And herein lies both an enigma and a warning; should the growing number of working-class graduates in the future also come to prefer security to money, come to prefer an employee status to that of the self-employed, one could feel apprehensive about the serious consequences of the contagion of latter-day middle-class affectations about hard work, profit and money having been passed on to the working class. This would be little short of disaster for the prosperous future of industrial Britain.

Education in Britain has not been seen as an important force for forging an industrial culture between classes which, in turn, could bestow greater social cohesion. The social divergences which are said to arise by being educated at public schools as opposed to at state schools are perhaps less significant compared with the content of the teaching in their respective schools. For it would be unwise to nurture the old-fashioned belief that any particular type of school has all the educational angels on its side. Schools still have wide discretion in setting their curricula, not all of them uniformly sensible; but with the introduction of a minimum central core curriculum, adequate knowledge for all is made possible in basic subjects. Some schools (and higher educational establishments as well) have put emphasis on marginal studies and neglected the importance of basics; perhaps they have put more emphasis on teaching the XYZs of knowledge rather than its ABCs—hence the number of illiterates in Britain, suggested to be 2.5 million, may not be far off the mark! As for innumeracy, three out of ten adults cannot do simple subtraction or division. Many schools are offering inadequate and unsuccessful teaching methods, sometimes by an inadequately qualified or trained staff. A badly structured school curriculum, without some emphasis on the requirements of the market place, and without satisfying the educational needs of the modern world creates a hazard for the future for student' careers. Yet, too many school leavers remain unequipped for an adult world since they do not possess the basic skills for the tasks required at work. By the very inadequacy of the curriculum in some secondary schools, and the often shoddy way of teaching, many a young school leaver's employment opportunities have been impaired.

Secondary school students would do well to study one or two subjects which would heighten the area of common understanding of subjects or ideas—comprising a cultural heritage of sorts. Artificially induced differences in secondary education subjects do not bestow on its recipients much 'diversity'—a term greatly cherished by the devotees of 'character development' at, what seems to be, the cost of imparting knowledge. This is where more recently some of the public schools have fallen short of the ideal. In their mid-nineteenth-century role, they were the vehicle of social mobility; they taught the trader's son the basics and the ways of a gentleman by enabling these 'parvenus' to rub shoulders with disinherited younger sons. Today, most public schools are not notable as agents of social change, and they survive in the minds of their scholastic adversaries as major class shibboleths. This is unjust, but the curriculum in some of them is certainly not going to catapult their pupils into the fourth quarter of the twentieth century with much zest!

The strength of the American and, to a lesser extent, of the European industrial culture is rooted partly in a mandatory, common curriculum for secondary schools and, partly, in the fact that more of their secondary school leavers go on to some type of institution of higher learning or to a recognized course at a trade school. Pupils at secondary schools in the United States or Europe are being instructed uniformly in basics, hence their better understanding of communal values and objectives. Pupils of all classes have many interests in common—the more uniform usage of the everyday language for instance; unlike in Britain, no revealing, differentiated class accents are cultivated or aped at school. No wonder the foreman and the company president have much more to say to each other, have much more in common with each other and understand each other better in the United States or in Germany than in Britain. A common language does not divide them; it still often separates us. The class element is ever-green in such a social-educational setting.

I would go so far as to suggest that cultural unity, class harmony and economic need will be better served by more and better uniform secondary education than perhaps by further expanding the number enrolled in institutions of higher learning. It is curious to reflect on the British recipe for improvement in output or quality in education. This recipe is ritualistically associated with the cry for more—more investment and more resources; when it comes to education the cry is always for more teachers, better classrooms, more open spaces; when it comes to industry, better tools, more up-to-date machines and more purpose-built factories. To improve education or industrial output, hoped for fulfilment always involves spending more money—and somebody else's (e.g. the state's by way of subsidies etc.) for preference. Yet, much can be achieved quickly, and without squandering extra money, simply by better utilization of existing facilities and resources. What is required is 'thinking to some purpose," to juxtapose functions or duties; in the case of schools, offering more intensive courses, changing textbooks or raising standards of teaching, could bring great improvements. In industry, machinery should be more intensively utilized. Much the same stock of capital equipment is available to the British and the German worker, much the same percentage of national income is spent on research but the output of the latter is substantially higher on account of superior utilization of plant machinery and better use of resources. Adult education facilities for trade unionists, for shop stewards, for instance, could be further explored by offering courses in business, some of these, perhaps, organized by the trade unions themselves. This would help workers to understand the business world at a level different from the one in which they work week in week out! A scheme to offer industrial employees more easily accessible education about business would be at least as important as turning out more graduates from Ruskin College, Oxford writing meaningful essays about the Taff Vale Decision many decades ago. To aid Britain's industrial future, educational improvements are more urgently needed at the secondary school and trade school level than at higher education levels. It is a matter of opinion; but it has been suggested that university education in Britain has become over-dimensioned by the Robbins agenda. The urgency in the 1990s is for more vocational courses and more business education below university level. For the accelerated progress of British business, for catching up in technology and in organization, for reducing employer versus union, or inter-union disputes, more deliberate educational objectives are necessary. More information in secondary school about money, industry, national finances, investments, would help create better understanding between employers and workers and their unions; a better understanding of the commercial world might also nurture a cadre of trade union officials with a better comprehension of their members' and their employers' long term objectives, beyond the immediacies of wage negotiations. To aid industrial progress the need for better educated, more knowledgeable and understanding trade-union hierarchy cannot be over-stressed. The existence of an education gap at the union level which needs to be filled was shown at the examination of candidates for appointment of general secretary to the Baker's Union in 1980. The president and the acting general secretary of the Bakers were among the candidates failing this examination because, *inter alia*, they could not calculate '5 per cent of 950'; to the question 'how much does the union spend on benefits annually?' one of the candidates would have bankrupted the union—his answer was in excess of the union's annual income. Numeracy has always been a weak point throughout the British primary and secondary education systems, yet the demand for accountants shows how much such skills are rewarded. Also, if education in secondary schools were a little more competitive, pupils would learn about good and not-so-good performance while still young—an effort partially suppressed nowadays in aid of egalitarianism.

Research—a new subculture of escape?

By contrast to the moonlighter or the entrepreneur, the educated elite still affects to disdain money—luxuriating in this cultural apartheid—and in the process frequently developing anti-business posturings. This upper-class affectation, for that is what it is, spills over into this elite's occupational preferences—and it's eager pursuit of employment in non-scientific research or in research-related activities in business reflects that affectation in seeking employment. It is suggested that research is an activity in which class attitudes to money and, hence, directly to business, register clearly. The propensity of many of the educated elite to pursue research in or out of the academies as a favourite occupation may well have no more positive motive than to stay aloof from the stigma of money-making. This is particularly relevant to research jobs in industry where the opportunities for high pay remain untainted with business in the employee's mind. To use the modern idiom for alibis—no guilt by association! Lord Rutherford is said to have remarked after his first successful experiment in splitting the atom at the Cavendish Laboratories in Cambridge, that it was a great day for scientific research, particularly as he saw 'no conceivable practical advantage in it to anyone'! This could be apocryphal—at least, I would like to believe it is—but the frequent repetition of this story and the all too whimsical emphasis on the absence of a profit motive convey a veiled anti-business, anti-money attitude, in this instance sanctified by one of the giants of science. But not all scientists are Rutherfords who apart from being a great discoverer also had a shrewd idea of the utility of purposeful research for the advancement and improvement of industry.

Because of the achievements of Britain's notable scientists whose successful experiments laid the foundations of much of modern industry, there is also a spin-off 'respectability' alibi in research—and if there is anything the middle class hanker after, it is a respectability alibi. Research of all kinds—from scientific to advertising—has become a 'recognizably useful pursuit' and in the universities an increasingly 'must' form of occupation. An enlargement of the range of subjects as 'a suitable case' for research has also left its mark on the universities. And, it is said, prospects are less cosy for those university teachers who neglect research as against those who neglect teaching. Academic boards inquire deeply about the research ability of a candidate for an appointment to a faculty in terms of papers and books published. Little attempt is made to ascertain if the candidate can teach—no test is taken—and in any case until recently there has been no recognized source of instruction for teaching as such. Good teachers, just like good prime ministers are born and not made? Luckily, prime ministers don't have to have formal qualifications!

There are other, equally telling reasons why so many candidates want to pursue research; for instance, one may suspect a hidden or not so hidden timidity in the better schooled when faced with the rough and tumble of commercial or industrial life, where performance is regularly monitored and reconciled. Research in business after all, is different from ordinary 'business' in its declared objectives and only more recently has it begun to be subjected more directly to the rigours of a profit and loss account; research is deliberately peering into the unknown, tyring to reveal hidden truths by building on quantifiable and known facts. Because an inquiry into the unknown, into the future, cannot be precise and is usually diffuse and tentative, the researcher is not expected, necessarily, to come up with hard, useful results and readily exploitable propositions; of course it is hoped he will. A significant chunk of all research effort usually turns out unrewarding, leads up blind alleys and resolves nothing. Much of research—particularly outside the natural and mechanical sciences or in medicine—is often couched in loose and woolly terms. The adage about ten economists having eleven opinions has much validity, and the accuracy and precision of economic and social research alike leave something to be desired. Thus, in much (non-scientific) research the results are imprecise; cost-benefit studies are rarely applied to its utility—all of which offer plausible alibis for likely lack of success. Aversion to the hurly-burly of business and preference for non-competitive pursuits such as research have a common ancestor in trying to ward off the social stigma of possible failure, less discernible in non-competitive occupations. This comment in no way denigrates research but indicates why certain persons have a propensity—an alibi perhaps—to engage in certain pursuits. The development end of research is outside this category.

Nor must one overlook the class origins of research workers; they appear, for the greater part to be from the better or well educated middle-middle and upper-middle classes—in contrast to entrepreneurs who stem largely from minorities and the working or lower-middle classes, with only a sprinkling of the aristocracy and the upper-middle class. Thus, as a species of risk-takers, the top and bottom of the social pyramid appear to be more entrepreneurial than the classes sandwiched in between—always with significant exceptions, of course. Apart from the predominantly non-working class origins of researchers, another characteristic prevalent among them is self-protection. Their middle-class respectability hopes to exclude, as argued, significant occupational hazards for fear of possible failure, resulting in loss of face. Could it be that the chances of failure in the real world anaesthetizes some of those who have been particularly successful at passing exams? Perhaps the fewer the exams sat for, the less inhibited the human being in trying out new ideas? Perhaps this is one of the origins of the primitive's courage? And in one way or another, entrepreneurs are primitives—some are even naive; it is their instincts, superimposed on their culture that makes them run.

Some research has become, largely, an end in itself. This applies particularly in large corporations where the existence of a research department confers prestige on the chairman and the board; apart from scientific research, research into economics or markets or advertising contributes little to the prosperity of the firm, but it's results sometimes act as a buffer between the board and the management; or they serve as an alibi for the board before the shareholders for not accepting or rejecting to pursue an idea or course of action. But, let us take another look at non-scientific research; should its fruits bring provable advantages to the firm, the translation of research into reality, the practical application of good research into better, improved or new products or know-how, again does not fall on the researcher but upon the socially less well esteemed ranks of society—the technologist or engineer; and finally, the risk of producing the goods falls on the man who makes the final decision—the businessman. Nevertheless, the researcher in a company may consider himself as a part of the decision-making team, hence he can well find himself in a position of authority as he often reports to top-management. Being considered important is a weighty social ingredient of a researcher's job. I am sure members of Mensa would endorse this contention. No offence intended.

Other attractions of research, apart from its social acceptability and non-competitiveness, are the difficulty of knowing exactly how well or badly the research worker is performing as the work cannot, ordinarily, be judged in immediate terms of financial benefits. For some of its devotees, the largely non-working-class connotation of research work— because research ability assumes a degree of education, hence upper-class allures of superior understanding—is a mark of distinction. There is a latent danger that the educated and self-conscious (petit) bourgeois in the research game may succeed in passing on their values—i.e. prejudices and guilt feelings about money, profits and the virtual absence of their accountability—to the educated, socially ambitious and self-conscious working class; and some of them may well be susceptible to such new, received wisdoms which appear to signify 'good form'—i.e. social embellishment. Is there another alibi here in the making?

Class and culture — the cult of the amateur

A broad definition of the functions of an elite is responsibility for supporting the changing needs and circumstances of society which is one of the preconditions of progress and success, and therefore of the stability of that society. The functions of the medieval elite in serving its community were carefully circumscribed and delineated, and change came only gradually over the centuries to meet new needs, demand, opportunities, threats and challenges. Elites, some hereditary some not, had to learn the necessary skills, be they clerics, merchants, lawgivers, craftsmen, or nobles. When elites no longer performed their allotted or expected functions adequately, or the *raison d'être* of their roles changed, the justification for their continuing importance in their role first declined and later disappeared; in the end, they ceased to be elites. But as there is always a need for elites, new groups replaced them—as the leaders of the state and of its society. Thus, the essence of elitism—which in the past often suffered from almost hereditary rigidity, while nowadays enjoying an almost total lack of it—is to be the fugleman; that is, to show the way, to take risks, offer example and perform well and thereby lead in the development of one's society.

In our professedly democratic age, the majority believes in elitism earned by merit— a meritocracy. But, are today's educated elites serving their society—the industrial society—with the necessary devotion and critical affection? Judged by the long periods of relative failure of a substantial part of British industrial society, irrespective of whether it is publicly or privately owned, this supposition remains unconfirmed. Too many of the educated elites hold themselves strictly outside the industrial culture. Yet it is the adequate performance of that industrial culture which nurtures this elite's living standards. There are several different classes of elites whose connections with the dominant activity of the day—manufacturing industry, or business generally—is non-existent or sadly tenuous, yet these same classes of elites would be the first to claim they are pace setters.

The real sadness about Britain's industrial culture is that its most talented philosophers, most gifted psychologists, or prolific novelists, to mention just a few, have not positioned themselves to assist in the economic or industrial revival of Britain; for the greater part they appear shy of even peripheral involvement with trade and industry. I hasten to disown any types of imposed social realism, a dirigistic obscenity wherever practised; but I do mean motivations for the common good and being aware in some measure of the work of the majority of people. The comfortable life everywhere hinges on the efficiency of the productive sector. Perhaps the envisaged imminence of post-industrial society is diverting creative energies to other, claimed, 'higher' social or occupational ideals; popular among these is an overgrown intellectual concern with distributive justice.

We are witnessing bizarre, twin developments: first, the rise of several elite classes, largely anti-capitalist in upbringing, education and spirit, and only marginally, if at all, motivated to pay even lip-service to an improved economic future, much less to aid it personally, yet certainly wallowing in its material bounties; and second, the rise of an industrial working class, vaguely anti-capitalist in spirit and often hostile in action and not noticeably eager to perform with discipline or enthusiasm. As a direct result of being ostracized by the intellectual elite and sometimes not in harmony with the workers, or their representatives, it is not altogether surprising that one type of elite, called industrial management, feel sometimes dejected; for lack of the appropriate support their productive enterprise fails to achieve what they know is within its reach. Here, then, is an elite which does not appear to have received over-much support from its peer groups, from trend setters from above and, equally, from the industrial working class and its representatives from below. If anyone has ever re-enacted the Labours of Sisyphus it is the elite in industrial management.

Much of class prejudice, and its deliberate or inadvertent cultivation by exaggeration in contemporary Britain seems to have its roots in all but the upper classes; active, class aggro is not part of their history. The upper classes have been resilient and capable of adjusting to fresh realignments of the social or economic forces: this tribute to their elasticity applies both to the old established members and, by precept, to the new recruits to their ranks. Disaffection with other classes appears to be more keenly felt by and among the lower-middle and the working classes, and polarized class consciousness is more discernible between the petit bourgeois and the working class: the curious characteristics of these verdant class differences is that they seem to be a source of enjoyment as well as a source of chagrin. Entrenched class attitudes can and do result in artificial rigidities, causing alienation. In turn, this compounds communication difficulties and brings with it more mutual suspicion, more anxiety and insecurity. The more segregated classes or communities remain from each other, the greater is the area of potential misunderstanding. Ghettos do not engender commonality of interests, they create objects of suspicion, scapegoats and firmly held alibis for personal and collective un-success. The self-congratulating propensities of people living in isolation from others knows no bounds. These are the negative blessings of ignorance.

The position of alienation is not irretrievable. The characteristics, attitudes and posturings of an elite or of any one class may well be softened or improved by constructive conflict and competition with other classes; both will change or bend a little by rubbing up against each other in a more 'open society.' Such co-minglings must be encouraged because contact among individuals between the different classes in Britain's industrial society is not sufficiently fraternal for such interaction to be as fruitful as the potential would allow. The lack of such sustained, amicable, constructive conflict between workers and most bosses—denying to learn about the other's ways and ideas—has predictable, unsatisfactory results. Work styles, views about work, attitudes and modes of living remain largely unexplored on either side—hence, in most workplaces of any size, particularly when a professional management elite is running the firm, the 'gaffers' and the men remain largely unappreciated by each other. Perhaps it is necessary to stress again that as the educational availabilities have not succeeded in introducing much of a common culture with shared objectives, the gap emerging in the schools has every chance of enlargement afterwards in real life. The result is that labour in industry is often restive and invariably suspicious even when giving the appearance of relative calm. This underlying restlessness has been more apparent in recent decades but seems less so since curbing trade union excesses. Class hostilities have become somewhat more muted since the British people have been given to more explicit reflection about the debilitating effects of their divisive posturings and affectations. The social and behavioural class compartmentalization has, on balance, diminished over the years as a result of only one manifestly affluent decade. The real success of the past few years has been largely educational in the cultural sense. The British working class is consciously aware of the 'treason' of so many of their class transferring to the middle classes in all respects—except perhaps in the retention of the fashionable working-class affectations! Rousseau said somewhere that to change the folk-memory of the people the statesman has to will it.

The question to be answered is how can Britain rid herself of these still thickly coated layers of affectation—misconceived clichés of class utterances, presumed superiority, bloody-mindedness—which inflinct injury? To have a better understanding of the underlying class issues between gaffer and worker it is helpful to get rid of the historical undergrowth which muddles a clear, direct approach to it. These areas centre on defensive class attitudes, which help define such differences. The inevitability of natural differences or conflicts of class interest, and their irreconcilability are long cherished concepts; the commitment to irreconcilability can only be described as a present-day affectation even if it once had its roots in sincerely held beliefs. Affectation steeped more in fantasy than in reality may be insubstantial, but difficult to disperse. In the armoury of working-class affectation, the apparent lack of desire to change, to up-grade, to merge from one class to another must still take pride of place. While in general the working class shows a desire for material improvement, the desire for up-grading in spiritual and non-material terms seems still a difficult jump for many to accept. Such a socio-psychological denial is not easy to grasp bearing in mind current-day patterns of consumption characteristics—an important determinant of class. For instance if the well paid working-class family move into a middle-class residential area, stocking their house with a battery of consumer appliances, owning an expensive car, installing double glazing and central heating etc.,—then by outside appearances they have become a middle-class type family. Their middle-classness will be encouraged and cultivated by their neighbours; in such a milieu it will be self-deceptive to remain working-class in mind and disposition, for the conditions and consequences of daily life have ceased to be working-class. Under such circumstances, exaggerated insistence on remaining true to one's original class can make adjustment difficult. A lingering belief that the working class is traditionally exploited, for instance, coupled with the enjoyment of a middle-class standard of living can set up conflicts. It is difficult to reconcile the present with the past. Thus, enjoying but not facing up to the consequences of an improved , changed life style, by rejecting a gradual watering down of existing class bias, the working class protagonist is falsely declaring the non-importance of riches—a mainstream self-deception if there was one. Money has been the principal issue over centuries and some working-class attitudes have been shaped by feelings of deprivation which a change for the better will shift only slowly. In dancing to the music of time, however, we must sometimes change partners. As emphasized, class cleavages have a spiritual as well as material platform, and class characteristics are bound up with the psychology of origins and pride; it may seem perverse to suggest, but the impression remains that class differences are still cherished—although less militantly than in previous times. There would be nothing wrong with that, if pride of achievement were as significant as pride of class in British society.

Class affectation is not a prerogative of the working class. The middle class variety—that of the boss clan—can be even more spectacular—affecting jobs, speech, money or social disposition. The middle-class consider middle-class postures as 'up market', hence to be admired, yet some middle-class attitudes are definitely undesirable. Less attractive middle-class affectations include the cultivation of amateurism, the simulated disdain of money and, arising from it, the cult of, the non-measurable pursuit. If working-class affectations of often false, studied independence —over-exaggerated pride of class, and until now a lack of incentive for general betterment—are weighed against bourgeois clan prejudice, it will be readily appreciated that much progress is still overdue from both sides despite discernible changes in recent years.

Amateurism, of course, has long been a cult of the middles classes modelled on that eighteenth-century gentleman who was well informed about the scientific developments, moral teachings, philosophical discourses and the literary occurrences of his day, who kept in touch with a large circle of friends by writing letters, and unexceptionally was either a successful landowner or farmer, a member of the professions, or a little later, perhaps a highly successful businessman. A major characteristic of the classical amateur was his familiarity—in a few isolated instances he excelled—with all or most of the cultivated pursuits of his day (and this is important) without having had to devote a lifetime and most of his energy to the study of them. Apart from conferring a measure of potted learning on such cognoscenti of the day, amateurism was an educational attainment, a social embellishment at a time when a wide range of surface knowledge was more than adequate to hold one's own in civilized society. Higher education was largely unorganized outside the classical universities, hence expensive, and for the most part accessible only to the well-to-do, that is, the upper classes.

The position today, some 200 years later, is the exact reverse of what was considered adequate education for the pursuit of business and generally for members of a cultivated society. Nowadays specialized knowledge is demanded for the mastery of almost any task and the degree of specialization appears to be on the increase. This trend is not without its hazards. The division of labour—that well ploughed Marxian field which brought in such richly publicized rewards in supposed alienation—applies to everyone in every class, from worker to the manager, from the petit bourgeois to the aristocrat. Specialization has long been the order of the day, and increasingly any man working at almost any level only sees a part, at best a substantial part, of the totality of the organization he serves. But, in general, specialization will allow managers and men to focus successfully on their allotted, limited, objectives in the business organizations —which is what they are supposed to do. A well turned-out graduate may have a chance to become a management trainee in a world-wide firm at the age of twenty-three and devote his working life to serving his firm. Forty-two years later, on retiring at sixty-five, he will know all about, say butter and fats, or all about metals and alloys, but the chances are he will understand precious little about business, as such, or even about the anatomy of his firm and how it works. The smaller the firm the more those working there will understand its dynamics and the nature of its operation. The man who comprehends all aspects of a business is the entrepreneur who started his own firm or has been brought in to put it right. Apart from entrepreneurs and their ilk, most managers have a partial vision of the world of business they inhabit.

A hundred and fifty years ago, when businesses were relatively small and much simpler to run, it was easier to see their fuctioning and purpose and the activities of firms must have been grasped more easily. Not so today, with the development of large and giant firms and their complicated manufacturing, selling and financial organizations. In past decades, even centuries, when the dominant occupations were clerical and governmental, reading and writing were essential tools of the trade. The dominant occupation in the industrialized countries today is no longer government or the church but business, yet little or no instruction is imparted in the schools about it. The largely conceptualized, theoretical notions about business, taught in the economics or commerce curricula of universities amount to little more than sophistries in grasping its essentials. Business schools are endeavouring to fill this vacuum at the top of the educational ladder but a much wider dissemination of knowledge about business is necessary. Curricula planners everywhere please note: the amateur in business today is an anachronism.

Another example of studied amateurism almost atavistic, which has had a bearing on the entire economic mechanism in Britain and on those who operate it, is the unwritten primitivism that men always overcome machines—a noble sentiment which is a variation of an earlier 'effortless superiority' complex. Contemporary epics about man beating the computer and other similar stories, some true no doubt, of replacing computers with simpler mechanisms or dwelling on the initial chaos born of installing a computer in the firm, are particularly relevant; though, I suspect the presence of the David and Goliath syndrome is at work here. A throwback example of the brilliance of amateurs and how they achieved so much with so little almost becomes a national epic in—significantly—an American film made perhaps with an eye on the British box office: *Those Magnificent Men in their Flying Machines*. Another durable and not manifestly beneficial or efficient pursuit of the originally upper-class notion of diffused general competence—another form of amateurism?—lingers on in parts of the world's diplomatic service. Only proconsular notions of infinite superiority and attachment to too much nineteenth-century history could persuade those responsible in the foreign offices of the world for shifting diplomats at shortish regular intervals around the world without good reason. The present is no longer an exclusively proconsular or, in contemporary jargon, 'generalist' age when work expanded to fill the amount of time available and specialist skills were largely unknown; the present is largely a technical age where trade statistics, industrial studies and competence in foreign languages comprise the basic strength of a foreign service. Hence, foreign service officers must seek to ascertain the technical requirements and market demand of foreign countries for goods and services and the nature of domestic and third country competitors. The really important 'generalist' approach in the transaction of political business is no longer invariably the province of ambassadors or even of foreign secretaries but is transacted, instead, between heads of governments on a 'hot line'; with the rise in importance of trade and commerce between countries, embassies today increasingly resemble superior chambers of industry and commerce. Hence, to transfer a highly efficient foreign service officer to Canada with language competence in Chinese, Japanese or Russian after a stint of three years or so in Peking, Tokyo or Moscow—when he is just about to become really useful as a linkman for British business and its Chinese, Japanese or Russian clients—seems like a triumph of an inflexible and antique rule book over common sense. The pursuance of such a staff policy is witness to an unbridled extension of the idea of the 'generalist', the amateur who it is claimed can operate efficiently any post in any country. This is a conceited, wrong-headed attitude and could be a remnant of an era when diplomacy enjoyed a lingua franca and conformed to a recognized pattern and conduct. The diplomat's industrial counterpart would claim that a trained manager can run a corner shop as efficiently as a steel mill. No doubt, there are highly talented members of the boss class who can straddle different industries with ease, but the majority will stick to managing companies whose output of products, structure of markets and pattern of labour relations are familiar. As for the entrepreneur, he may stay with his firm for a lifetime.

Finally, the pervasiveness of this attractive, aristocratic cultural pretension of amateurism among members of the middle and working classes is illustrated by their adopted class disdain of good housekeeping, of valuing effort and of respecting the sums that come out of the counting house. In the nascent industrial age of the mid-eighteenth century such posturings by educated aristocrats did not amount to much: and it could not have survived among the aristocratic-industrial pioneers of the eighteenth century! But for the working class to ape similar attitudes two hundred years later in an interdependent, industrial culture is nothing short of calamity!

Aspiration at work

Is it possible to isolate different approaches to work and to the work place by the working and the middle classes as elements of class difference? Beyond the customary genuflecting to working-class rights and ideologies and the hopeful arrival of a New Jerusalem—by realizing the aims of Marx, Trotsky, Benn, Heffer, or of the Militant Tendency, according to disposition—working-class aspirations give the impression of being short-term. Expectations seem to run to more cash now, a reduction in the standard working week—but not of overtime—and, increasingly important, improvements in working conditions. The primary duty of working-class representatives is to secure increasing collective benefits and recognition for their members. This is a strictly limited vision of the immediate future. Broader horizons of self-improvement for members of the working class, within or without the union movement—demanding better education and training, upgrading skills and imparting new ones, participation in management to help improve the business of the company—do not seem to constitute a widely recognized or consciously realizable part of general working-class aspirations; nor have such ideals been a significant part of trade-union catechism.

Middle-class approaches and aspirations to work differ widely from those of the working class—both individually as well as through their representative organizations. A common middle-class objective—starting in the home—is to improve on education and training, competence and performance. Another revealing difference is that in the boss class—including the self-employed, the professional and the bourgeois generally— the question of reward i.e. the rate for the job, is left mainly to the individual to determine, to bargain and to obtain; for the greater part, pay or rewards are not determined by their professional organizations, if indeed they belong to any. Even in the civil service and in large companies there are grades of payment for the same work with room for manoeuvre. For the working class, negotiations are left to their institutions, the trade unions, and not to individual workers. Another important institutional class difference is that a major plank in the task of middle-class organizations—i.e. institutions—is to be vigilant and to enforce standards of probity, maintain professional standards, demand competence by examination, define and guide professional conduct and keep discipline among their members. Such positive practices as professional associations are designed to offer—a minimum standard of performance by its practitioners—the trade unions have not sought to emulate. The reason may be traced to divergent class approaches to work. The middle class in general wants to supply or offer advice to its clients and serve customers' needs and wishes to offer satisfaction so that they may come back for more. Middle-class survival hinges on testable consumer acceptability for the goods or services offered. The industrial working class, in general, especially its militant members, is not, on the record, intimately concerned with the welfare of the firm, the employer or its customers—as the uncompetitiveness of such a wide range of British-made goods or services offered bears witness. The objective of too many is not how to perform well or better or to greater all round satisfaction but, rather, finding ways of investing tasks with the least personal participation and involvement in energy, effort or thinking. This is not a blanket description, but examples abound to give this assumption validity; a substantial element in working-class thinking still believes that the employer always wishes to exploit workers. How far such an old-fashioned attitude to the employer and hence to work is still widely held is difficult to determine, but such attitudes and approaches are clearly visible. In describing class attitudes in a general, illustrative way, I want to underline the plethora of individual exceptions within all categories in the application of effort to their work. None the less a comparison of the work ethic offered here depicts manifestly contrasting preferences in the approach of the working and middle classes and of their associations to the organization and performance of work.

Working-class employment opportunities, hence attitudes to competition, are both different from and more circumscribed than those of the middle class. Among those without specific discernible skills, knowledge or experience to offer, that is, the unskilled working class, competition remains in a minor key—the element of competition barely exists. At that level of employment there are limited opportunities for competition, for preferment, for excellence, except for pride in the job. It follows, therefore, that the commonplace negative attitude held by the diminishing number of the unskilled industrial working class to its work is not necessarily a perversion—but simply a corollary of the nature of work and the milieu.

Perhaps there are good reasons why strong mutual protectiveness (expressed also in trade unionism), sometimes justified and sometimes mistaken, among those without discernible skills to offer (i.e. much of the unskilled working class) is inward looking and particularly emphasized at the *individual*, social level; while among the highly skilled and highly motivated (i.e. much of the middle class, plus many artisans), solidarity and protectiveness are more emphasized at the professional (or craft) performance level. Taking this idea of a perceptible additional class difference a step further there is no gainsaying that social solidarity between individual trade unionists is likely to be much greater than, to choose examples, among consulting engineers, stonemasons, works managers, chartered accountants, judges or managing directors. Qualities of protectiveness, solidarity or kin feelings differ between social and occupational groups—and these may be inferred to represent different class attitudes. As already suggested, competition among numerous working-class occupations hardly exists, and this is accounted for by the nature of many such occupations as well as because of the developed, mutual protectiveness of fellow workers towards each other. All these impulses lead to a reluctance to outshine the other worker and to the belief that willingness to please the gaffer is a form of sell-out. How different is all this among the middle classes! In most, if not all, middle-class type occupations, individual social protectiveness towards each other hardly exists, and competition for work between individuals is strident. I am not simply arguing that 'life at the top' or 'near the top' is uncomfortable on account of built-in competition, but I would go so far as to suggest that the edge of competition gets gradually sharper with rising job responsibilities. An increase in responsibility also implies an increase in pay, and in the higher echelons of pay, competition is keen and brutal. For those climbing the management ladder in business, competition starts quite early. Here I am thinking of those who are competing for partnerships in professional firms or for preferment in management positions within the corporation. But the corporation or the firm has first to be established—and that is where the entrepreneur comes in. The entrepreneur has none of the 'in-built' social protectiveness which is so characteristic of the classes from which he has traditionally emerged. It could be argued that to become an entrepreneur any semblance of self-protectionism must be first abandoned. Competition between entrepreneurs is axiomatic at all stages in their careers; they compete against each other collectively in all aspects of business, and when they have made good, they compete with each other personally. The price of survival for the successful entrepreneur is unceasing competition.

More culture—less class

What does the future hold for class-conflict ridden Britain? By the continuing fuelling of class differences, in their different ways, all classes share in the responsibility for the incomplete liberation of the nation's energies. While class rifts and disaffections alone are not a complete catalogue of Britain's troubles and tribulations, they are a material ingredient of them. The increasingly polarized, political allegiances of recent years also encourage a social discord; their bitter fruits have affected national purpose. Radicalized ideologies, sustained largely on illusory conflicts of class interests, are still being acted out in gladiatorial displays in the industrial arena; but with the reduced role of the trade unions and their increasingly divergent philosophies towards work and their place in the industrial machine, disparities have declined, confrontation has decreasingly become the norm only a very last resort; reconcilable differences—and differences there must be when two parties are negotiating—though still too often couched in the language of stern invective, have shown moderation. Though durable co-operation between boss and worker is still largely *démodé*, former macho methods have not continued as the chosen alternatives to rational negotiation; and most important, industrial disputes no longer escalate unnecessarily as they did for many years. Such developments are symptomatic of a decline in class rebellion against consensus; by acting out such latter-day anachronisms as self-enervating industrial disputes, until recently neither the worker nor his union have been offering a workable policy for a co-operative approach to the social and economic challenges of Britain's industrial culture. Judged by the continuing if more sporadic turbulance of the labour scene— dissent and discontent are still on the surface in the daily lives of a minority of the working people. However, some of that discontent and militancy has been channelled in recent years into inter-union disputes. Here may lie a problem for the future–the delineation of different aspirations and the interests of different unions. Fastening sights on a successful past offers a safe world-view and tends to reduce the need for remedial action; satisfaction with the past has resulted in developing a new fondness for a neo-Edwardian outlook, almost irrespective of class; the old, comfortable excesses of historicism have become an intellectual opiate, as have, in a less cerebral way, the popularity of old films, of music-hall, and of television serials like 'Upstairs, Downstairs'. Such a backward glance is agreeable as it allows thinking of Britain as an idyllic land—remembering her as she probably never quite was—a country of great pioneers, of mighty industries, of fashion and elegance, a founder and ruler of a great empire, and with endless accumulation of wealth among its people. Though, admittedly, wealth or power are not now as endless as they once were, many want to continue to believe that Britain still can play a significant role in world affairs and continue to have an important say in the comity of nations. This is to believe that British influence *and* power are still supreme. With such lingering thoughts the delusion can easily persist that the crises and difficulties of this country are just passing phases which have always been overcome in the past, if in no better way than by 'muddling through'; the sun is hiding behind the clouds but clear, blue skies are only just around the corner. For almost four decades such escapist thinking has helped to avoid necessary and often unpopular decision-making on a long-term basis, allowing the nation to work out its problems in more settled calm. Because we have not been notably successful in doing just that, we are apprehensive about the future, despite our collective sang froid; but to remedy recurrent conflicts in labour relations or to generate durable enthusiasm in wealth creation, we have been trying for shortcuts instead of thinking more radically and well ahead. In no sphere has the lack of success of a short-term outlook, and the absence of clear-cut longer-term decision-making been more apparent than in trying to establish greater social cohesion—a 'preliminary must' in facing the industrial and economic challenge foisted upon every country by the rest of the world.

It is appropriate to re-emphasize that a more settled and widely accepted relationship between classes and their institutions is a prior condition for a successful political and industrial working partnership. An approach which can help achieve this aim is the evolution of a specific cultural unity between the classes. It is a matter of urgency, therefore, to encourage also the appreciation of Britain's industrial culture—not the literary, not the artistic alone: this industrial culture must become more diffused, thereby becoming the property of all classes. It must encompass those working without as well as within the industrial framework—manual labourers, chartered secretaries, cabinet ministers, social workers, typists and shop superintendents must have a better understanding of Britain's industrial heritage. Working in industry does not automatically inform the worker of his industrial culture—while working outside it ensures his automatic exclusion. While the pursuit of business as the major source of wealth might nowadays be less widely misunderstood, is it also more consciously recognized? A vital role of a dynamic industrial culture is wealth-creation; in post-1945 Britain, this vital role has not been properly recognized, or examined or discussed as an important part of the dialogue between the working and managerial classes, indeed between us all. Perhaps the wealth-creating role has been obscured, but there is every reason for it to be rediscovered now.

The subject of wealth creation has not been much pursued and analysed through the educational process. Having lived in a country of great wealth for many decades—supplemented by an overseas income—the facility for wealth creation has been taken for granted, alas, mistakenly as it turned out. Equally mistakenly, the focus of class interest was and remains concerned not with its creation but with its distribution. Elementary knowledge and experience informs us that efficiency and profitability are vitally necessary for a successful industrial culture–which is at the base of sustained, successful wealth creation. These simple notions have for so long been put on ice that the act of wealth creation only rarely underpins class relationships into a common purpose at or after work. Failure to understand the imperative for wealth creation goes a long way towards explaining the blatant inefficiency of so many British enterprises, privately or publicly owned. For many, trade and industry means only a source of the weekly wage or monthly salary. They are not a central concept to them in the determination of their individual living standards which is also a marker in the collective economic power of a nation.

The result of misunderstanding the importance of the wealth-creating process through industry and trade is that at all social or occupational levels many will refrain from taking an intelligent and purposeful interest in the problem of the business employing them; yet, it is in their power not only to take an interest in but also to improve on it. Some will desist from action because they have been taught that it would only make the boss richer; perhaps the saddest comment on this economic illiteracy is that it is far from being confined to the industrial working class. It also militates for taking an interest in the demand side of business activities alone—such as wages paid and working conditions enjoyed—and not the supply side of the business—output produced, sales generated, invoices paid, and profits earned. Such ingrown beliefs of mistaken self-interest are still fanned by some worker's representatives who continue to believe in a form of primitive class relationship which teaches that hostility against the boss class and taking advantage of it must work to the unions' and the workers' advantage. Of course, such attitudes remain the best ways to perpetuate the 'two nations' concept, and then engage in the luxury to rail against it! But the fault does not lie solely with the working class or their representatives. The capitalists, the bourgeoisie, the boss class have been only rarely aware of the need to explain the implications—moral as well as commercial—of the industrial system to the working class; though it must be realized that not many have a wider appreciation themselves of the industrial culture in which they live. None the less, I consider this a dereliction of their duties as leaders, as spokesmen for their work and their beliefs and as communicators. Nor have many entrepreneurs been gifted in analysing publicly their own important contributions to wealth creation and the industrial culture, or in marketing their own corporate achievements instead of just marketing their products. Their teaching role has not been a manifest cultural success. Some are and remain incredibly gauche at explaining themselves; others wish to keep their role in obscurity; yet others still wish to deny any serious involvement in the wealth-creating process, which is a form of denigrating it. One is, ocasionally, astonished to learn that there are not a few owners and managers in industry who are not, themselves, particularly exhilarated by their own activities or successes. Though members of the boss class, they strive to give the impression of not belonging there—they are timid about their sources of wealth or of associations with business. Some industrialists or businessmen, especially the second or third generation, undoubtedly, would prefer to be engaged in rather more gentlemanly occupations—or such is the impression created. Surely there must be good reasons why such businessmen exhibit a preference for more 'genteel' pursuits?

The lack of enthusiasm of numerous bosses for their own industrial or commercial pursuits is, I suspect, an echo; it is a repeat of the voices of the intellectual elites, the opinion makers. But is it surprising that intellectuals in the academies, in the media, in institutions or in politics take little active interest in the realities of the industrial civilization around them when so many of those engaged in it and working the system have manifestly come to undervalue, some even disdain, their own contributions? Is it possible that to be in alignment with the social snobberies of the age, which understate the importance of industry and the bosses' role in it, some members of the boss class have been acting out an intellectual, now redundant strictly upper-class affectation by undervaluing business as a pursuit? Is this the price extracted by the contemporary chic for conferring acceptability? If so, representatives of the boss-class can only blame themselves for being misunderstood about industrial wealth creation and their honourable role in superintending it.

The majority of opinion-forming intellectual elites in the schools and universities, in government, the institutions and often in the professions have not been much exposed to the pains and pleasures of business; so is it all that surprising they have put business in the isolation ward? Most of the intellectual elites in the professions dealing with business engage in it piecemeal—as advisers on a limited front—on tax, accountancy, law, science, technology, etc. Hence, few of them gain a view of business as a whole, as an integral part of their own culture. There are several reasons for this lack of knowledge, hence interest, in business, but one of the most important, if not manifestly idealized cause is the dismal lack of interest of modern English literature in industry or business. I cannot think of many books of the imagination in which industry or the boss of the company plays a role of focal importance, as opposed to a mere backdrop to events or circumstances. Nor has the entrepreneur himself been a favoured hero in the novel; the bosses' exploits in power or sex—not usually slanted sympathetically—are mentioned from time to time, but that is not quite the same as explaining the 'nimbus' of business! In recent years, there has been a slight rise in interest about businessmen among the younger generation of novelists.

Now take the other side of the business coin, the working man—he has always attracted an immense amount of literary attention. In many of the arts, certainly in literature, the worker has often held the centre of the stage, sometimes as a profound performer, but just as often as an exemplar of soulless exploitation. I have seen a plethora of public statues of statesmen, soldiers, poets, writers, painters, and revolutionaries who made good; I have never seen a public statue of a businessman, erected for the simple purpose of immortalizing his achievement in business; yes, I have seen monuments for his contribution to philanthropy—yet the public benefit in as much as we all live on the profits of businesses. Why no statue? Such a relegation of the capitalist, of industry, of successful effort, such a jaundiced view held by the literary intellectual or the creative artist, offers little choice between Soviet or British social realism. I remember reading Simone Weil, an over-rated French philosopher of the thirties and forties, commenting on her working experience in a factory; she could not comprehend—intellectually I suppose—how a man engaged in dirty, heavy foundry work could sing cheerfully while toiling. She could only perceive the horrors of the workshop and within her framework of understanding, happiness in that pursuit of work and under such conditions was not plausible. Decades if not centuries of accumulation of such maladroit assumptions may account for art and literature being more interested in depicting the misery of toil than the joys of achievement in good performance. Communists disclose a better understanding of economic needs, hence of their industrial objectives. Work, whether manual or mechanical is glorified and so are its workers and managers. The constant glorification of communist industry is the result of 'official' directives not, one assumes, of overwhelming artistic or literary desire. Yet there is no obvious reason why the nobility of work should not be joyfully depicted—with or without directives from politicians. It is amusing to contemplate that while Renaissance artists have painted scribes in untold different postures and showed them as persons of importance, modern painters and sculptors in the West have not discovered much interest in immortalizing his contemporary counterpart, the clerical officer or the shorthand typist, the tax inspector, the auditor or the company secretary. The neglect of particular types of work by artists and intellectuals also reflects their lack of interest in that genre of work. The malaise of educated disdain about industry in Britain runs deep. Two hundred years after the Industrial Revolution, with Britain building up an empire and enriching herself on the output of her industries, industrial culture has not yet passed sufficiently into the bloodstream of general British culture to become of general interest.

Working-class culture on the other hand has long since entered the mainstream of cultural currents in Britain. Strands of working-class culture have been woven into the general culture and some of it has been absorbed by the middle and upper classes. Have the 'two nations' begun to merge into one, spawning numerous related sub-cultures *en route*? It is a sign of the times, and not sheer inadvertence, that Willie Garvin, one of the two major characters in the clever and long popular Modesty Blaise *London Evening Standard* cartoon, is depicted as a U-working class type who has made good but refuses to lose his identity—hence his recognizable working class speech. Willie disports the best kind of working-class shrewdness and strength, physical and moral prowess, which all classes admire and would wish to identify with. Then there is the dress sub-culture of the working class—discarding ties, wearing open-neck shirts and jeans. The widespread adoption of such sartorial habits by all classes exerts a levelling influence on class by leading to greater all round uniformity. But like all traffic, cultural influence of class travels both ways. While, sartorially, the middle classes have tended to dress down to the working class, the more successful and adaptable members of the working class in turn have been increasingly emulating middle-class sartorial habits by dressing up, wearing waistcoats, coloured shirts, and fashionable ties. No wonder the old cloth-cap image is largely memory (it was originally an upper-class head gear), except in working-class political lore or during protest meetings or demonstrations, where such crass transparently manufactured class distinctions are deliberately exhibited.

Working-class traits have evolved for reasons which had validity at a given stage in the past; and while some of them no longer bear much or any relevance to the present, they have been retained as class markers. Their forced retention may well signify a deliberate wish to express class belonging and retain class identity, to hold on to something familiar, perhaps, in a society undergoing rapid change. One such characteristic is the ritual wearing of soiled, tatty and torn overalls while working on a job—in the engineering shop, even more so in service stations, on building sites and road construction. Why this indulgence? Since many manual workers wear clean overalls, there must be a reason why some deliberately keep on wearing soiled ones? Another anachronism is the strict observance of the tea break. I would go as far as to suggest that a well-nigh atavistic insistence on the punctilio for set tea breaks has become a ritual with a triple purpose—first, such an intermittent activity, different from routine, reduces boredom; second, the tea break as such may well be another form of determined class expression; and, third, simplest of all supplementary explanations, it eats into the working time.

What will help overcome class animosities inside and outside industry is the simple realization that for the working class to maintain its dignity, and its improved living standards, it is no longer necessary to assume a militant class stance against the capitalist and the middle classes. Though industrial turbulence still continues, hopeful signs for a more tranquil future are not wanting. Rising working-class incomes for a generation, coupled with supporting social services, and progressive downscaling of income taxes have brought the income of the working class nearer to that of the boss class. Considerable redistribution of incomes has taken place. Differentials of income continue—lower in Britain than in most Western industrial countries and much lower than in Communist countries—and must remain to give weight and reward for education, self-help, effort and risk-taking. Interchange of customs and of code of conduct between classes has always been fluid; but now it is accelerating. Wine drinking, fashionable clothing, foreign holidays, and expensive, centrally heated homes have become part of working-class culture. While at the boss-class level, do-it-yourself home decoration and 'militantly' working wives have become accepted norms.

The forces mentioned so far contributing to a reduction of class hostility have materialistic connotations. But there are other, equally significant pulverizers of class differences—non-materialistic inventions of the industrial culture. Some may consider them as anodynes—but socially they are immensely helpful. The plethora of occupational titles and designations, unleashed on an unsuspecting business world, particularly since the end of the Second World War, are undoubtedly important. Until relatively late in the nineteenth century, there were few titles of authority (as opposed to designations describing skills) on the industrial-commercial scene; there were managers and clerks or masters and men, and a foreman if the organization was substantial enough. Nowadays, hardly any employee fails to merit a designation of some sort, not only on the administrative and clerical sides, but on the manual and supervisory sides too. It could be quite rewarding to write a vocabulary of inflated pharaseology about jobs. Equally, it is difficult to judge if these high-faluting job descriptions have any substance—though some probably do. But let us not get bogged down by 'bourgeois simple-mindedness' in believing that what is unimportant to the 'inner directed' entrepreneur at the top of the heap, cannot be important to others in his organization under him; though none can bestow class, 'the gaffer', the management, can confer designations which enoble status. Thus, titles and designations have a therapeutic effect on dignity and, as I know from practical experience, they have an impact on performance. Reflecting on the value of such designations both to the donor and recipient it is not difficult to comprehend the growing self-importance of the race of professional managers. Management—whose representatives are of mixed origins, but stll mainly working class or artisan—has become a middle-class occupation because some managers have made it their business to emancipate themselves vocationally, many others socially, and a few culturally. The example of their successful transformation is a harbinger of normalizing relationships between those working in industry. Many managers stem either direct from or have had origins in the working class; hence their actual experience or folk memory of working class conditions may have a significant, practical effect in endeavouring to improve the physical and psychological conditions of workers under them as well as propagating the 'good neighbour', democratic attitude of business relationship between managers and employees.

Signs are not lacking that a more general diffusion of industrial culture in Britain is about to gain speed, hence there is a good chance of reducing class conflict on the industrial labour front in the short term. For the present however—and notwithstanding the greater permissiveness nowadays allowed at the workplace, and the enhanced social responsibility assumed and discharged by management in business—I doubt if business or the businessman have ever been less cherished in social esteem than they are today. The business of business has not become more alluring during the late 1960s or in the 1970s, and this can be accounted for largely by political and not by social distortions; however, times are signalling a change. An incipient recognition that boss-class and working-class co-operation is a precondition for preventing Britain from becoming an industrial wasteland is token of an improved relationship. The mutual interests of working and boss classes is being fused more firmly—despite such aberrations as the continuation of unsuccessful, protracted strikes, sit-ins, sporadic militancy, illustrated by flying pickets. It is in difficult business conditions that the qualities of a successful boss class can best be judged and such a testing time is upon us now. A better understanding or appreciation of the boss class, and its objectives, in turn, must also blunt working-class prejudices. If this assumption is valid, the continuing efforts at the coercive proletarianization of Britain by a small minority of dedicated working-class militants and their well-off and often over-educated middle-class leaders, will gradually become redundant.

The continuing radical aim of class militants in widening the cleavage between the classes is unlikely to succeed because the underlying economic or social assumptions for validating such regressive ideas are no longer extant. The working class in Britain is not a 'lumpen proletariat', suffering the exploitation of a grasping upper class, with a single-minded revolutionary devotion to bringing about deeply desired radical changes in society; the working class is not even a homogeneous class any longer with common priorities, identical objectives, shared values and monolithic facade—not even for a week or so each year at the annual union conference. A growing if still hesitant realization of the need for putting an end to compartmentalized class notions in Britain augurs well for more industrial peace, more wealth creation, more co-operation and more success as a nation. The moral and economic failure of imposed elites in dirigiste countries professing but far from practising socialism, underscores the potentially more promising British market economy solution which while improving living standards is also helping to reduce crass class differences; note—not to eliminate them completely, since classes will remain as staging posts of success in the recognition of merit and performance, now more than ever open to all the talents.

Quality of life

Men and women seek and increasingly find agreeable, worth-while occupations, and, if opportunity offered, would work as civil servants, were said to work in the nineteenth century, from 10.00 to 4.00—just like the 'pigeons in Trafalgar Square'. Such are the desired ultimate fruits of living in an industrialized country: but most jobs nowadays leave time for men and women to develop their talents, enjoy learning, explore the world, cultivate the arts and read books; all these plusses come under the omnibus heading of 'the quality of life'; all classes—the middle-class more vocally perhaps—express much condescension about other countries where they believe the quality of life does not equal that of their own.

'Quality of life' is a currently trendy esoteric expression enjoying wide currency among the 'middle-brow' cognoscenti; as a declared attitude towards everyday life, it radiates divisiveness by assuming superior postures about the importance of certain values. It is also one of the current-day smug slogans seeking sanction for a state of affairs by assuming—sometimes erroneously, sometimes not—such values to be more widely shared than they are. However, and to begin with, what is supposed to be the quality of life, must be, at least in part, different for different classes and sharply different for different people in any given community—because incomes, housing conditions, medical facilities, educational preferences, transport conditions, job opportunities and other miscellanea are not uniform but divergent. Horse riding, hunting, country dancing, brambling, javelin throwing, or practising for the pentathlon, are probably outside the urban middle-class intellectual's definition as contributions to his quality of of life. Nor would pursuits such as chamber concerts, pre-Raphaelite paintings, poetry readings, visits to Venice or art galleries be of magnetic appeal to an average sixteen year old working-class lad, apprenticed in the toolroom and deploying his spare time for study at night school, who must be up early enough in the morning to clock in at the factory gates at 7.30 a.m. A country man, in turn, could not comprehend how any middle-class intellectual might enjoy urban life and a noisy town. How come, then, that the quality of life so dear to one should be so totally lost on another? Have we stumbled here on a real cultural gap as divisive as old distinctions of class?

But wait: the quality of life could be described as the spiritual values and material goods we yearn for; this could be amateur dramatics, a mechanical toy like colour television, a racing car, offer of voluntary service, taking a camel ride across the Sahara or spending a night with a sensationally beautiful, voluptuous virgin in Thailand. But whether it is culture or commerce, the possession of goods or the availability of services that we desire—we think of them as constituting our brand of tastes, in fact, our quality of life; we are thinking of images we cherish, material and spiritual. Images are less transient, none the less, and they define shifting values at all times.

It does not demand much of a leap forward in cerebration to suggest that our scale of values is much influenced by our milieu and these in turn are a determinant of class, all of which combines to reflect national attitudes. Our milieu, like our lives, is in part real, in part escapist, and imagery plays an important role in forming it. Thus, our variegated attitudes to class are in different degrees also an expression of these images—the way we see ourselves, our work, our life, or other people's—and they contribute another aspect to the perennial class conundrums. The media, particularly the Sunday papers and their supplements, cultivate a species of supposedly upper-class type escapism in the sense that they carry a good bit of brilliantly produced, sophisticated, fantasy-life advertising, dropping tokens of the unrealistic on the readers' doorstep. White horses galloping through pages of mist, revealing bottles of whisky or expensive wristwatches worn by tanned, macho men best fitted for scuba-diving in exotic places or for driving fast, expensive motor cars and displaying

numerous revealing signs of superiorities; all this revealed—are we
back to encouraging upper-class values again?—with a dash of
English whimsy, the usual cool understatement and an icon or two
thrown in to indicate the 'now' of the message. Then, think of the
wartime dash for freedom epics and tales of heroism, repeatedly
carried by the media—all staples of middle-class fantasy. Whichever
way we turn, some or many of our values are escapist; they flourish
among civil servants probably as much as among entrepreneurs,
clerks or seamen, society is permeated by it. The question is whether
cultivating such a diversity of escapisms—i.e. individualistic
fantasies about the quality of life—might have been a partial cause for
avoiding facing up to divisive differences and attitudes staring at us for
so long? Perhaps we have been anaesthetizing ourselves into an alibi,
wanting to believe that class conflicts were just another form of
fantasy?

Rediscovering money

Pride of class, conferred by types of employment, is another source of
social and occupational sensitivity, tending to bestow class
differences. The image of different types of work—we are back to
images—with their diverse grades of dignity has class implications
sufficiently important and potentially destructive to warrant
mention. Different jobs, and the broad categories within them, have
come to represent degrees of esteem. Aspects of snobbery are involved
in this durably sensitive issue. In the legal profession, in the popular
esteem at least, the barrister is more highly placed in the hierarchy of
occupations than the solicitor—though the latter is usually more
prosperous and contact with a solicitor is more likely than with a
barrister; hence esteem often conferred on members of the Law is
unlikely to be based on personal knowledge or experience; a county
court judge appears to precede in rank a master in chancery yet they
are considered to enjoy parity of esteem in the legal hierarchy. A
barrister's clerk does not rank very highly in the public mind, but
without his activities the bar would suffer a standstill, barristers could
starve and solictors' businesses shrink. In industry, in the public
mind, the position of the chief scientist is undoubtedly considered
more glamorous than that of his managing director, without whose
approval of the research budget the chief scientist and his team would

not have been engaged in the first instance. An upper-middle-class valuation of an occupation may also hinge on its divorce or distance from actual money making. This is a form of inversion of the apocryphal nineteenth-century boss class's attitude to the poor which suggested that there was nothing undesirable about being on the breadline, as long as they also enjoyed being in the fresh air! A barrister's clerk in chambers certainly has a higher income despite his lack of recognized status than any young barrister or a good many old ones; and managing directors excluded from *Who's Who* are invariably much better paid then their boffins, who are often included. But this divorce of the esteem in which a job is held from the income it commands or from its importance in the scheme of things—we are back to it again—is a class affectation; it is a sign of sobriety that such value judgements have not yet been appropriated by the working class who are more dedicated on improving the rate for the job than to being paid in added glamour. Whatever happens elsewhere, inside the factory gates pay determines class!

To become competent at any task and then to progress 'up the ladder' demands application, extended study perhaps and, always, energy. There was a time, not so long ago, when the foreman was God in the factory—he was the backbone of industry. Skilled men graduated to their jobs through apprenticeship plus, often by home study, through evening school. By investing time and effort, thereby acquiring above average skills, they enjoyed their rewards in higher pay. The gap in the pay packet between the skilled and the unskilled worker was significant. The skilled worker enjoyed pride of class over the unskilled—as well as superior pay. Notwithstanding the traditional higher social esteem and the enhanced economic utility extended to those with more deployable skills, the position of the skilled industrial worker *vis-à-vis* the unskilled worker appears to have deteriorated in recent years, both in recognition and in rewards. The differentials—which in plain English, non-trade union parlance means higher pay for higher skills—between the skilled and unskilled have shrunk probably due to the fashionable political exaggerations of equality in the 1960s and 1970s. The end-product of such generosity to the unskilled caused—a good example—a decline in the number of apprentices striving to become skilled workers. Such developments contain a warning about the hazards of artificial telescoping of wage differences where higher pay rewards higher skills which, in turn, puts the skilled worker in a higher class. The practical consequences of shrinking differentials—and hence the erosion of status differences on the factory floor—are unfilled vacancies for skilled men in industrial engineering centres through Britain, at a time of still high unemployment. The surrender of private and public enterprise to trade union persuasion and to exhortations of social justice by granting higher 'fairer shares' to the unskilled—unsullied by substantial contribution in return—was bound to recoil. If there has ever been an overworked adjective in today's trendy vocabulary, that word is 'comparability'. For equality to have any meaning in the workplace, as elsewhere, it can only be extended to equals in skills or performance—parity of esteem has to be merited; no extension of compassionate sensibility, forced social egalitarianism or enforced comparability formulae can bestow equality—it must be visibly earned and deserved. Just like the role of gold in an inflatory world, so skills in short supply must be paid for and their rewards upvalued as necessary. Deflating the twin rewards of skills—pay and status—will not call forth the enthusiasm needed for the hard grind to acquire them. It is an intuitive sidelight on the need for qualified apprentices, that a foreign chamber of commerce in Britain has set up its own training courses for training anew for members' companies.

There is a conflict of ideology about the juxtaposition of different skills in the workplace and the price of their skills. Neither the rate for the job nor the status of the work remains the same for ever; the reality must be faced that over a period differing rewards may be paid even for the same work, which in business terms means that supply and demand are not always in equilibrium and —the dreaded words—the market for labour is 'imperfect'. Even the most dirigiste must recognize that occupations can become less or more important or even redundant because the demand for them changes—hence their rewards must also be adjusted accordingly. In fact, the most classless of all mechanisms, the market, will freely determine what rewards any work should carry. That union pressure may influence the market price is another factor. There will always be aristocrats of labour whose high earnings are justified—at chairman or chargehand level. But there are no fixed roles; relative earnings i.e. differentials of either may change, improve or deteriorate. It all depends on demand for specific, easily delineable skills. Take the case of the American, Red Adair, the only man who has been successful in capping oil well head fires. His reported wage in Britain for a few days' work was a hundred times the average wage of an industrial worker for a year! The oil company needing his type of skill could not afford not to employ him!

The apparent distancing from money-making by many of the middle and upper-middle classes—often second or third generation descendants of successful capitalists but no longer with any roots but with possibly a shareholding in productive industry—had a retarding influence by endeavouring to separate job—i.e income—from class. Their disdain—which I term anti-money, but not for a moment anti-wealth—often nurtured in comfortable financial security, has a two-way influence. First, it belittles the focal importance of reward for work, by rejecting money as a gauge of success; and second, by inference, by affecting to diminish incentives, it managed to make money—the reward of work—look vulgar. Fortunately dispositions to earning money and enjoying its fruits are undergoing an apotheosis in the 1980s—to the advantage of national financial health. But let us not forget that decrying money as a valid yardstick of reward has for long been a favourite battle-cry of those wishing to manifest a 'genteel disposition'—the manifest bearer of upper-class values. The hypothetical question frequently posed to high salary earners, in important positions—'would you work any harder if you switched jobs for higher pay?—is supposed to elicit a conditioned, similarly pseudo upper-class answer of a resounding 'no'! Such a negative reply about the role of money would still be judged good form by some today; in real life the exact opposite is true—though, of course, the terms and conditions of pay are not the sole determinants of job desirability. Those who have been asking such questions have not usually been averse to militating for or just accepting inflation-proof pensions, grabbing opportunities for promotion and, given a chance, for changing for better pay in sheltered occupations. None of this would matter much, but affectations of this variety have in the past led to positive downgrading of the dignity of work and put obstacles in the path of workers to feel socially useful and financially satisfied!

A sensible choice of occupation is 'also' guided by potential rewards, though some elegant egalitarians may declare this philosophical stance wholly mercenary. But many of those feigning to ignore 'income' (as a premier consideration in job selection) are manifestly among those who would assiduously shop around to get the best value for their own 'expenditure'. This seems a little contradictory in terms of value judgements. Simulating a disregard for rewards (perhaps in favour of other—class?—factors) is a self-imposed constraint about money inconsistent with intelligent thinking—which attributes different cultural or class values to the demand side (incomes from jobs) as opposed to the supply side (expenditure from earnings) in personal money management. If ever there was a distorted affectation of class values—paying lip-service to this income syndrome is one of its best examples. What would Plato have said about this sort of logic on his way from Syracuse?

Many people seem to have developed both guilt or envy about money, and some do not even consider it as the logical, major culmination of reward. Such thinking is a good illustration of class reflexes, enshrined in the knowledge that in Britain some of the most prestigious and interesting jobs are not all that well paid; it follows that to compensate for lack of sufficient reward in such jobs, the importance of money must be relegated as secondary to the job. This then is a good example of a comparative exercise in class values versus material values. Transposing this contest to the 'social' side, the superiority of non-monetary values is asserted in the scale of snob values by a more ready social acceptability of an untalented hereditary peer to that of a successful industrialist, or chartered accountant. Worse still, the uninformed working class could fall for the long discarded upper-class canard that hard work, good pay and success, in a taxing but not prestigious job are not as desirable as less money in the right sort of desirable job. I remember a young Indian, a fledgling merchant banker who insisted that, after training, he would only join any one of the half-dozen or so 'clubbable banking houses' in the City. What this definition is supposed to mean is probably buried deep in his libido; but, equally probably, he meant those merchant banking houses with a respectable pedigree and not the new if often equally successful but also perhaps more brash firms. This is a good example of firmly bequeathed English, upper middle-class type of occupational snobbery still lurking around and perpetuated by some schools and universities and being passed on to unsuspecting young men; how pervasive such vintage Edwardian snobbery must be for a young Indian to be repeating it in the 1980s.

How many graduates will nowadays contemplate their occupational choices largely in terms of financial rewards on coming down from university? My gut feeling is most of them, and manifestly more today than even a couple of decades ago. All the same, on having acquired their first degrees in the liberal arts how many would contemplate that opening a retail shop, as opposed to entering a profession, may be a smart move so that fifteen years later they might have built up a small chain and become successful entrepreneurs and made a fortune? Not too many, I would think. A liberal arts graduate's choice according to his 'received' occupational catechism would run to non-profit making or a non-exposed 'staff position in a larger firm in business or in a non-participating institution'; becoming an 'economist' in a large organization, appointed 'personal assistant' to the chairman or managing director, signing up as a journalist preferably on a London daily, or taken on as a writer on the BBC; or seek a foreign service appointment or, as an increasingly unattractive last resort, become a teacher. A very few may become yuppies with its attendant risks. I would submit, in a non-snobby way, that none of these acceptable or even desirable occupations are any more or less interesting, exhilarating or boring than that of a skilled shoe salesman—and, being a shoe salesman has the added merit that the job can develop entrepreneurship and hence lead to founding a firm which, if successful, will in turn lead to greater wealth creation, the accumulation of personal capital and greater individual independence. But the gap between the great majority of British university graduates' unflinching choice to join the salariat or the ranks of independent professional firms as against becoming a huckster selling shoes, is still a veritable chasm—induced by actual or assumed social influences, circumstances and prejudices. In making these choices we are back to the assumed aristocratic affectation of disdaining money. Would it not be more realistic to acknowledge the importance of financial rewards as a prime impulse in job selection —as the Americans and the Europeans have done and as the City of London has been practising more recently? The result would be more young people making straightforward occupational choices, unclouded by social mist and esoteric value judgements of class variables. Highest paid jobs would, for the most part, carry the highest status and their attributed class component—where snobbery can easily be converted into a personal subsidy of the job—would, therefore, largely disappear. Those who would seek, in their eyes, the more absorbing, but traditionally less well paid occupations could in the absence of genteel snobberies press for and obtain higher pay; and no hazy prejudices of social desirability would be used as a moral subvention for under-payment in such a job—considered as conspicuous investment in 'class belonging'. Such a shift in occupational values to the American or indeed the Russian pattern—where the same view, too, obtains about prestige and pay going hand-in-hand—would also offer all classes of workers a direct and unclouded view of effort, achievement and reward. The more closely Britain has been approaching a less class-influenced society in the 1980s, the more important monetary rewards have become in relation to the rate for the job. Other outlets are being found for non-monetary satisfactions and rewards.

Nationalism—an antidote to class?

Class, in Britain, exists at many levels and lurks in many corners. I have endeavoured to explain that the subtle and not so subtle differences and insinuations about class are more apparent in this country than in any other comparable Western-type democracy. Several reasons have been advanced for this class-ridden ambiance growing increasingly anachronistic as we are nearing the second millennium. Suggestions abound on how to reduce conflicts of class—open and concealed; undoubted progress has been made to lessen such conflict. But beyond the historical causes of social distortions, I have been seeking other explanations for the tenacity of class feeling in Britain even in the present age, which has so successfully removed the prison bars of the social compartment in other countries. I want to suggest that one of the most weighty reasons for the prevalence and, occasionally, for the intensity of class conflict in Britain can be found in the British variation on the theme of nationalism. For this reason class affectation while diminishing, will retain an innocent allure; and why not?

As already mentioned, nationality is a modern concept invented by the French Revolution. The forces liberated by the revolution under the banner of liberty, equality and fraternity were relatively quickly afterwards assembled for war, conquest, and oppression. A major consequence of the 1789 revolution and the pursuit of wars for glory through Napoleon, was that nations in general conceived the idea of nationality as a form of defence or attack; this happened in France under Napoleon, first of all, and later in the countries he attacked—Prussia which rose in defence of its people to defeat the invader, is an early example. The forces of nationalism were galvanized by the French in the countries they invaded and this, eventually, led to the conscious development of nationalism throughout the world during the nineteenth century. Nationalism has become and will remain perhaps the most important force in modern political history for some time.

Of course, the idea of national belonging, born of the growing cohesion of nationhood, was formed, embryonically, by the evolution of central government in late sixteenth-century England and France. But, while Christianity remained the ruling passion in Europe, and Latin the language of communication, that is until the revolutionary wars in the late eighteenth and early nineteenth centuries, people at large felt themselves belonging to a community that was Christian and European first, dynastic and tribal second, and national—such as Prussian, Austrian, English or Russian—as a remote third.

With Napoleon's European invasions, the French wars of conquest changed all this. In particular, it changed the disposition of the Germans who, first believing in the victory of freedom and humanity, as declared by the revolution, soon found themselves at the receiving end of the French armies plundering their territories as they were marching through them. The numerous and fragmented German states—first dominated by Austria for centuries as the leader of the Holy Roman Empire and after Napoleon by Prussia—were not passionate in their nationalism until the French invasions changed their minds for them; and, just like the French, they too became enamoured of nationalism as a successful means of defence or riposte. In the history of the nineteenth and twentieth centuries the rise of nationalism first in Europe and then elsewhere takes the centre of the stage with its twin—imperialism. Even the Americans were to acknowledge its contagion—in terms loftier than most—not unconnected with their own efforts and success in gaining independence and nationhood by a revolution earlier even than that of the French. Within half a century after the rise of Napoleon, by

1848, nationalism was in full swing in Europe, and in the United States. The idea of nationalism became even stronger in the twentieth century when the rights of small ethnic groups to gain their separate identities proved to be the principal victor at the conference tables at Versailles and Trianon in 1919 and 1920. The problems which such derived concepts of national determinism brought to the fore during the inter-war years did nothing to assuage its strength . The displacement of numerous minorities after the dismemberment of Central and Eastern Europe after the First World War and the rise of Successor states fostered a particularly virulent form of nationalism—i.e. irredentism—with clear revanchist overtones, as manifest by Hitler in Germany and in a different way by Stalin in Russia, Beneš in Czechoslovakia and Admiral Horthy in Hungary. Nationalism brought up-to-date was the real cause of the break-up of two durable, ancient empires—the Austro-Hungarian in 1918 and the British since 1945—after the First and Second World Wars respectively; the march of nationalism continues unabated all the world over, as the rapidly risen membership of the United Nations signifies.

An interesting consequence of nationalism in modern times —witnessed in virulent forms in Russia, Poland, France, Germany and Hungary to mention some of the most notable varieties—is that nationalist sentiment has served as a lightning conductor for moderating and partly dissipating the forces of class hostility; thus it diverted energies, which might have been stoked by class prejudice and social disaffection, to other issues. Hence, issues other than class assumed greater importance, foremost among them being the real or assumed threat by external enemies for the nation. Though class issues in these countries were just as intractable, as crass and as diverse as in Britain—perhaps more so—they did not become as divisive and destructive as they did in Britain. Nationalism, and not class claims the major role in post-1918 European and world politics—except in Britain. This is not to say that some of the revolutions, particularly since 1945, have not had a class bias. It is all the more remarkable, therefore, that the victory of socialism in Russia—said to be the victory of the working class—has not succeeded in delineating and inflaming class differences in other countries even more. Class antagonism during the past few decades seems to have waxed more in Britain than in other lands, yet until quite recently she has been the least Marxist of all developed countries.

What in the years to come may undermine the 'compulsive' desire for nation states, willingly imposed on peoples by nationalism, is that nationalism itself is also beginning to fragment. The increasingly bellicose stance of small ethnic groups, the exploitability of religion and of religious differences, the difference of language and indeed of colour—all these notions augur unfavourably for the future of nationalism as a coagulant of the nation state. Should the hitherto unifying characteristics of nationalism decline, the likelihood of social and class issues coming to the fore more strongly in countries experiencing such a shift is very real. The result will be a further fragmentation of the nation state into smaller component parts.

Political systems have changed in the recent past in Germany, France, Hungary, Poland and Russia, to mention some of the more important European lands: but, however vicious political infighting may have been to change these systems—representing as always a measure of class interest—and however pressing the social issues awaiting resolution, the divisive nature of neither compares with the compensating, cohesive qualities of their nationalism, which allows everyone to focus on an urgent common objective. All this is a long way from the British experience. Britain is an old country—long untouched by foreign invasions—whose national figure, not surprisingly, is not a fighting hero of legend, a king or the mythical founder of the nation, but the 'gentleman'. Being cut off from land by a strip of water, the British are not well positioned to imagine what it is like being involved most of the time with real enemies on the other side of the border—a recurring experience for the continental countries.

The experience of invasions and wars had welded nationalism to the folk memory of the European people long before the twentieth century legitimized class wars, and emphasized class differences more starkly. Not so in England; naked nationalism is not and has never been a great, persistent force —though the English are patriots and are known to be jingoists on occasions. Patriotism is a much older and more civilized trait than nationalism. It means, of course, a love of country, celebrating the kind of feeling which must have prompted George Bowes in the 1740s to build a column to British

Liberty in Co. Durham—the mid-eighteenth century having been a period of exuberant patriotism, of 'God Save the King' and 'Rule Britannia'.

Nationalism in Britain is certainly not strong enough now to inject a lasting dose of such adrenalin into all classes, thus exhorting them to make common cause at home in matters of substantial importance—and certainly not in peacetime. There was a substantial element of national unity in response to the Falkland episode—but this was the result of an attack on British sovereignty—i.e. a small defensive war. Not many years after the First World War, the elite of Britain's universities became so nationalistically *déraciné* that some turned against their country by identifying with the policies of Hitlerite Germany, the aggressor on the European scene. Others became so terrified by the insidious nature of fascism and the apparent failure of capitalism at the time that they deserted democracy and became communists. It did not occur to many of the intellectual opinion formers in pre-war Britain that it was possible to be anti-fascist without having to become a communist. These then were two polarized indications of the British and, more particularly, of the English way of thinking. Such thinking plumped for imported political fashions more than for developing national unity. The political polarization which has come to exacerbate class differences increasingly during the last forty years confirms a remarkable national propensity for vindicating new divisive orthodoxies, as opposed to taking joint action in the national interest.

The same type of disdain of patriotism was brought to the fore more recently by the Blunt spy affair. Though the high cost of treachery was fully understood, few condemned him for having been a dangerous spy and recruiting agent for the Soviets. Most people judged Blunt as a man, who may have expiated his sins, and not as the traitor setting a bad example to the young and one whose activites may have cost many British lives. There was no nationalistic outburst—save one or two isolated instances—about his anti-nation activities, spread over so many years. One need not wonder long about the likely reaction of the French or of other Europeans or even Americans to such revelations as those to which we have been entertained about Blunt. I am not making value judgements or expressing relative preferences, just stating the difference in nationalistic reactions.

The Scots, the Welsh and the Irish tend to think of themselves more in national terms than do the English, though this has not blunted their typically British class feelings. A explanation may be that the English have been the dominant nationality in the British Isles, the state-composing element in modern times—interestingly enough, the original colonizers. The idea that stirrings of national unity in the face of great danger stifles class conflict even in Britain, is underlined by a marginally improved relationship between the working and other classes during the wars. The hatchet of class conflict was largely put out of sight, but not buried, between 1939 and 1945—a period when not a few of the best books and films had a happily mixed class flavour. The suspension of much class hatred in the face of common danger was buttressed by the necessity of common sacrifices—equal shares in misery—and shared experience of hazards, defeats and victories. Were these the alibis needed for galvanizing the people? And the notion and reality of equality of sacrifice were competently carried out by the government by the proper allocation of resources during the war—and for a time afterwards. Perhaps the British are partial to this kind of egalitarianism? Or perhaps they pay only lip-service to it and remember the period as one of those romantic interludes. Though after 1945 peacetime governments continued their insistence on 'fair' distribution for a time, this gesture did not materially contribute to a decline of class friction—if anything the class war was exacerbated after the immediate post-war euphoria had died down.

Conclusion

What is the outlook for greater social cohesion in Britain and can it be realized without the opium of emerging nationalism? There has been, for instance, a short-term rise in national togetherness for a section of the British people as a counter-sentiment to the Common Market. In a direct sense, the enmity created by belonging to the EC has given rise to mild shades of nationalism. The successful Falklands expedition commanded nation-wide support, transgressing class or politics. At that time, unity of national purpose was momentarily restored. Such feelings are unlikely to be durable, however, so I do not think we can forecast a rise in nationalism, to serve as a tranquillizer for the British socio-occupational scene. No, we must evolve our own brand of togetherness, without the claustrophobic compulsion of pressing external enemies!

We are in the process of discovering that while in Britain we have had much class affectation and friction in the past, there has been no radical class confrontation—and that any such confrontation soon collapsed. There have been attempts more recently to exploit class differences and endeavouring to radicalize and to polarize them through the instrument of politics. None of these attempts will prove durable or successful as a more educated and increasingly sophisticated working class has a better understanding of Britain's real problems, and as partners join hands with the boss class. This is exactly what has happened in Britain during an unprecedented period of unemployment and inflation in the 1970s and 1980s. The boss class has not run away from confronting organized labour with rational and telling practical and intellectual arguments resulting, in the end, in determined action—because in any circumstances and in all places and at all times somebody must be boss. The important corollary to giving orders is not only that they are being given, but also that they are seen to be in the general interest. The boss class in Britain has acquired that great working class vote winner—a healthy capacity for indignation. The causes of friction have been brought into the open. Friction between workers and bosses will be better resolved if capitalists went out of their way to explain their position. In recent years, capitalists have been a little better at this task and as a result, the artificially inflated working-class hostility against 'the system' reaching its high water mark between the mid-1960s and late 1970s, shows distinct signs of receding.

What would be remarkable is discovering a novel British solution to reconciling class differences or animosities—many real, some imaginary—without external pressures, such as wars or, still worse, defeats. Improved co-operation between the working class and the boss-class will, I hope, be ensured not by threat of starvation as with the Germans after 1945 or by rabid nationalism, imperialism and civil war as in the USSR, especially after 1935, but rather as in the United States by wide ranging internal political debate followed by appropriate action 'between consenting adults' irrespective of class.

Of course, this is one possible scenario, where the British gradually shift their attitudes to class—and class in this ultimate context must be viewed as a comprehensive notion of a way of life. It is also possible that nothing of the sort will happen, in which case we shall continue in our bumbling way to live out our lives until there is enough dissatisfaction for a social explosion to occur—the outcome of which remains unpredictable.

There is yet another scenario, perhaps even more likely, that our EC partners will themselves become enervated and class-ridden by their new security from external attack. These nations in an eventual United States of Europe will gradually forget about nationalism and following this line of normal progression they may rediscover and re-embrace class, involuntarily perhaps, as a necessary source of conflict. If this state of affairs comes about, we have nothing to worry about any longer. We shall have succeeded in exporting the British class disease; it has prospects and will travel!

ON MANNERS AND CIVILITY

Books on manners do not seem to be much in vogue nowadays—yet, to suggest they are superfluous would be a bold inference. Excepting Norbert Elias's *The Civilising Process—The History of Manners*, a monumental study on the history of civilization, published in English translation in 1976, I cannot remember any book in recent years dedicated to an 'intellectual' discourse on the manifestation of manners, their impact on everyday life and shifts in their importance and meaning. Discourses on manners, how to behave and to conduct oneself in different situations and how to acquire courteous ways, have a long history. Such writings can be traced as far back as the twelfth and thirteenth centuries, among them Hugh St Victor's (one of the schools which founded scholasticism) *De Institutione Novitiarum*, published in 1141, and, a hundred years later, Johannes von Garland's *Morale Screarium* in 1241. Even a saintly fourteenth-century mystic like Meister Eckhart had distinct views on appropriate manners; he is quoted as suggesting to 'avoid especially anything remarkable whether in dress, or food or speech, high flown language . . . eccentric gestures which serve no useful purpose. But all singular behaviour is not forbidden thee, far from it. Many a time and with many people one must take an independent line. An extraordinary person will do extraordinary things very often and in various ways'; Eckhart was certainly celebrated by contemporaries and his writings enjoyed much acclaim. Straddling the fifteenth and sixteenth centuries, Baldesar Castiglione, in the service of the Duke of Urbino, wrote his celebrated book on manners *Libro del Cortegiane*. Translated as *The Courtier*, the book had immense vogue throughout Europe, and it dealt with etiquette, social problems and intellectual issues. Castiglione foreshadowed the sixteenth-century humanists and Sir Philip Sidney, considered a model of Renaissance chivalry, was said to have been much affected by his writings. Another Englishman, Francis Bacon, also had the wisdom to impart on manners, but the English intellectual contribution to this subject has not been particularly notable—then as now.

However the first highly popular and widely-read book on manners was published during the late Renaissance, in 1530. That was the year in which Erasmus of Rotterdam, the outstanding humanist of his age published *De Civilitate Morum Puerilium*, a guidebook on manners and civility in children. Erasmus's text 'lived' for over two centuries as a source of enlightenment on manners and it is reputed to have gone into 130 editions and been translated into several major European languages—including English. The success of the book was due not only to the outstanding and durable moral authority of its author but, equally, to the rising importance attributed to the subject of manners. What perhaps also deserves approbation is that while Erasmus was recognized as a leading man of learning of his age, he did not consider it too trivial or frivolous to write on manners—a subject which current-day sages have, apparently, contemplated with little interest or affection. Education, aimed at general improvement—including manners—was a cherished objective in the sixteenth century and vigorously disseminated. An early legacy of the Reformation was the encouragement of the spirit of inquiry—even common soldiers were exhorted to improvement, and in *Euchiridion Militis Christiani*, Erasmus again offers them advice.

Since the late nineteenth century, several notable attempts have been made by Americans in publishing primers designed to instruct, supposedly, aspiring or extant upper-class devotees of the Social Register about 'practical' good form: Miss Emily Post's *Etiquette*, a practical guide to social behaviour published in 1922, enjoying its twelfth edition by 1969, was and remains widely acclaimed; she wrote copiously, particularly for the American woman; *The Personality of the House* was another of her efforts at good taste. Writing in America at the turn of the last century, Thorstein Veblen discussed manners as ceremonial attributes of the leisure class, as devices invented by the upper classes who then inveigle others to conform to them. This would give hostage to the notion that good manners are imposed—rather than as many believe, emulated by osmosis. In *The Theory of The Leisure*

Class, a classic of its kind, Veblen may be right in suggesting that manners are held higher 'in the esteem of men during the stage of culture at which conspicuous leisure has the greater virtue . . . than at a later stage of cultural development'. To put simply, he suggests that 'manners have deteriorated as society has receded from the patriarchal stage'. Certainly, the ceremonial content of manners has become thinner which has syncopated their use—in many instances for the better. In nineteenth-century America, *The McGuffey Reader* was indispensable for the young; and the notion that one cannot start learning too early is proved by an amusing but helpful mid-twentieth-century booklet *Tiffany's Table Manners for Teenagers*, also published in New York, in 1961 by a former president of that famous store and which enjoyed its seventh reprint in 1964. One of the most insightful commentaries on American manners was written in 1840 by Alexi de Tocqueville in his second volume of *Democracy in America*. American influence on manners has even invaded Britain; a new edition of Debrett's *Etiquette and Modern Manners*, published in 1981—a widely respected arbiter of good form—is in fact edited by an American. She tells us in refreshingly unstultified good style how to accommodate those unmarried guests, how to announce births in one-parent families, and instructs hostesses on how to steer dinner table conversation. We should betray no surprise when we find an American instructing the British at such proprieties. Americans—some might find this surprising—are very polite to each other, because it is one of their praiseworthy 'social compulsives'; hence their civility to each other is considerable. Deliberate bloody-mindedness and studied bad manners, English specialities since the nineteen-sixties and further refined in the eighties, are not among the cherished national sports in America. I hasten to point out that all published efforts to lubricate social intercourse should be considered as admirable attempts to carry on a tradition of civility and politeness or to examine reasons for the need for good manners. Any improvement in day-to-day relationships, whether this enshrines courtesies towards one another by greater civility or ways of conducting ourselves by an improvement in manners, must be and should be welcome.

At the other extreme from *Debrett*, the impact of the machine on the manners of a mature industrial civilization should, too, be a critical subject for study—after all, we are living in an increasingly scientifically oriented industrial society; unsurprising that one of the most important observations in modern times on this phenomenon on manners and industry should have issued from yet another American. With standardization, batch production, and mass production in factories and workshops, with the omnipresence of the machine in our mechanical epoch, a revealing viewpoint on manners was put forward by Lewis Mumford in his *Technics and Civilization* in the 1930s. He contemplated that 'Without standardization, without repetition, without the neutralizing effect of habit, our mechanical environment might well, by reason of its tempo and its continuous impact, be too formidable: in departments which have not been sufficiently simplified, it exceeds the limit of toleration. The machine has thus, in its mechanical manifestations, something of the same effect that a conventional code of manners has in social intercourse: it removes the strain of contact and adjustment. The standardization of manners is a psychological shock-absorber: it permits intercourse between persons and groups to take place without the preliminary exploration and understanding that are requisite for an ultimate adjustment.' Again alas, the new agreeable role of the machine envisaged by Mumford has not crystallized. Alas, the machine has not been a great unifier by inventing and harmonizing a code of conduct because individual machines are increasingly replaced quite rapidly, and operatives may be shunted to different machines too frequently before they become sufficiently familiar with them. It could be argued that the pace of change is too rapid; operatives no longer work at a specific task or one specific machine in the same way for very long—at least long enough to develop 'attitudes' which could translate themselves into communicable—and agreeable—manners. Instead, we have evolved new brands of unmannerliness among which latter-day Luddism is one and football hooliganism another form of divisive behaviour. This attitude, again, applies more in some classes, communities and countries than in others.

However, what I am hoping to show, and not much more is claimed, is the impact of manners as a personal expression, and civility as public conduct, between people and groups respectively. Such conventions as have developed over time are an important part of the day-to-day social or occupational intercourse; most of these can be conveniently grouped under the omnibus expression of 'manners'. Hence, manners recognized by a *coterie* serve as an alibi for extending recognition, acceptability, on comaradeship according to social positioning. A useful consideration of manners from my vantage point may include two aspects of the subject: first, an analysis of certain current-day practices—actions and reactions which tell us a great deal about ourselves as people; and, second, an examination of changes in manners over a period—that is changes in their application when passed on by one class to another. The number of different ways of looking at the importance of shifts in manners is legion. Perhaps the only observation I wish to make in this respect is a rider, inasmuch as no one is responsible for the use to which manners of a *coterie* or class or community may be put subsequently by its other users. Manners, like ideas, have legs!

Britain is rich in literature about manners; the reason for this may be found, partially, in the long history of the court, strongly entrenched in the affections of the people, and of a durable and renewable aristocracy which transmitted courtly values and conduct, democratizing them en route; that's why the rising middle classes in the nineteenth century found it far from difficult to adopt and share them. The main reason, however, for this abundance of written sources on manners has been the generous supply of moralists, particularly in Victorian times, but also in the preceding century: for moralists are dissecters of and commentators on manners. Moralists and novelists delivered themselves on this subject—as reflected in their novels and tracts. For most of the nineteenth century, technical and economic progress and social changes were rapid—for comparison, probably as swift as the changes occuring in Britain in the 1980s. All changes lead to the mutation of manners and tracing them allows glimpses into a society in transition. In a state of flux, traditional morality is sometimes under siege and contemporary manners mirror this defiance of tradition.

Good conduct, good style, good appearance are virtuous in themselves, as Lord Chesterfield insisted in his *Letters to his Son* in 1774—illegitimate alas,—when he wrote to him about how to enter the fashionable world in which, he insisted, manners counted for more than morals. Anthony Trollope was a keen observer of manners, and his Barsetshire novels are a microcosm of mid-Victorian society at the middle and upper reaches. His mother Frances Trollope examined the difference in manners between the English and the Americans early in the nineteenth century—a continuing source of interest, charm and sometimes embarrassment. Reading the *Domestic Manners of the Americans*, published in 1832, one becomes aware not only of transatlantic conduct a century and a half ago but can, too, gauge the immensity of change since then. Mrs Trollope remarks of men and women not supping together in American society 'as gentlemen liked it better this way'. The movement from a patriarchal to a matriarchal society in the United States with its attendant change in manners has in such and in other aspects been dramatic; after all, America has been transformed into a womens' world perhaps more than any other land! Emily Eden contrasts the manners of a dying squirearchy in England with those of business in *The Semi Detached House* (published in 1860 but written 30 years earlier) and her anti-business, anti-rational, anti-semitic comments are not untypical of the morals and manners of her class and period. Her narrative describing the erosion in the cohesion of the 'establishment' classes and commenting on the upwardly mobile, thrusting, primitives are filled with nostalgia—a potent force in people and classes involutarily descending the social pyramid.

From Mrs Beeton to Disraeli and from Matthew Arnold to George Bernard Shaw to James Joyce, hosts of writers in England commented on manners and the civilities. In the twentieth century members of the Bloomsbury Group exerted a strong, if not particularly durable, influence on manners, not so much for what they espoused but mainly because of their established social position—they were well-off, well connected and very sure of their values. Virginia and Leonard Woolf, Clive and Vanessa Bell, Roger Fry, Duncan Grant, Lytton Strachey, Desmond McCarthy, John Maynard Keynes and E. M. Forster exuded social complacency—their insularity, over-enlarged self esteem and snobbism enjoyed a vogue until just before the Second World War. Their influence on morality—hence on manners—might have been significant in the roaring 20s, which did reflect their hedonism and self-love.

Undoubtedly the most influential book on manners in recent years was published by Nancy Mitford; in *Noblesse Oblige* she invents the U and non-U concepts as measurements of good or indifferent conduct. Not so long ago such rights and wrongs were expressed as 'done and not done' but the U concept has brought it into sharper focus and made it more readily understandable. But like all good books about manners they are particularly relevant for the times in which they have been written. Such a limitation of relevance is even more apropos in today's fast changing world than perhaps in any previous times—except at a time of successful revolutions which impose new manners instead of allowing them to evolve gradually.

Books on manners have in recent decades become more rapidly out-dated; no wonder the only remaining source in general use, I suspect, is the Ten Commandments, which most of us take with mother's milk—not that absorption through the nipple has, on the record, made it all that effective. Again, many of us are aware directly or vicariously—perhaps depending on age and circumstance—that 'it was not always like this'. Upbringing at home, instruction at school, and the social constraints imposed by milieu taught the basics, and adult life at work or away from home further shaped conduct according to circumstance. Being aware of and adhering to some sort of recognizable standard form of manners is always useful for easier communication and for better understanding; in the more 'structured' past, adherence to recognizable forms was more urgent and necessary. Former generations have published printed works containing instruction on manners, some of them all-embracing social brail—a recognition of their importance. 'Acceptable' good manners were acknowledged as part of the necessary bag and baggage in qualifying for a better station in life. Until relatively recently—perhaps only a generation or two ago—it was not beyond the aspirations of the less tutored to want to learn about good manners so as to conduct themselves more like their betters; or, for the better educated and courtly to leaf through a checklist spotting means of betterment. Improvement in general, was a recognizable and cherished idea and one approach to individual progress and indeed to preferment was an improvement in manners, and, in its public multiplier, civility.

To diagnose a lack of contemporary interest in manners —studying and comparing them, as opposed to passing superficial or sometimes derogatory comments about them—is not difficult. This is not a criticism of the times nor of the manners of the times in which the social scene is being played out; it is just a statement of fact. Without heavy-handed and subjective value judgement and without an authoritative stance, it is still possible to suggest that though 'traditional' good manners—reflecting the respect of one person for another (humanism?)—largely survive as part of our tolerant culture, they have not been embellished. Civility, *per contra*, has been on the retreat. It is difficult to be categorical, but a measured decline in respect and in courtesy has been a particular corollary of the post-1945 period—the years during which Britain went through the turmoil of a lengthy and inevitably confused social upheaval which may be described as the latter part of the British revolution. Perhaps this discernible lapse in traditional courtesies is only a phase. A higher degree of individual impatience with certain aspects of life, such as a speeding up of technical achievement but not of political fulfilment; or greater opportunities for misunderstanding between people on account of widening polarizations and their increasingly radical expression—these are but two developments conditioning manners and civility; conflicts may also have arisen from more people being in contact with more people (the inevitable residue of greater all round mobility), many different from each other, some away from their own locality and with a differentiated background or cultural pattern. But whatever these newly enjoyed problems, many of which stem from success, particularly since the Second World War, these bear no resemblance to Talleyrand's lament after the French Revolution that those who had not lived under the ancient regime had no comprehension of the '*douceur de la vie*'. Pre-1939 England was never like that!

Manners—a consensus about values

One is tempted to think it a little bizzare that, while a wide-ranging examination of the nexus between people has become a much vaunted achievement of the social sciences in recent times and has endowed us with more knowledge about them, the relationships between them—as individuals, classes, income groups, occupations, races or nationalities—have not noticeably improved thereby; if anything, the élites and their camp-followers now live in a larger number of different and often less friendly ghettos than previously, and certainly in Britain. What seems like a double paradox is that the mid-twentieth-century social ferment, which had and still has as its objectives a reconciliation of social differences and a radical lessening of material differences between people, should, instead, have tended in many areas to reduce mutual tolerance and to enhance antagonisms; perhaps too much familiarity results in greater intolerance. Has the effect on the comedy of manners been deleterious?

The maintenance and, if possible, the extension of civilized conduct between human beings is a measure of consensus about values; generally acceptable manners, leading to improved togetherness and understanding, must not be taken to mean those gaped at superficialities practised by the photogenic personalities and enshrined in their eternal and, by definition, insincere smiles. What one may call manners in a wider context can and does serve as a lubricant in social relations, and this is likely to be more beneficial the greater the area of shared history, past or current experience or futrure expectation. Manners are conceived and gradually developed and, as though by 'transference', shared as such in general civility: and thereby they endeavour to add an extra dimension to opportunities for mutual understanding.

The age, in which we live then, puts less emphasis and, for the greater part, takes less pleasure, in the public comedy of manners—hence confrontation is more often preferred to negotiation or called by its unattracrive name—appeasement. Relationships between old and young, employer and employee, black and white, majorities and minorities, have not noticeably improved, indeed in many instances they have noticeably deteriorated into aggression. Whether or not such a change in civility is to be applauded, condemned or merely condoned—according to taste—it must be admitted that it does not create a milieu in which there is a demand for more enlightenment or better instruction or greater effort for social synchronization. Hence, it is unlikely that anyone in Britain today would wish to write a standard guide to desirable conduct in a narrower (manners) or in a wider (civility) context, according to some generally recognizable criteria; much less is one likely to discover an eminent contemporary thinker, like Erasmus in the sixteenth century, who would undertake to write such exhortations or suggest definite rules. It is one thing to write on manners for a narrow 'society', which *Debrett* attempts with such elegant and commendable 'cool'; and quite another when writing a manual of more or less general appeal in this highly differentiated epoch when the obstacles are distinctly more intimidating.

Collective lament—individual torpor

There are several good reasons why a latter-day Erasmus, writing on manners, is unlikely to arise in our midst. Manners as such, while many are physically transmitted or exhibited, have humanistic aspects and spiritual expressions, inasmuch as they bestow dignity of conduct on and between individuals. The need for such dignity is probably less highly valued in today's atomistic class relationships, though continuing lip-service is paid to their importance in collective relationships—in reference to countries, or communities, particularly minorities, or bands of aficionados, or when referring to the human race. But like many expressions of the collective spirit, they idolize generalities or abstractions as these cause no great pain and cost little effort; those most indignant about global wrongs are often not the most charitable to their next door neighbours. It is easy to be complimentary and concerned about the courage or suffering of the oppressed or the hungry of this world. Such general sentiments are often, but not always, of course, a 'safe' way of contracting out, they reflect conventional wisdom—a commonplace alibi for actually doing little or nothing about such matters individually. Lament about the collective is a pretext for inertia by the individual.

However, looking for a silver lining, we might console ourselves that while currently there are few books of any merit on how one is to *conduct* oneself or improve one's manners to embellish civilized society, there are literally thousands of books published on how to *do* things. These volumes are the building-blocks of a materialistic age. The torrent of 'do-it-yourself' literature shows every prospect of waxing further; the increasing popularity of doing things oneself is buttressed not merely by the easy availability of purchasing suitable DIY equipment but it is, too, the inevitable corollary of the shortage of trained tradesman and, when available, the surprisingly high cost of employing them. This uninterrupted trend over the past two decades, of working hard at ameliorating the individual's own physical surroundings and comforts at home, but not paying anything like as much attention to the individual's personal relationships within his wider milieu, constitutes a recognizable strand in current cultural changes in Britain. If it is true, as is sometimes suggested, that significant political changes can first be discerned in a people's culture, then latter-day changes in manners would suggest that

Britain is in the midst of important political developments. I think my guess is probably not wide of the mark.

The effects of this materialistic revolution in Britain are, in some respects, as predictable as, in some other, they are unexpected; naturally, they are influencing private and public attitudes about such notions as contentment or envy; but as can be commonly observed, they have given rise to dissatisfaction with the possession of purely material riches—despite or as a result of a much more widely diffused improvement in living standards and life-styles. John Stuart Mill said in his book *On Liberty* that 'success reveals infirmities which failure would otherwise have concealed'—and there is more than a trace of this truth in the present state of the nation. Rising individual living standards, coupled with thorough-going, deliberate social levelling seems to have evoked more instead of less social abrasiveness. Conflicts are positioned between those whose traditional interests—as folklore would have it—are supposed to be antagonistic to each other, such as the nexus between employer and employee; but, and here comes the rub, abrasiveness in manners is also extended to those whose interests would appear to be similar and often identical, as between members of different trade unions or the employees of a nationalized corporation. Higher real incomes, greater social justice, enlarged social and occupational mobility, intensive care units for social or occupational misfits and immensely improved opportunities in general might have been expected to cause relationships—expressed in manners and civilities—to improve or at least not to deteriorate between the same or even different layers of society. When the opposite happens—as it has since the late 1960s—the causes of discontent must run very deep.

Manners as mirrors

The sad truth is that manners—mirroring as they do shifts in thinking and in attitudes—reflect all changes, good and bad alike. The sudden, absolute enrichment of one class, the sudden, relative impoverishment of another, the 'no change' in the position of yet another—all these manifestations of change bring with them social fissures which take time to heal. Or, to take another aspect of the same phenomenon : the loss of British hegemony over a quarter of the globe—all compressed in under forty years—has not improved the

Britisher's *bella figura* of himself either. The effects of the infusion of several different ethnic groups over a relatively short time into a socially cohesive population, however tolerant, can only be overlooked by those who do not want to see. The erosion of the authority of an old established ruling class—and the delayed arrival, so far, of a new élite capable of taking charge—have given rise to new uncertainties, generating hostility and leading to a deterioration of manners, such as mutual respect, consideration and tolerance, between individuals and groups. The Houses of Parliament have similarly reflected and transmitted a deterioration in conduct.

And now a few commonplace examples applying to the British scene. A good illustration in socio-occupational relationships evoking indifferent manners, is afforded by the position of being a waiter. To many a Britisher, waiting at table implies a servile relationship between the patron who pays and the waiter who serves. One generous reason that may be ascribed to this social friction is individual pride—no longer considered a deadly sin; another less generous reason is that the client commands a sufficient surplus of money to spend in a restaurant and will, therefore, consider himself 'superior' by being able to pay for this special, personal service-relationship; it follows, therefore, the waiter must feel—and perhaps be—'inferior'. Yet another reason could be that the kind of servile manners which a client thinks a waiter should be extending to him is the sort which he—a proud Briton—might have demanded, had he lived in the colonies in the old empire days; or, perhaps, this veritable client—this average Brit—just considers such roles fixed in his mind—of foreigners to be generally servile and the British to be generally superior. (This actually fits the bill as most waiters are foreigners.) One result of this coloured or contorted occupational-ethnic view, when applied to a particular occupation, in this instance to that of the waiter, is to reduce a British waiter's expectations of the value and hence his competence in his job. The sad moral of such topsy-turvy reasoning is that it would rarely, if ever, occur to that waiter to think of making a career out of his occupation in the hotel and catering industry: to realize that being a waiter need only be a first stage and that he can up-grade himself by study and good example to become a head waiter and eventually open his own restaurant and thereby earn a substantial income. I wonder how many British waiters have observed the success of the Chinese in selling unfamiliar, foreign food to their clients under strange names they fail to understand and then proceed to make a fortune?

A greater propensity for bad manners—expressing a dislike for an idea or for certain types of person assumed to hold certain beliefs—is particularly discernible in the devotees of casuistic beliefs. The detestation by one person of the ideas, notions or disposition of another and the resolution of such detestation by taking certain steps, is, of course, often not based on any experience of such ideas or of what they may stand for. After all, some people can hate others across a crowded room, without ever having met them, simply because of discernible differences in educational standards or social adjustment, such as ease of conduct or conversation, or—manners again—in ways of dressing or presenting themselves—manners as a form of style. Striped trousers and black jackets still symbolize some workers in the City—the disliked counting-house type—yet the garb is donned only by a fast diminishing band of elderly gentlemen. Is this an example of one person thinking he is recognizing another type of person whom he suspects may be endowed with particular 'unloved' or unfamiliar characteristics or ideologies? Is this recognition of an image which is 'different' and the reaction to it almost predictable, i.e. combative? I think it is. This aggressive and vindictive reaction expresses a type of prejudiced bad manners which, in the end, is calculated to impact on people not even remotely associated with the activity conveyed by the offensive image, idea or deed. But here lies the classical alibi for aggression.

A particularly telling example aimed at raising the temperature was the demonstration of American graduate students in central London some years ago, objecting to ex-President Nixon addressing the Oxford Union. They clogged up even more streets of an already chaotic metropolis, inconveniencing its population unconcerned with Nixon and uninterested in the imported, civic disaffectations of politically motivated American students in England. Vietnam has brutalized American student thinking, yet it was Nixon who put an end to Vietnam! Strikes and demonstrations caused by demarcation disputes by a rival union fall into a slightly different category since it is the haunting fear of one union pinching members of another union which is the trigger mechanism. However, the end result is the same, they inflict discomfort and sometimes damage on a defenceless public who are no party to the cause of their discontent. Furthermore, the inconvenienced public are in no position to help remedy their grievances. The trade union's conduct in such a situation is hurtful, specifically to those without a stake, authority, or influence over the issues to be resolved—hence three times removed from helping to resolve the conflict. In these examples, there may or may not be a legitimate or chimerical grievance resolvable by negotiation, but two observations may be in order; first; the conflict is likely to have been sparked off by a shift in manners—arising from a different or changing attitude or stance; and second, while the conflict is being resolved it is likely to have inconvenienced others, outside the quarrel. If that's not the nadir in manners and in civility, I don't know what is.

Simplistic approaches

Casuistry, oversimplification and polarization erode civilized manners and their effect may result in the reverse of those intended. Good examples proliferate when the indignation and activities of vocal and muscular environmentalists and other similiar groups are reported. I am at pains to emphasize the overwhelming importance of an agreeable and healthy environment and its preservation; but I am hostile to those mouthing a lexicon of clichés in search of conflict—and sometimes with motives other than those confessed. A momentary reflection will reveal that environmentalists' chosen actions—i.e. manners— in some cases may be self-defeating, and could bring disadvantages and not benefits to those on whose behalf they agitate. That such acts may even destroy their own credibility does not occur to them. The uncivilized manners of the Greens to each other in Germany has reduced their parliamentary effectiveness and has resulted in their partial eclipse as a political party. Abrasive manners, born of casuistic beliefs, are self destructive. For instance, environmentalists maintain that people are entitled to live in a hazard-free environment. They have in recent years increasingly opposed the building of more nuclear power stations—an ever-ready whipping horse! Exaggerating a minor accident at a nuclear plant in Harrisburgh, USA, illustrates their genre of concern. This accident might or might not have been potentially serious, but it turned out not to be because adequate safety regulations and good monitoring prevented it. Their alibi for their over-zealous concern appears justified by the tragedy at Chernobyl—or is it. The nuclear power station out of control at Chernobyl was a safe installation until unauthorized experiments were carried out on the reactor by nuclear scientists and technicians too drunk to know what they were about. To fight against building nuclear power stations, some are prepared to go to any lengths. After all, are they not on the side of the angels? Perhaps not, if one takes the Polish example; when the Polish minister in charge of the nuclear electricity generating programme was attacked by Western environmentalists his curt answers posed one question—have you ever felt cold for a whole winter? Chernobyl was unrepresentative of nuclear hazards—it was representative of low grade professionalism slovenly monitoring, inadequate safety measures and half drunk inspectors. Too onerous limitations put on the development of nuclear power generation may retard industrial and economic expansion—certainly in developing countries or regions. Militant environmentalists invariably enjoying the fullest range of comforts and benefits can safely inveigh against atomic power stations because they live in well functioning industrialized countries (where all such hazards have been reduced).

The importance of being too earnest has rarely deserted environmentalists—to take the case of a modern British composer/conductor; he apparently cancelled a series of concerts to concentrate on composing a piece about the nuclear dilemma. His enthusiasm was unleashed by his local electricity board's plan to drill for uranium in the Orkneys. Since uranium is used in nuclear fission as well as in medicine, he implies it might well be used for other than therapeutic purposes. If Haydn could compose *The Creation*, a celebration of the birth of the world, or Beethoven a celebration of the divinity of man in his ninth symphony, is it too unrealistic to invent a work for the nuclear dilemma? However, composing 'universal' music about the nuclear dilemma, liberation theology, the demise of capitalism, or working class solidarity seems hopeless unless accompanied by suitable words. Belief that music exerts an influence is firmly held by the authoritarian mind and Rachmaninov's works were banned by Soviet Russia as 'especially dangerous on the musical front in the present class war'. At all events, the composer has gained publicity for a cause dearly held, a view honestly pursued; but mining uranium in his vicinity may in fact bring local benefits! The intolerance shown by environmentalists and others, apparently deeply motivated, during their well publicized demonstrations brings into focus two notions—the spectacle of a belief becoming contorted into dogma; and ignoring the choice or perhaps the preference, indeed the need of others and thereby denying due consideration to those views or aspirations. This is an abnegation of good manners.

Manners and radicalization

Dogmatic protests can degenerate into fantasy when the individual convinces himself that some sort of higher cause or compelling intellectual argument validates his belief in taking action—however harsh its effects may turn out on others. This must be a large part of the explanation why those besotted by ideology find it easy to deny the usual courtesies to those holding different views or electing to seek alternative solutions or even compromise solutions to reach the same objective. There are some telling examples to hand. A fundamental, *avant garde* belief of the past half-century has centred on social amelioration; and since socially ameliorative thinking has been given 'official' warrant by political sponsorship, in recent decades all plausibly socialized thinking or socially inspired action has been considered as both desirable and as being in the van of progress. When *avant garde* ideas are eventually fused with political respectability they can easily slide into dogma. Yet, as the history of ideas has shown, dogmas have very rarely delivered the hoped-for ameliorative results; also, their life-span has shortened as new dogmas are produced in greater profusion. Was one of the most widely acclaimed, benign nineteenth-century dogmas, 'greatest happiness of the greatest number', of such unalloyed success? Was it likely to lead to a better relationship between the governed and also between them and their government? It is difficult to measure, but if happiness were pursued so dogmatically it would lead to tyranny, certainly of the minorities; but this would occur only in democracies since in dictatorships the minorities rule absolutely. Taking another look at this Benthamite dogma, has it not incited the notion, and overpraised the virtues of, intransigent individualism out for itself? Such eccentric individualism results in a constant asking of the question 'what's in it for me'? When, over a period, this attitude becomes a part of manners, it results, as it has become manifest in current-day Britain, in a denigration of the common good. Plato would not have endorsed it.

A critique of pure 'unreason'

There remains an element of Rousseau-esque, nature-loving simplicity and romanticism in much casuistic argument in Britain today; disarmingly charming, perhaps, but only marginally relevant to the real world. In this desire for a return to the simpler life in the escapist image of a Christmas card-like 1850s village life—for 'caring' relationships in suitably integrated communities—are manners and civility staging a return? Or perhaps luxuriating in a new revelation that only 'small is beautiful'—a vision of updated nuts and bolts technology or eating only organic foods—maybe, such and similar notions can be so sincerely held as to fuel hostility, and result in ill-manners towards the unconverted, not readily or uncritically sharing such visions. No one is more astounded and not infrequently disenchanted, therefore, than the *avant garde* political dogmatist when he realizes that even the political masters of a socialist state, ostensibly sympathetic to such convictions, cannot always, or even often, countenance progressive or deserving ideas; it is hard, if not impossible to deliver idealism intact; only political virgins could aspire to such fulfilment! Such obduracy of the socialist state, in not wholeheartedly and without regard to cost furthering the dogma of miscellaneous, desirable, socially harmonious existence is nothing short of heresy. Non-socialist governments, of course, are better known for being perversely, reactionary—recognized by their love of market mechanics and desire for freedom in general, dismantling dirigism, large dollops of *laissez faire* and diminished sensitivity about social needs; and they must be fought at every picket-line, at every demonstration for not promoting actively socialist ideas. The irrational, professional ameliorationist's awakening—and I am using the expression as an omnibus term—that some or other of his desirable aims are frequently unrealizable because they cut across other desirable objectives or because resources are not unlimited,—must turn to disenchantment. The relationship between such a casuist and his community must sour since the man with the dogma cannot accept the economic or political limitations of the modern state; how can he consent to such reactionary negativism when socialism has been declared scientific, i.e. predictable, and the modern state has been declared all-powerful? It is the realization of such limitations which is likely to upset and offend members of pressure groups; they will, in response, reject civility as an ingredient of protest in their relationship with others whose posture is neutral or, worse still, opposed to their own ideas.

Disenchantment with institutions, organizations, ideas, policies or actions leads to their criticism; all these are a natural corollary of civilized life. But life and affairs do not consist of censure alone. It is a fact of life in today's Britain that criticism of all kinds has run amok. and the effects of such torrents of unceasing censure on manners is significant. Again, take politics as an illustration. The two main parties have criticized each other's policies and their underlying philosophies with such venom and rancour that on numerous vital issues consensus has largely disappeared about the governance of Britain; its concomitant, the democratic parliamentary system, may have been weakened. There has been radical criticism of the performance and organization of industry but surprisingly, unlike in politics by politicians, there has also been much constructive self-criticism by industry. Criticism of everybody and everything from the Royal Family to the Trades Union Congress has become one of the absorbing social rituals in contemporary Britain. Nothing succeeds like failure.

The verbalization of over-much self-criticism of Britain by the British has been taken at its face value by a world unaware of the social rituals, i.e. manners, concealed behind this well-developed national pastime. A not wholly unexpected result of this primarily English whimsy for destructive self-criticism has been to imply that, technically, British industry really is antediluvian; that industrial relations are a shambles and worse than anywhere else, and that the record of industry in satisfying its customers in respect of price, design and delivery is execrable. The same cultivated voices of the 'lumpen critics' would add that British industry variously has short-changed its shareholders, customers, managers as well as its work people. In a word, British industry is 'punk'. Have these worldly censors realized that it must be a highly competitive British industry which annually exports billions of pounds worth of goods?

At the other end of the spectrum, the pursuit of the under-statement—still often practised, I think, as a cloak of concealment—can be equally misunderstood. Are such statements a manneristic social ploy or are they well thought out alibis for underperformance, for not achieving what is demanded? In the same way, criticism can be a decoy alibi to conceal weakness and errors. Too much of it can lead to the assumption of hidden ulterior motives.

Much confused criticism about the role and the ends of education, has befogged the real pedagogic issues of what offers the most adequate education for children of an industrial society in the twentieth century. In keeping with love of ritual, the form of education to be offered—state financed or privately supported—has long been more in dispute than its content. And if anything did need revision it was the curricula in secondary education. Insistence on the introduction of a core curriculum goes some way towards ensuring that the basics of education will be more or less properly and uniformly taught. In the final reconciliation what is being taught largely determines success or failure in preparing young people for living and building up their own and their country's future.

As for the arts, convoluted mannerisms prevail; the criticism of many writers and reviewers has become so elitist in this, advisedly, equality prone, socially levelled Britain that they have developed an 'in' language which may have meaning and message for their esoteric inner circle, but hardly any significance or guidance for ordinary readers of literary reviews or for musical audiences. Such reviews are not designed to enlighten or instruct the general public. The conduct of such studied, in-grown toe-nail type exclusivity must be construed as undesirably manneristic for an art appreciative public which has limited choice for artistic guidance and, hence, must endure such shoddy esotericism. Such writers' shop-windowed social or political consciousness and *avant garde* approaches cannot help their readers towards more knowledge and better understanding. Why should such—I think—destructive type criticism be so prevalent when the chance of bringing art to a better educated general public today is the first, real opportunity in making art widely popular? Is it because so many critics are *manqué* performers? Is it because quite a bit of British art in the twentieth century—visual and auditory—has been homosexual? and not immediately comprehensible due to their highly differentiated mannerisms? Or is it because artistic gurus and critics look down upon the uninitiated spectator, listener or reader? Are many critics really reviewing art as such? Or, are they increasingly preoccupied with reviewing art in a social, political or personal context only? In such instances, their uncivility to their respective publics cannot be overlooked. Can there be no more art appreciation without trying to discover hidden psychological springs? Luckily, there are some critics who understand their art, and remain unconcerned with political or social science postulates in their output.

Espousing radicalization

Conflicting critisms, lack of clear political leadership over time, a glorification of the past, coupled with a clouded outlook for the future, the short-term antics of political parties and a long period of lack of political or commercial success in our affairs—over two or three generations—has made many of us increasingly self-destructive. We criticize one another with Jesuitical fervour, almost to the point when written or spoken words of censure become an acquired feature of manners and thus as end in themselves; often the central issue, the object of criticism or comment, is lost in the invective. Being bitchy has become smart, a voguish characteristic which elevates studied bad manners to premium merchandise—and this not only by rogues, untalented trendies or ineffectual, bitter and disappointed men, but also by many 'honest', 'to-the-point', 'down-to earth' thinkers. The trouble is that too much virulent criticism short-changes us all; criticism over-played fails to correct, and too much practice at this art may easily wilt the capacity for admiration. Thus, the new British propensity for censure is not matched by like propensity for admiration. But to admire—the other side of the coin of censure—men must recognize and adhere to values they cherish and against which they can usefully measure standards, performance, achievement and themselves in general.

Acclaim, then, rarely boils over at a good performance—except perhaps in sport (not excepting football) where the abstract has not replaced the concrete. The moral for manners here is that, perhaps, it is not so safe or at least not such good form to admire anyone or anything when recognized standards of good or bad manners have become less discernible. Hence, it is in accord with the manners of the decade that, for example, one's elders and betters are less admired, or that one's teachers or bosses are less cherished; they have all come in for rougher treatment perhaps than before. Are all these changes in civility not different species of deteriorating manners, symptomatic of the individual's hesitance or insecurity over the validity or relevance of established values and standards? Are they as well a sign of a cultivated impermanence, an educated obsolescence of cherished ideas? I suspect here a contemporary desire for 'accelerated depreciation' of 'pedestalized' persons and lofty ideals whose sustained admiration must be diminished! The social-occupational mobility of the age has, if anything, encouraged a belief that permanence of values is suspect, that admiration of all sorts is mostly misplaced—hence, the flux is the thing. From such a start, it is only a short way to a vulgarized revelation of such beliefs which is crystallized in the notion that 'anything goes'. This assumption disposes of the need to judge, on the basis of some consistent value or standard, about individuals or relationships or actions, or to examine critically the issues of the present against those of the past or the likely future. It is submitted, then, that the cultivated disdain of (socially, emotionally, occupationally or politically) cherished values—more characteristics of those rapidly uplifted by greater social mobility—leads to an erosion of those much needed fixities, which I shall call a 'comedy of manners'; by which we can take bearings and which in helping us to understand our milieu allow a more integrated and coherent way of life for us all. Contorted manners, in this context, are additionally fuelled by intolerance which, if sustained, denigrate dignity and encourage brutality. Because in the contemporary Western world, individuals as well as society often feel shaky about their values, people can less afford the generosity of 'give and take' which stems from a feeling of security. Failure to reach a workable, broadly based consensus over so many relatively straightforward objectives will only fuel our well reported and, perhaps by some, admired gladiatorial performances. Daily confrontation at Westminster in politics, weekly riotous football matches in London and the provinces, permanent, over-strict demarcation lines at the workplace, or warring trippers at Boulogne are expressions of inner violence, symptomatic of inner confusion and uncertainty about values; all these examples are an expression of manners we have locked ourselves in. They are an unfailing mirror of social, economic and political upheavals and obscurities in settled values and indicate a failure of new, more permanent values being forged to emerge in present-day Britain.

It would be difficult to conceal that much of current comment and criticism—artistic, vocational, social or political—has overreached itself. Instead of being forthright, direct and constructive by comparing values, offering new insights and wisdom, or propounding new ideas, they have become a new blight—speaking a private language and insisting on perfectability which is a species of Utopianism. In seeking an explanation for this, one cannot divorce much of the unrealistic and forceful criticism of man and affairs from the growing politicization and radicalization of important and less important issues of the day. This is unfortunate since unbridled censure must lead to deteriorating relationships—again, shrinking opportunities for the 'comedy of manners'. Politicization and radicalization of issues are likely to engender brands of fanatical beliefs and lead to distortions of meaning or varieties of heresies which are difficult to accommodate.

Politicizing straightforward notions often leads directly to distortions —such, as for instance, the much bandied about nineteen-thirties' term—the 'means test'. This expression has for decades conjured up a detestable image of indignity imposed on the unemployed (by defination, working class) on the dole during the 1930's depression; hence the expression 'means test' endowed the words and the people to whom it was to apply with inferiority, second-rateness, or just denigration. This image transfer continues to linger in the minds of young and old alike though those under 55 years of age could not possibly have direct experience of conditions in the 1930s, nor could they have been ever touched by it; but the British talent for historicism has taught them either from their parents, their trade-union organizers, their political leaders, or from books of its association with unemployment relief. The words 'means test' have gained an unsavoury, humbling inference—as for instance going 'cap in hand' for unemployment benefit and having to prove the validity of one's claim. As a slogan, the means test has become a rallying cry against the indignities assumed to have been heaped on the working class; it has not occurred to the British worker or to his mentors that there are several varieties of means test and they apply equally to all classes and coteries. Away from loaded slogans, hire purchase contracts, mortgages, bank loans, personal credit, credit cards, etc., are all obtained by a form of means test, a form of financial yardstick used for establishing the credit-worthiness of borrowers. However, this point may be made—if words or expressions such as the 'means test' awake continuing Pavlovian responses of memories of unpleasant experience, there must be political capital in dredging them up.

The aim of politicization and radicalization of any convenient issue is to bring about change, and preferably radical change, by violent criticism. The inference is that the process of radicalizing society is aided by shrill censure. Radicalization enshrines that ideological ingredient of the critic-idealist who insists that if a need, an ill or an error—real or assumed—is diagnosable then it is automatically remediable. Of course, the fuglemen of such deserved change don't pause too long for confirmation. Such and similar assumptions give rise to Utopian notions. Hopes and aspirations could be perhaps more easily realized if such efforts were contained more or less within the context of civility; but this is increasingly unlikely as the successful changeover to militancy has shown by—hospital workers, among civil servants, or even school-children, not to mention undergraduates or certain highly unionized workers and more recently by the coloured minorities. And places of unrest at Toxteth, or Brixton, the pitched battles at newspaper publishers offices, the flying pickets at the coalfields and fighting at the football pitch are varieties of radicalized beliefs being acted out—not only by hooligans, trouble-makers or psychopaths but also by decent normal people insanely radicalized. The insensible radicalization of school-children during a recent school janitors' strike when eleven and thirteen year olds were asked to say whether or not they approved of the caretakers' strike for higher wages, would have qualified as a shining example in any 'cultural revolution'—British or Chinese—except the latter have abandoned this perversion. How far away is this example from Herr Hitler's radicalized school-children who ultimately reported their parents deviation from the true creed to the Nazi Party officials? The fight for readership encourages the media to diligently feature radicalization. No wonder, newspaper typesetters have probably been persuaded to believe they live in a topsy-turvy world —and behaved accordingly!

Civility in the governed

Such divergent examples of overkill by criticism and radicalization reveal a decline in natural good faith and the trust of people in one another. Take that threadbare old British pastime, the class war, much of which has been so sedulously cultivated by the self-appointed upholders of social engineering in the collective. There is little to go to war about in the class issue, as such, in current-day Britain, yet the deliberate over-emphasis of such tribal divergences can and have led to artificially inseminated friction between people, and hence to serious lapses in civility as well as bad manners. The existence of inequality is often attributed to a residue of class differences, thus it is axiomatic that the demise of class, as such, must be sought by social and political radicals to reduce or eliminate inequality. But no political system—irrespective of its claims or successes of egalitarianism—has been successful in eliminating elites, which would be tantamount to extirpating class or stamping out inequalities. It is just a farrago of nonsense to imagine elites can be eliminated by radical action, without new ones always taking their place. Such ritual incantations for the illumination of 'elitist' concepts remains the hallmark of still credulous levellers in free societies—not, remember, in dirigiste or unfree societies.

Take other polemical, current issues which continue to attract radicalized solutions—unemployment or inflation. Unemployment or redundancy cannot be solved by marches, sit-ins, strikes, all attractive radical recipes, all ineffectual. They may help win elections and popularity contests but will not create jobs. Practical solutions are not improved by radicalization. Unemployment has been, as it must, a political hot potato, yet it is an economic and industrial issue; coping with it successfully depends upon rational solutions and not on fashionable or conventional political wisdoms. Nor are monetary issues, including inflation, resolvable through dogmas fervently held. However omnipotent latter-day politicians imagine themselves to be—though Conservative governments of the 1980s have prudently rejected playing God in this respect—in 'managing the economy', real success in this respect has eluded the dirigistes in every country. But this has not prevented them from promising to impose economic 'management' since they realize that, if in the short-term at least, such devices would stabilize the economy, this would also stabilize their electoral support. Thus, in the problem-solving exercise over the many social or economic issues preoccupying governments, the less radical and dogmatic the approach, the easier and the more likely it is to find an equitable solution. Equally, it would be foolish to disregard the political orientation of governments in their approach to such matters of the moment. But not until there are realistic alternatives for solving economic or resolving social issues should political preferences influence the choice of means. Here then are suitable good examples for which it is worth working at civility, trying to ensure consensus thereby.

Promises of a better life for all have been a popular, if not so secret, 'weapon' of all political parties in modern Britain and elsewhere. Politicians have invariably been ready to promise 'a little more' than they could conceivably 'deliver', and particularly at election time. In Western democracies the modern version of being 'let down' by over-promises is manifest in a way such as this: after elections, politicians want to put on the line that 'little more' so sincerely promised, but to turn promises into reality causes overheating in the economy, hence consumer booms, inflation, increased wage claims, upsurge of imports, balance of payments crises, and much else. Several British governments during the 60s and 70s overspent by budgeting for more from 'non-existing' real resources—although neither prime ministers not their parties had been pressurized by the electorate to take such steps. But it is a wonderful feeling to play God by promising plenty and to succeed temporarily by printing money and thus satisfying sectional interests. And it must be remembered that the less even handed a government, the more it fuels a lapse in civility. The chosen favourites of the state are always arrogant. By promising more than the economic machine is capable of delivering,—except, perhaps, selectively—the ripples of disaffection are only widened. No wonder then, when the promises of a better life remain only partly fulfilled, a lack of trust by the electorate in their governments can be discerned.

Unfulfilled promises undoubtedly radicalize—the residue of three decades of fickle politics. This is my primary explanation for the present disturbed state of the nation which shows such uncomfortable signs of a lack of cohesion. Bits begin to loosen, though they have not yet fallen off, as in the case of the now buried Welsh and Scottish devolution proposals, or—in a more hostile way—Ireland. Is there, perhaps, a conscious parallel between the demands of the ethnic minorities in Britain today with those of the aspirations of the minority races under the Austro-Hungarian monarchy not so long ago? The separatist impulse among ethnic groups had been made respectable by the invention of nationality, a radical residue of the

French Revolution in the eighteenth century, and by the hothouse notion of national self-determination in the twentieth century—the latter, a well-rehearsed American espousal.

The map of Europe has been redrawn several times since 1918 as a direct result of nationalist aspirations. Yet these changes, bringing the succession states into being, have not ameliorated conditions between or indeed within them. The vacuum caused by the break-up of the Austro-Hungarian monarchy after the First World War was filled, first, by Hitler's German Reich and subsequently by Stalin's Soviet Empire. The conquest of the succession states has scarcely fulfilled the radicalized aspirations of their founders who clamoured for national self-determination and thus were largely responsible for the break up of the monarchy. This is but one significant example of steam-heat nationalism not conferring hoped-for benefits: nor has it been much of a success in two other countries—whose nationalism led to the demise of Austria-Hungary—as the history of Italy and Germany has illustrated. Neither centripetal nor centrifugal nationalism led to durable political stability in the regions covered by these three countries. But to condemn nationalism as wholly malign would be too sweeping; after all, there were laudable elements of nationalism in the American War of Independence and in Mexico's fight for freedom. The radical hate of the other nationality—the sign of bigoted nationalism—that of the British by the Americans in this example, was absent. The American colonies' revolt was a positive step to enjoy more liberty, and not a negative step to extirpate all that remained of the former culture—and thereby enjoy 'exclusivity'. Perhaps there was also another difference in these transatlantic examples; they enjoyed the therapy of distance between their respective imperial countries and themselves. Is this one of the reasons why nationalist separatist movements have been and remain fraught with such difficulties when opposing forces are territorially adjacent to each other? Here. the difficulties may well be exacerbated by close living, but, perhaps the more so by speaking different languages. Ireland, the Basques, Wales, Tyrol, Scotland, are all appropriate examples. However, I suspect that strenuous attempts at separatism rarely arise when the central nationality, the main state-composing element in a country, is dynamic and successful. Consistent endeavours at separatism by nations comprising a nation state are a sign of overt weakness of the state—and lead to quarrels. The differences are not usually reconciled by well-mannered discussions.

What leads to lack of civility between dominant ethnic groups and between the majority and minorities is also relevant to pressure groups. The rise in the number and importance of pressure groups with political or social motivation and the tensions between many of them is a further symptom of the loss of the 'stable state'. While elected representatives of the people, i.e the government, consider they are pursuing appropriate policies for implementing their promises and putting legislation on the statute book, the central reality of British politics in recent years has been too much compromise to mollify recalcitrant pressure groups. The history of the Labour Party and of Labour governments in and out of office are good examples. The game of political football, of one government repealing the legislation of another, has led to uncertainties and abrasive political stances and has been a contributory factor to why Britain has been lacking greater political unity. Attempts to erode the central authority of government in a country as centrally governed as Great Britain will not lead to less friction. The past timidity of governments, their inadequate belief in and display of democratic authority to govern, has led to such deterioration—and to bad manners—between employer and employee, between the trade-union leadership and the rank and file, and between those professing different political faiths or holding divergent beliefs about the causes of social or economic ills and their remedies.

The promise of politicians—particularly in their election manifestos—would not lightly stand the scrutiny of the Office of Fair Trading (don't abolish it just because of this!); the gap between politicians' promises and performance in the 60s and 70s has widened with every general election which has not contributed to mutual respect between governments and the voters. Issuing false prospectuses was not that uncommon, to which the public responds with apathy and hostility; if a similar offence were committed in busines as in politics this would result in a businessman being put behind bars. Much important legislation in Britain has become political football in the thirty years or so since 1945. No wonder there has been an erosion of confidence in the elites in and out of Parliament. This has also created confusion about values and blunted their certainty: in turn, this blurred the frontiers between right and wrong, rewards and punishments, justice and compassion, and has led to an imbalance and often confusion in spiritual and material values and beliefs. The result of such confusion leads to lack of courtesies and civilities, and even nodding acquaintance with psychology will reveal that when uncertainty takes over, aggression abounds.

A lesson for working-class mannerists

I would argue, that a major reason for the lamentable anti-business educational stance in schools and universities was the misdirection of the initial great changes in the British educational system taking place in the nineteenth century; introduced, accidentally as it were, at the wrong moment in the country's social and economic development. The reform of the ancient universities, the need for more and better instruction at secondary school level in the arts and sciences and their application to trade and manufacturing, and the necessary broadening and gradual lengthening of the educational ladder—all these major changes occurred around the mid-nineteenth century, at the height of the Romantic Movement. It should be remembered, that the Romantic Movement was born out of hostility to material progress and industry. Thus, the epoch did not favour a better understanding or nurturing of industrial capitalism, by progressive educational measures which a policy of economic growth should have demanded—hence, the inevitable decline in British industry's competitiveness since the 1870s. On the contrary the mid-nineteenth century saw a rejection of business, and a disdain of industry; in its hazy primitivism to return to arts and crafts, extolling the merits of neo-Gothic architecture, a cult of ancient civilizations, and a newly-found Wordsworthian love of the 'country', it simply retreated into the past. Matthew Arnold's espousal of education was echoed by William Morris in the arts, and the cycle was completed by the anti-industrial spirit of the English novelists—especially of the women novelists of the first half of the nineteenth century. These inhibiting forces were the direct influence of the romantic element in an age which also extolled fourteenth-century aristocratic values, the real—manneristic—fly in the ointment. A romantic approach in this context entails a worship of courage and courtesies—so useful in knightly jousts or in vice-regal governance—fuelling the participants to great achievements, however impossible; such visions have also invented an aspect of magic, as the romantic imagination demands that any performance must seem effortless in order to rank as excellent—an intriguing expression of manners! Thus, with its roots in the romantic imagination, it was only a few steps away to establish the genesis of a cherished mid-nineteenth century upper-class 'belief' in the 'effortless superiority' of the British. There was much substance to it, for quite a while, since Britain carved out the largest colonial empire the world has seen and was responsible for starting the Industrial Revolution.

There was no misunderstanding about the value of education and the purpose to which it could be put at an earlier part of history, at the end of the eighteenth and the beginning of the nineteenth century. Education became increasingly important at that time to exploit the inventions and discoveries of science and to make Britain the leader of this new industrial age, this machine civilization; this period was also an age of optimism, in which the future looked bright and the progress for mankind well-nigh limitless. The diffusion of education became recognized as part of the mechanism for progress. It was 'the done thing'—it became a part of manners to be informed. There is little doubt that ever since, or perhaps even before the Enlightenment, the middle and upper-middle classes in Britain took their education seriously. Such instruction as was imparted at the time may or may not have equipped a tyro with significant, up-to-date, industrial skills, but it celebrated industry as new and enriching; by the middle 1800s such education, as was received, was certainly not in focus with the needs of a country in a fast developing industrial world; to suggest that the study in the better schools of subjects that could be useful for trade or industry were not contemplated is a commonplace; but the study—particularly in the upper echelons of society—of classics, coupled with doses of athleticism, became (as explained in another chapter) a part of Victorian ethos.

While Victorian optimism combined with hard work demanded by the Protestant ethic made the upper-class and upper-middle-class mid-nineteenth-century student diligent, alas, often only in non-intellectual pursuits, simultaneously, mid-century romanticism also subjected him to a mannerism inducing him to try and hide his propensity and desire for sustained diligence. The ritual worked in this way: strain every nerve and muscle to master your chosen subjects and pass your exams with distinction, excel in sports, if possible, but never betray you are working hard—to give the impression that you do, would be 'bad form'. The detestation of the 'little swot' probably dates from around this time; the sentiment has stayed with us since. This, I suspect, is how 'look, no hands' notion may have found its origins, almost imperceptibly perhaps, as an unpredictable by-product of high romanticism. Such and similar upper-class affectations, also related to the 'understatement' syndrome, culminating in the 'stiff upper lip' stance—both of them being an extension of romantic good manners—gathered too great a momentum to stop after either school or university; they were carried into the routine mannerisms of adult life. The 'effortless superiority' of the educated colonizer in the far-flung parts of the Empire was a natural continuation—to mention just one of its implications—of school life. But never let the notion of effortless superiorty be underestimated. Social affectation or no, this spirit brought fourth immense strivings for achievement by those who believed in it. That during the nineteenth century this 'superiority' could not be harnessed to an exploitation of Britain's industrial strength, but was largely devoted to managing an empire, is all the more regrettable.

The self-confidence of the Victorian age was consecrated by the notion of innate British superiority. This was all very well so long as it could be imposed on a docile or recalcitrant world; but after Britannia no longer exclusively ruled the waves it landed her in trouble in an unexpected, indirect way. This singular convention' to work assiduously but to conceal the effort, to simulate idleness while labouring hard at, say passing exammiations successfully (another form of hypocrisy?) or to achieve other aims and objectives, might have remained just another piece of upper-class attitudinizing. Like so many other fashions in manners' it could have easily disappeared, having outlived its usefullness or its appeal. I believe this is exactly what would have happened if this affectation had remained confined to the upper crust of society. After all, such an 'earnest' attitude to effort and achievment was a little contrived and might easily have mellowed or disappeared—its appeal declining with the retrenchment of romanticism and, in this instance, leading to a return to more naturalness, as was undoubtedly the case in the arts. After all, was not the rise of the Pre-Raphaelite school about just that? It set out to correct the 'corruption' in art, the heavy manneristic styles, and to purify artistic sensibility, delivering art once again back to naturalism.

One could speculate that a gradual change by around the *fin de siècle* might have occurred in upper-class attitudes but it did not, and these manners prevailed; the 'little swot'—i.e. the hard worker—still enjoys pejorative connotations and the acceptable manner of success, (as well as failure), is still appropriately represented by a 'stiff upper lip'. But neither the pervasive nature nor the appeal of this upper-class social affectation to other classes could be foreseen. This attitude of misleading aristocratic hauteur, extolling idleness and denying the need for hard work to ensure good results, seeped through, gradually, to the middle and lower-middle classes, who in turn bestowed it, involuntarily alas, on the artisan and the working classes. The texture of the social pyramid in the nineteenth century was most probably more 'porous' than now (in terms of the lower class wanting to emulate their 'betters' even more) and values and manners were more readily, perhaps even eagerly, transmitted and adopted. The inhabitants of 'upstairs, downstairs' all had their respective dignities, but the impact on downstairs was continuous.

Of course, values often change their meaning in the process of transmission, if only slightly. In the event, the consequences of adopting the 'look, no hands' mannerism, not in the least among the industrial working class, proved significant. One of the mid-twentieth-century manifestations of this, trickled down, 'effortless superiorty' inherited from the Victorians was the belief that the British were 'natural engineers'; after all, did they not create the machine age, a new industrial civilization and have they not been excelling in invention and science? The success reaped for a century beginning in the 1750s, made the British insensitive to the need for a wider ranging technical education at all educational levels—increasingly adopted on the Continent and in North America—to harness technical and applied scientific knowledge for the benefit of industry. Why did this not happen in Britain? The great success of the new machine age, the Industrial Revolution, was brought about in Britain by practical men; this made largely redundant a more earnest consideration of whether or not theoretical grounding should supplement the pragmatic learning of a trade or craft on the job. Thus, the insistence and long duration of practical training, in an apprenticeship system, and not only in the mechanical arts but also in some professions. The sentiment that in general to be severely practical is a necessary as well as sufficient condition of success has only been challenged since 1945. Theoretical training possibly at a university was associated with intellectual studies and probably affections, and an age which worshipped the empirical continued to disdain the intellectual. It could well be argued that such an approach also nourished latent anti-intellectual sentiments in general, a notion still not extirpated in current-day business. It seems to me that upholding the illusion of 'effortless superiority', coupled with the long enduring mood of anti-intellectualism, was quite a price to pay when witnessing the long list of dying industries in today's Britain. Such are the unwanted and unexpected fruits of misunderstood manners.

This attitudinizing by the Victorian upper classes, simulating apparent idleness while striving hard to achieve their chosen objective was, in the end, interpreted (or misinterpreted) in a slightly bizarre way, as the idea spread through the different layers via the Edwardian, neo-Georgian and neo-Elizabethan periods. What, in fact, happened is that by the middle of the twentieth century most classes adapted to the mannerist, aristocratic and upper-class affectation of not working particularly purposefully or very enthusiastically—but this mannerism now became a reality, not a semblance. The artisan and working classes who aped the upper classes in this respect were not, unexpectedly, sufficiently sophisticated to appreciate that the effortless superiority, the 'look, no hands' syndrome was an illusion, an attitude of sham sophistication, masking hard work. The twin results, as far as I can judge, of the wide diffusion of this upper-class mannerism over several decades are that many among the British working class suspect—some are perhaps convinced—that their (upper-class?) bosses do not really work hard (largely untrue) and, as a result, they are keen to emulate their 'suspected' conduct (largely true). Who knows whether a century later, the residue of this nineteenth-century upper-class mannerism has not contributed, inadvertently, to work-to-rules, to go-slows, to wildcat strikes, hostility to the boss and to latter-day Luddism?

Language shaping manners

Another telling illustration in the development of manners is the way they influence the use of language. Because the English are a literary race, with the richest vocabulary in any language, there are many different ways of speaking it. This gives rise to cultural differences which translate into class distinction. Sometimes, these cultural differences based on language are sharpened to reinforce feelings of identity or to provide an alibi of class affiliation. In no other country can the individual's position be pitched so accurately in the social pyramid as in Britain by the kind of language he or she speaks. Manners are a development of social and occupational conditioning and impact on language. Curiously it can work also in reverse—language impacting on manners. It's effects can be well grasped in a multi-lingual or multi-racial state, where language can develop into a social tool for better understanding and possibly for peace. The examples offered by the Austro-Hungarian Empire until its demise in 1918, and by the British Empire until only yesterday, of the effect of language on manners, are highly relevant in this context. Both empires contained a *mélange* of people speaking diverse languages and with different national prides, sensibilities, sensitivities, prejudices and history. The languages spoken by the dominant nations were German in Austria and English in the United Kingdom; all developed domestically anodyne linguistic formulations, used widely, with ease and elegance at home and abroad which probably materially contributed to social stability and an emulation of manners as long as the empires endured.

The example of the Austro-Hungarian Empire seems particularly interesting, since the indigenous language groups in the different parts of the monarchy were clustered together in Central Europe, while in the British Empire they were all overseas (except the Irish and the Welsh). In the case of Austria-Hungary, the empire included many different nationalities—Serbs, Croats, Slovaks, Slovenes, Romanians, Poles, Italians, Ruthenes, Czechs, Germans, and Hungarians; in terms of religion, the state religion of the Monarchy was Roman Catholic—not for nothing were the Habsburgs Holy Roman Emperors—but there were numerous followers of a diversity of faiths, made up of Protestants, Jews, Muslims and Eastern Orthodox, around the Empire; in fact, the earliest fifteenth-century Protestant believers were to be found in Eastern Hungary and even earlier among the Hussites in what is now Czechoslovakia. The centre where all races and religions converged and mingled was Vienna, the capital of the Empire—for centuries a vast clearing-house of humanity, the centre of culture and a meeting place between East and West. The two professions open to all of the Empire's nationalities were the army and the civil service; through them, people from any part of the Empire could rise to positions of great power and influence—with representatives of many different nationalities serving under them. Thus, the commanding officer of a regiment stationed in Austria could be a Croatian or a Pole, and the head of the foreign office in Vienna a Hungarian. Not for nothing was an Irishman, Count Taaffe, a childhood friend of the Emperor, Chancellor of Austria in the 1890s.

Because of the inevitability of close living and unavoidable social intercourse between nationalities, the need for good manners to breed tolerance became imperative, so as to avoid offending each others' sensibilities—and to promote maximum peaceful coexistence. Hence, the immense capability developed by the Austrians, and the Viennese in particular, to talk endlessly about nothing in general, by the men and women serving in the shops, by the soldiers in the army, by the policemen in the streets, or by the clerks in the counting house. In an endeavour to avoid giving offence to 'other classes and other nationalities' the Austrian cultivated a blandness which spilled over into relationships between members of the same nationality and class. Circumspection in their language to avoid wounding or snubbing others thus became the accepted part of manners—widely practised in Vienna and emulated in other parts of the Austro-Hungarian monarchy. This verbal consideration for one another did not result in a weakening of individual national sentiments, as the chauvinistic break-up of the monarchy in 1918 has shown: but for a long time the tolerance acquired through adjustment in manners helped to avoid giving offence and lubricated and eased the social and ethnic problems of the 'minorities'. Arising from this, it could be argued that the development of considerate manners by the deliberate use of language probably extended the life-span of the Monarchy; after all, the Monarchy was suspected of being an anachronism long before its dissolution.

A not altogether dissimilar situation was extant in Great Britain and the British Empire. Like the Austro-Hungarians, the English in England mixed with many different races—the three early, major experiences being the Scots, the Welsh and the Irish; the need to mingle with many other nationalities increased vastly as the British Empire expanded; indeed, much of the subsequent mingling in the Empire overseas was carried out in tandem with the Scots, the Welsh and the Irish. The colonial world visited England, and colonial and foreign communities sprang up in London and in provincial cities. To ensure that as few hackles as possible were raised either when talking to the people from the Empire in England or when meeting them in the Empire, in their own countries, an inoffensive sub-species of the English language was invented which eventually matured into and became known as 'small talk'. Contrary to popular (foreign) belief, small talk was and remains the property of all classes in England, not only of the upper echelons.

Perhaps the most important residue of the invention of an inoffensive language has been an enhancement of tolerance in general. Not for nothing has Britain been such a tolerant country for so long. One might wonder if the extension and maintenance of tolerance in Britain—in the face of large scale immigration in recent years—was made just that little bit less difficult than in some other countries because for centuries four different races have been rubbing shoulders in the UK and they have also mixed widely with peoples from other countries. And, certainly, as long as the Habsburg Empire endured, tolerance remained an ingredient of daily life in the monarchy, as, equally certainly, it declined after its collapse. Nevertheless, in the dual monarchy of Austria-Hungary the people never enjoyed the degree of tranquillity which the inhabitants of Britain took more or less for granted during the long high-noon of their empire. Being at the crossroads of Europe—as was the monarchy—with its wars and invasions could not inculcate security. For this reason the tolerance exhibited in manners and developed by language was all the more remarkable in Austria-Hungary. The rise of intolerance, coincidental with the end of the monarchy, and its deliberate cultivation in the successor states after 1918 scarcely needs documentation. By then, the civilizing influence of an old and once successful empire had vanished. Barbarism in manners gained the upper hand in parts of Central and Eastern Europe—which shows little sign of abating today. A similar descent by some of the succession states of the British Empire is also on record.

What happened to tolerance, based on temperate language and mutual consideration in post-empire England? While 'small talk' continues to reign and has become general property, tolerance has lost some of its fullness. One telling reason to which it could be ascribed is the loss of the empire, and with it the trusteeship of its people who expected leadership and good example from its British rulers. The British did hope that nearly half a billion people should admire their domestic way of life and native traits and culture, since such emulation facilitated the rigours of governing them. The question then arises, why have good manners and civility deteriorated, so relatively quickly after the loss of the empire, say by the mid-1960s—all in two decades?

Since the post-empire phase, many in Britain had their stock of sympathetic energies dissipated. Previously these creative energies were, to a large extent, focused on the Empire and its people. The purposeful channelling of this care and attention came to an abrupt end after 1947. The cynic would maintain that it is easier to be concerned about people and events a long way away than about one's neighbour—especially for the British, who are so keen on privacy, which in itself is a significant expression of preferential manners. Even so, they continue to show concern, whether or not such concern is expected from them.

Perhaps there is too much familiarity in the air. Open government and disclosure about virtually everything has led to much enlightenment—but equally, it does intrude. More people are 'into each other' and such close living is likely to spark off more mutual criticism. No wonder notions such as inequality, civil rights, homosexuality, women's liberation, to mention but a few, have become hotly contested issues. We have reached a stage where the vocal representatives of the population irritate each other probably more than ever before for holding divergent views .

Ultimately, such problems are probably irresolvable, either by idealism or by revolution—but they can be mitigated by cultivated manners and tolerance. However they are virtually irresolvable, because after the 'intolerable wrongs' have been righted, the smaller ones left behind loom all the larger. It was de Tocqueville who put forward the sophisticated view of human beings' insatiable aspirations in *L'Ancien Régime et la Révolution*—in effect emphasizing that in social and political relationships one cannot reach a state of bliss, only a state of compromise. The true remedies for injustice and cruelty are not hatred and fanaticism but, as we all know, kindness, tolerance, and their residual good manners. The agreeable qualities of tolerance, kindness and exemplary good manners have been the property of the British people for a long time; the absence of any great national cause in recent years could work towards dissipating this heritage. Post-empire Little Englander-ism is an inward-looking doctrine, nurturing narrow sectionalism or even nationalism, not proud patriotism. Britain's acceptance of the need for European unity and her Common Market membership will fortunately change this scene. Political developments furthering an expansionist view and encouraging an outward-looking desire for cooperation must be supported. Much of the recent barbarism in Central and Eastern Europe stems from membership of politically and socially sealed systems. To paraphrase Dean Acheson, 'Britain has lost an Empire and has not found a role', but will have done so by her alignment with Europe. Europeanizing the British will prove to be a long haul but a start has been made with signing the Treaty of Rome and with membership of the North Atlantic Treaty Organization.

Manners admired—manners adopted

Thus, with blemishes only too apparent, and excluding incorrigible protagonists of dud dogmas who pop up in every age under a diversity of guises—and whose bad manners are part of their armoury—manners and civility in Britain have changed materially in the past forty years, and not always for the better. Manners and civility, inasmuch as they represent a *Weltanschauung* express the shifting fortunes, preferences, and relationships between individuals, classes, government, occupations, members of the family and the impact on them of the outside world. Perhaps more than in any previous historical epoch, manners in current-day Britain have been prone to the quicksands of change and pressure, for the simple reason that for several decades we have been in an agitated state of flux about values—impacting on the individual and affecting the community (state). There are certain hopeful indicators, however, that much of the fashionable experimentation in life-styles and desired changes in social, economic and political relationships is about to 'firm up' in form as well as in content. Such a development in my opinion could well lead to growing social and political tranquillity; this, in turn, could trigger a more widely desired consensus about admissible attitudes—hence to a range of manners being more generally accepted and enjoyed as a reflection of our changing disposition to each other. The foundation of a new political party, the SDP, offering middle of the way consensus has however run into the sand. Does this indicate that a new consensus will be built on a reconciliation between polarized beliefs?

I welcome such likely devolution in attitudes because it will indicate a slow return to a new normality and stability. With manners less fragmented by attitudes growing less tribalized, and with civility more naturally expected and extended, the renewal of our currently still divided society in the British Isles could be invested with more unity. It could be assumed that the endlessly talked about breach in British society—the 'two (or more) nations syndrome', a much bandied about expression, often fraudulently used for emotional, special pleading—is not irreparable. The notions which started the British social revolution in the 1880s, a thirst for redistributive justice, greater fairness and equality, the idea of making colonial dependencies self-governing and eventually independent, attempts at greater occupational and social mobility, equal opportunities, all these high hopes have been largely accomplished. Every section or class of British society participated, and actively or passively helped to bring about this revolution. Having realized far-reaching economic and social changes on a wide scale, the natural and inevitable inequalities between peole will once more be respected and accepted and not distorted, exaggerated, envied and exploited. Conscious recognition that we are about to arrive at this next stage in development is beginning to be more widely shared. The dubious alibi of the class-war mercenaries for fuelling conflict no longer seems to hold. This is progress!

My task in this essay has been to draw attention to the important role of manners and civility in general and to indicate how by impacting on the relationships between individuals and groups they deeply affect and influence everyday life. The essential core of manners and their application can and does change over time and older generations will, invariably, find a little wanting in the manners of those following them—hence the chasm between ancients and moderns. This is natural and desirable since nothing stultifies the individual and society more than perpetuating inflexible rigidities in manners and in form of civility. All manners change and develop over time. By discussing and analysing them we shall perhaps exert useful influence over them; this will lead us to understand better their importance and their intrinsic role in helping to bring about the 'good society'. Thus it would not be amiss if some day soon, a latter-day Erasmus were to compose a new primer about manners—would this be feasible in a multi-racial society?—because, by upholding humanistic ideals, such influence would be pervasive in successfully disseminating desirable conduct. Of course, manners must enjoy elasticity; changes in milieu, recognizing limits to self-interest, realizing that some obstacles cannot be resolved easily or quickly or at all, and acknowledging the influence of external pressures—that is, they must recognize the need for interdependence of peoples and communities—all such and many more similar considerations influence the continuing evolution of acceptable and desirable manners. In the end, and after periods of vicissitudes, men have always endeavoured to better themselves, if only for self-protection, and this they accomplish by accepting improved or different but agreed codes of conduct—more agreeable manners and greater civility. Remaining an optimist, I have always believed that people will adopt the manners of people they admire. Should we not be more careful about our choices of heroes?

ON INTELLECTUALITY
AND THE MARKET-PLACE

A changing milieu for businessmen

The English woman, said the American-born Lady Astor, the first woman elected to the House of Commons in 1919, has three important qualities: platitude, rectitude, and high hatitude. Many British industrialists could be said to be still suffering from two out of three of these frailties. That no hatitude, low or high, comes into the businessman's purview is simply a matter of fashion rather than of disposition. But platitude and rectitude have long been valued accessories in most industrialists' armouries—and their outpourings about their firms or industries or the world around them reflect this preference. There is little cause for complaint to such an approach in explaining business life, providing that it leads to the successful execution of the industrialist's tasks and responsibilities as a public person. Businessmen must be aware in this increasingly vocal age that the searchlight is focused on them more strongly than ever before. They must also be aware of having been often buffeted in recent years by familiar and unfamiliar forces, which has made them less sure-footed than they ought to be. Business in Britain has been unceasingly under attack for a century or more, and has laboured under a variety of specific disadvantages, particularly in the last few decades. Thus, one is compelled to conclude that the industrialist's or businessman's approach to his vocation and his rebuttals to the critics of the results of his efforts have not been entirely rewarding or successful: businessmen have not devised satisfactory ways of coping with them. The British businessman has not been able to secure fully the recognition which is offered unreservedly to his counterparts elsewhere in Europe and particularly in America. There are many reasons for this, many of them historical and extrinsic, but some generated by the businessman himself. One of the surprises is that, irrespective of being leaders or laggards of businesses, particularly in manufacturing industry, businessmen are often taken unawares and are perplexed by what is being said about them or their firms. Too many industrialists fail to notice the pace of change which, in a relatively short time, may affect for good or bad, the conduct or the direction of their businesses. However, as private sector business provides the surplus on which, in one way or another, we all live, it is to be assumed that even the meanest intelligence or prejudiced adversary must want to keep this engine of wealth creation efficient and profitable. Unhappily, this has not been always the case.

Living in an age of often contorted motives and much mutual misunderstanding, we have seen more than just glimpses of energies which seem to be directed towards weakening enterprise and profit-making. The initial, simple misunderstanding in the life of the businessman begins when he is baffled as to why so much of political or social comment should be so hostile to industry, its owners and managers. Such attitudes may be lacking in logic but have been widely and successfully disseminated. A realistic appreciation of much unexplained hostility must serve as a starting-off point for examining where the industrialist's credibility in public affairs has failed to demonstrate his own and his creation's general utility. Are there ingredients for a fuller understanding missing, of which the muscular businessman is unaware? Is there a 'Formula X' which ensures success? There does not seem to be. The businessman's failure to bother about a clearer understanding of the roots of this hostility to business enterprise continues to impair his status in modern society; it has an impact on the social esteem in which he is held and may act as a brake on the potential of industry or business to do its best for the nation. Equally significant, it can debilitate the optimum functioning of the businessman in his daily domain—the corporation.

An analysis of the two major types of British businessman will not reveal much that is contrived or conspiratorial. The chairmen and directors of substantial and prestigious companies nowadays are frequently graduates, often with wide cultural interests. Such men are unlikely to have built up the company over which they rule, and their presence induces more confidence than dynamism. Perhaps these are the precise qualities which large companies need at the helm when they become mature corporations; or perhaps not, as some may argue; it is debatable that large corporations could be better served by civilized men of combat as against men of complaisance. The founders or directors of small family firms or newly-founded entrepreneurial companies, are unlikely to have had too much schooling. This had been their background until, perhaps, quite recently: such men are severely empirical and especially proud of calling themselves 'practical men'. Curiously enough, the notion of the 'practical man' is often offered, with pride, as a manicured expression for lack of higher learning, understanding, or qualifications—particularly in the manufacturing industries. However, this lack of guile, the simplistic viewpoints and the so-called 'practical man's' unsophisticated approach to industrial issues, are not the sole property of the owners or managers of smaller firms; such characteristics can also be observed within a more educated directorate in larger, more substantial companies. The visibility of such native or acquired primitivism in some businessmen makes him vulnerable to attacks on his job, his company, his industry and his ethical aura which validates his way of earning a living by employing scarce human material resources to do so. Implacable among his adversaries—the noun is used deliberately—are the only too commonplace intellectual critics of business. Intellectuals in Britain are still rarely found working in business, but they hold positions at opinion- making intersections in numerous occupations—government, universities, foundations, the media, civil service, and the professions. It should be said at once that the alienation of the intellectual from industry and the industrialist's dislike of the intellectual and, even more so, of intellectual notions, has led to yet another form of separation of elites from each other—which has been an English rather than a British speciality. This in turn has given rise to a less efficient industrial society in Britain. There are signs however that a greater mingling between businessmen and intellectuals has started.

Intellectuality in business

To counter his critics, today's progressive businessman must develop a degree of intellectuality when approaching the growing number of variables encountered in managing his firm and in ensuring its profitable survival in an economy growing more competitive every hour. However, an important warning is in order here. The businessman must not turn himself into a shadow intellectual; this would be counterproductive and that way lies disaster. By definition, most intellectuals are not great decision-makers or risk-takers. Their gift is to dissect ideas, to analyse them, to generalize and to bring new insights to prevailing circumstances. The basic role of the intellectual in society should be creativity—though only few intellectuals possess this quality and manage to be creative. More important however, there is also an 'intellectual way' of looking at things and it is in this context of cerebration that businessmen would do well to school themselves; but they must never discard the more muscular, direct action side of their nature—which is every bit as creative as that of the intellectual's—i.e. optimism, self-confidence, risk-taking and decision-making. To bring forth the best results, the primitive and sophisticated forms of creativity must coalesce.

Latter-day intellectuality appears to have been more passive than active, more critical than creative; yet, intellectual conduct was not always such. It was an intellectual, rational way of approach and speculation which supplied the motivation for the scientific-technical-industrial revolutions and their practical application in the seventeenth and eighteenth centuries. It might be asked what happened to that stream of intellectuality which powered the transformation of industry into the machine age and exploited new technology by introducing it into the manufacturing workshops? Indeed, where are today the type of intellectuals who became entrepreneurs themselves and founded firms? What changes have occurred for over a century to distance the intellectual (and intellectuality) from the founding and running of businesses in Britain, and from the profit motive? And why has the businessman been encouraged in his belief that practicality and not intellectuallity is and must remain the dominant characteristic for success in business? Why has this polarization occurred? Does British society tend to polarize more than other societies?

The progenitors of England's first industrial age, with its genesis in the early eighteenth century, were largely the Nonconformists. The history of the 'chapel people' is closely woven into the fabric of industrial progress. Industrial activity, such as machine-building or the production of metal wares, was taken up by many of these self-taught, ambitious men who were excluded from official positions, or from the professions, under the 1662 Act of Uniformity. While the dominant strain in striving for advance in the mechanical arts was Nonconformist, tracing its progress further will reveal that its cradle was in the North of England and the Midlands, where their numbers were most substantial. By the eighteenth century, Nonconformists and Jews and Catholics, comprised the majority of the English people, and manufacturing and trading became a major avenue for their occupational and social fulfilment, and a pathway to wealth. As industrial work offered conditions superior to those of agricultural work, manufacturing and trading became enviable occupations. From the 1750s to the 1850s, business was the dominant occupation for Nonconformists, who comprised a significant part of the country's workforce, and their successes by the 1820s and 1830s began to attract middle-class indignation. This bustling age, tailor-made for such zealots with energy, eagerly embraced a working style which can best be described—not too accurately, perhaps—as the Protestant work ethic. Nonconformist work ethic would describe it more accurately.

The exclusion, between the mid-seventeenth and mid-nineteenth centuries, of such a large number of aspiring, hard-working Nonconformists from full citizenship, challenged its votaries to prove themselves financially since socially they were not fully acceptable; they suffered or, better, enjoyed the psychologically combative disposition of a politically and socially oppressed minority—though they were, in fact, in the majority. But it was their dogged disposition which made the chapel people strive for success through hard work, and through their strivings they acquired a perceptive intellectuality. The unfolding of intellectual attitudes, coupled with single-minded hard work, offered success to many Nonconformist entrepreneurs. It was this development which gave England the industrial substance upon which to build a wealthy homeland and the largest empire the world has seen.

These aspiring parvenus who applied intellectuality to industry and worked with such frenzy, scored great success in business, and some accumulated great wealth; their subsequent political and social liberation was brought about by the repeal of the Test Acts and the passing of the second Reform Act in 1867; Nonconformists compromised the majority of voters in England by this time.

With enfranchisement however, came an inevitable decline in enthusiasm. The pressures demanding success via business, a major route open while disenfranchised, were relaxed as other, socially superior avenues of employment were opened up for them and these were enthusiastically embraced. Manufacturing and trading occupations gradually lost their lustre, particularly for the progeny of the Nonconformists. Concurrently with this decline in interest in industry, it is salutary to note the receding social, cultural and economic importance of the quasi-Nonconformist manufacturing cities in the North of England after the mid-1870s.

What became of these newly emancipated chapel people, many of them comprising the new type of intellectual businessman? In which direction did they channel their energies? Once they had been accepted as members of the establishment, and all positions opened to them, two important transformations took place in their 'world view'. Many of the more successful Nonconformist businessmen became gentrified after accumulating sufficient wealth; their children emulated the values of their social superiors—the upper middle class and the aristocracy. In practical terms this meant that owning and cultivating land, service to the state, or the practice of an established profession became preferable to manufacturing or trading. Manufacturing, in particular, became a grimy occupation, but earning money on the same scale in the professions, or in the universities was well-nigh impossible. Hence, it was inevitable that the act of setting out to make money in business should, at first, have a reduced status. As time went on, it was considered a rather coarse pursuit, not to be encouraged by the socially superior—the better educated, the rich and, of course, by the descendants of the recently financially endowed gentrified *arrivistes*. The ability to earn money and accumulate wealth remained, doubtless, an enviable pursuit to be emulated with great circumspection and perhaps not too visibly. This attitude has survived until very recently in a variety of ways.

Thus, the better or well-off, socially emancipated Nonconformist intellectual came to prefer a non-industrial career. So, this intellectually-minded new and rising middle class, formerly nurtured on industry, became gradually isolated from it, and from the industrial working class. They were seeking a plausible alibi to reject their past and the instrument at hand was the well documented inhumanity in factories and workshops, resulting in the exploitation of workers and the enrichment of the capitalist entrepreneur. Luxuriating in this theme and its variations, twenty years after emancipating the Nonconformists, by the mid 1880s their critical intellect coupled with the rising political force of socialism developed an enduring social conscience, worn as a badge of honour. Thus, many of this previously disenfranchised group which by its intellectuality had exploited science and technology through founding firms, running them efficiently amid the rising importance of the new professions and accumulating wealth, now began to assume establishment, anti-industrial postures in their changed circumstances, after the social pressures were removed and they were declared clubbable. Their renowned enthusiasm and intellectuality could not be annihilated—but these were now often channelled towards non-business endeavours. The unfolding of such changed manners in respect of business success was, and remains, a good example of that virulent kind of self-destructive fashion which is sometimes generated by a desire for acceptability. A similar but reverse transformation from non-establishment to establishment status for business and the businessman did not need to occur in the United States because business has always been held in high social esteem—and the Nonconformist spirit of hard work has for long pervaded it. With no long-established upper-class tradition excluding business from among the suitable avenues of fulfilment, it flourished.

Perhaps the *élan* that left business in mid-nineteenth century England may be reappearing now. When a rising number of the offspring of today's leaders and opinion-makers reject the civil service, the professions, or the universities, as the first choice employment opportunities in favour of joining industry or financial services or, even better, establishing their own firms, then a hopeful beginning will have been made for a second Renaissance in British business by the participation of the intellectually minded!

The sad and unsatisfactory results of the intellectual impoverishment of British business by the conscious desertion of an intellectual middle class need little chronicling; it has contributed to a declining share in world trade, the under-exploitation of inventions, tardy application in industrial reorganization, reduced enthusiasm for industry, recurring balance of payments crises (now partly masked by oil revenues), and, most lamentably of all, a decline of the entrepreneurial spirit. These are all valid examples of the paucity of intellectual input into business: until North Sea oil began to flow, Britain was the mendicant of Europe. The *trahison des clercs*—the intellectuals' abandonment of participation in the wealth-creating process for a good hundred years —was concealed for a while by the rewards of colonial empire, by falling back on reserves, i.e spending accumulated wealth both private and public, and by outside help. All classes participated in an Indian summer of British prosperity. They enjoyed a living standard to which they became accustomed without earning it, but accepting it as a birthright—until the sobering world economic difficulties of the 1960s and 1970s revealed Britain's fundamental economic infirmities. The country's economic and industrial problems were further compounded by an absence of the required social cohesion between employer and employee to overcome them with less damage.

Only widely shared and understood vicissitudes can hope to re-enlist the sympathetic co-operation between classes, including the intellectual elite, for desirable objectives: in the interests of comfortable survival, business must be the first beneficiary of such common understanding. This has been partly accomplished more recently by the revalidation of the profit principle. The anti-business, anti-profit stance of socially over-concerned intellectuals is slowly losing credibility as the nation is facing testing times. Hence, for the remainder of this century at least, it will no longer be recognizably fashionable to decry the profit motive. Togetherness in industrial aims is all the more vital, as immeasurably greater effort and application are needed today to 'keep alive' in competitive industry. Superimposed upon our reluctance to apply intellectuality to improving business there has been a reluctance to change. But at least the truth of the British industrial situation has been revealed, hence it became remediable;

removing distortion in employment has helped to convert overmanning into what it really is, i.e. redundancy, resulting in unemployment. Thus the financial burden of paying for surplus labour has been transferred from the companies to the state, and placed on taxation instead of (ultimately) prices—on the general public and not employers.

A strong hope for involving intellectuals in business lies in the fact that, like everyone else, they dislike being short-changed by life and circumstance, and ultimately will want to co-operate by taking action to stem the erosion of their influence.   In the halcyon days of the Nonconformist intellectual's involvement in industry, he looked upon his work as an instrument of universal and social utility; to rekindle his interest in business now, nearly a century and a half later, the intellectual needs to have another mission. Such a mission is difficult to invent; but the intellectual must be made more fully aware that his social withdrawal from, and lack of cultural orientation to, business will not contribute to solving his Utopian vision of life. His intelligence should be aroused to realize that a society which for some decades had concerned itself with social and psychological needs of people primarily and only with satisfying them with goods and services secondarily can only lead to everybody's detriment. Playing poor Richard has become an unattractive stance and it becomes a little hammy with too many actors. In England, people criticize each other, while in America they criticize the efficiency of the goods they purchase.

The businessman's view of the intellectual

When examining the reasons why the businessman often suspects and sometimes dislikes the intellectual, it must be realized that he encounters him rarely and when he does largely in the world outside business, away from his usual routine; no wonder the businessman feels at a disadvantage in dealing with intellectuals. The intellectual's distaste for business and the businessman, at least until recently, hardly needs asserting, but the realistic comment must be made that such dislikes are reciprocated and, usually, mutually nourished. This, of course, is a generalization, but it does broadly hold water when considering the undeclared hostility between them.

Intellectuals who impinge on business as critics and commentators are not, for the greater part, revolutionary wreckers, would-be abolishers of the monarchy, notorious labour agitators, representatives of radical students' unions, paranoid fanatics, Marxist teachers or misguided members of the 'caring' professions. Intellectuals will be found among politicians, members of government, trade unionists, civil servants and many others—even among businessmen. *Vis-à-vis* the intellectually minded and with significant exceptions, businessmen suffer from diverse inferiority complexes. The industrialist visiting a ministry to plead his firm's or industry's case is surrounded by condescending ministers emboldened by good patter and an impressive retinue of civil servants, who speak with exacerbating fluency and supreme confidence to a well-rehearsed brief. When it comes to the press, most businessmen are hostile to journalists, believing they want to catch them out; and they are surprised by the pertinent questions asked by pressmen with minuscule experience of business. Few businessmen achieve mastery of the situation in such encounters and, having failed to gain any mileage for their firm, they also feel not a little foolish for failing to get their argument across, however sound. Often, the result is skewed up reporting. Such troubles are compounded by the businessman's indignant belief that intellectuals have failed to grasp his 'practical' points. The sobering fact is that businessmen do have grounds for disaffection with the intellectual's approach and attitude to his problems. From the inadequacies of the Foreign Office policy over the years in placing suitable officers in sensitive commercial appointments abroad, and the ostrich-like qualities of educational institutions in failing to serve the needs of business adequately, examples abound where the businessman's indignation about intellectual attitudes and pretensions is fully justified.

The intellectual's view of the businessman

The intellectual's view—as a social critic—of the businessman is similarly scathing, but different in substance. To begin with, intellectuals generally hold much better opinions of themselves than even the most conceited businessmen. Businessmen often wish to masquerade as simple chaps, while intellectuals are keen to give the impression of being tortured spirits, motivated by elevated ideals, constantly confronting dilemmas and engaged in incessant creativity; intellectuals are over-romantic and businessmen over-pragmatic in their evaluations of themselves. The intellectual's chief weapon is conceptualization, not decision-making; here, perhaps, lie the roots of the intellectual's disdain for the decision-maker, particularly in business, who is merely concerned with reconciling competing preferences and opportunities to make a profit. However, one may suspect another, not so oblique, reason for the businessman's disdain—and this is the result of the little, direct impact intellectuals have made on the business world. Whether or not this is partially accounted for by the practical man's distrust of the theoretical, is less important than the fact that industrialists view intellectuals as indirect, hesitant, indecisive, as well as 'uppity' and illiterate about trade and industry. The suspicion that intellectuals hold the view that making a success of business is easy while their own, diverse occupations are taxing is again not conducive to mutual applause. And the businessmen looks down upon them still further because (in his terms) intellectuals are non-risk-takers. However, this does not imply that intellectuals are not fighters—indeed thay can be; the quality and degree of in-fighting between dons at universities, for instance, is far more vicious and contorted than any quarrel between businessmen in different companies or within their own. The reason for this is simple. In business, the game is largely, but not wholly, about an easily understood commodity—called money; in the intellectual's sphere, the game is not primarily for money, it is for preferment, reputation, recognition, political or other influence, authorship, and their appropriate symbolisms. And most intellectuals have their own conception of the good and the beautiful—whether in society, economic organization, or national politics—which they cherish, defend and proselytize with religious zeal. The ferocious espousal of their beliefs does not offer, nor necessarily presage success; it does, however, often create trouble and animosity.

In addition, the intellectual has observed—alas, accurately—that there is little room, except in some of the larger establishments, for the deployment of an intellectual approach to the problems of business. British business prides itself in having always been severely pragmatic—the 'practical man' syndrome raises its head again in the collective. By extolling practicality, British business has taken a different approach from that of the European or American where the consideration of intellectual notions are a staple for progressive thinking by businessmen. Whether or not this state of affairs in other industrial lands has been aided by encouraging attitudes in education and in the home towards business as a career, and by a genuine recognition from the entire educational system of the importance of business, is similarly a matter for contemplation. For the native British intellectual—less so for the imported variety—much of industry and trade remains deliberately *terra incognita*. It would be interesting to contemplate—if only one had the facts—how many politicians, civil servants, or highly paid professionals (whose income depends largely or wholly on working for business), who preach about the need for well-run and competitive British industry, do in fact encourage their own children to seek employment there. Perhaps it would be a sophistry to press the question further and ask how many of the children of such men have, in fact, found employment in busines, or perhaps started one of their own? I do not think it is difficult to guess!

There are other factors which militate for the rejection of direct involvement by intellectuals in industry. Business in Britain has not, until more recently, been a much esteemed career; it suffered and still does from vocal critics in schools, in universities, in the media and even by (some) businessmen. Perhaps the underperformance of business for many years has contributed to this. Few businessmen have enjoyed durable, high public esteem in the past, and for the budding intellectual recognition and endorsement are important motivations. Also, industry—engineering in particular—cannot afford those extravagant starting emoluments which even smaller professional firms in the law, accountancy, banking, journalism, or even the universities and certainly government departments, can offer—often coupled with exceptional fringe benefits. Not so in industry! Added to moderate pay and little status, are the not so occasional 'unsocial' hours; as for place of work, the factories and offices are often based on the edge of a provincial town or within a suburban cluster of an industrial estate. As a general observation, most aspects of employment in industry are less attractive and more taxing than those in many other middle-class occupations.

Intellectual failure

The worlds of the businessman and those of the intellectual have been divergent and largely separate for a long time. This separation has been induced by diverse forces—by an educational system, which has consciously rejected the preparation of the young for business until quite recently; by a social system which put a higher snob value on employment outside business with a higher second-hand value for future employment; by a lack of respect for the profit motive; and by an atavistic political sensibility which has viewed Britain as the political centre of a commonwealth instead of an efficient industrial and economic centre (which, if only encouraged to function better as it has recently, enables the country to wield world political influence once again).

For centuries, legends have abounded about the nation's political success but there is little folklore about industrial or business achievements. In *A Study of History*, covering nearly six millennia from 4,300 B.C. to A.D. 1947, Arnold Toynbee fails to mention a single businessman—he must have made a conscious effort to conceal them—yet some of them must have influenced the course of civilization more deeply than many princes or their political acolytes. With the historical and moral heritage left by the Toynbees of England and their precursors and successors, can anyone wonder that, with few exceptions, British politicians since the late nineteenth century have largely failed to comprehend the economic sources of the power which they enjoyed and unhesitatingly applied in pursuit of their aims? Institutionalized British politics on the right or left certainly revealed no real understanding of the need for buttressing the roots of its power—industry. This is why the first fully-fledged industrial nation of the modern world—enjoying unequalled supremacy for around a century—failed to be encouraged by the leaders of its political society to keep up with industrial progress elsewhere; thus, the long enjoyed position of this country as a world power was undermined in a relatively short time, and the ground was laid for innumerable internal social and economic stresses and strains—some still unresolved.

The erosion of Britain's industrial power had several causes—but the most important destructive agents in the process were largely non-material. A century of rising prosperity for all classes between the Congress of Vienna and the First World War, made the accumulation of private and public wealth seem almost effortless. One of its results—buttressed as it has been so often by a little intellectual guilt of money-making—was that intellectual concern quickly shifted from the production of wealth to its distribution. Since the late 1800s, distribution and not the creation of wealth has been the subject of protracted debate in universities, in politics, in the professions and among the ruling intellectual elites of the day. With an almost paranoid disdain for the productive process, and a dedication to distributive justice, i.e. the redistribution of wealth, the day of economic reckoning could not be indefinitly prolonged. Yet, during the leaner times of the 1920s and 1930s, intellectual effort did not, as logic would have it, return to a contemplation of how to increase the production of wealth more successfully in order to increase distribution. No! The opinion-making intelligentsia conceived the deprivation of some, and the difficult conditions of life for many during the inter-war slump years not as imperfections of their political objectives—more socialism, more welfare state—or national educational aims, or of their simplistic views of the merits of wealth creation, but rather as the result of a yet unsolved defect in the distribution of national wealth—i.e. soak the rich! The impression left behind is that the ruling intellectual gurus were more concerned with dividing rather than enlarging the national cake. Their own often well-off background, with their unearned incomes, deluded them into believing that the resources, the wealth, were there.

For a country nurtured for several generations on industrial success—from which flowed economic and political success—it seems to have been unthinkable for its intellectual leaders to inquire into the reasons for creeping industrial obsolescence and recommend solutions for its reversal. Not too many of the country's intellectual leaders would have understood the fundamental industrial challenges confronting the nation. The most widely held view until the mid-twentieth century was that Britain might have lost her way momentarily, but blue skies were around the corner. This false security—underpinned by inherited individual and corporate wealth, which for long subsidized living standards—was not to run out until the mid-twentieth century and even then its consequences were not correctly grasped. Few of Britain's politicians, trade unionists, or any one group of its assorted intellectuals warned businessmen consistently of what will happen if the country's industrial competitive position were to be further eroded: as different power groups, they were busy with attempting to maintain their own position and failed to act and think together. The philosophical heritage of eighteenth-century individuality needed rejigging! No wonder, to take a contemporary illustration, that for several decades the economics of wage bargaining in Britain were not focused on a firm's ability to pay, as many of the nationalized and private sectors of industry bear witness. The unions' alibis for higher pay were based on ignorance of economics. That is no basis for prosperity.

That a chaotic state of industrial affairs was allowed to ensue in a highly civilized country like Britain must be attributed not only to the treason of the intellectuals at that time—uncaring about the state of the nation's business—and even hostile to it—but businessmen too must take a goodly share of the blame. Industrialists and trade unions alike were not fully aware of the run-down state of British business, hence little defence was taken to repair its deterioration, or to influence those who had the power to make conditions more conducive to invigorate this potentially great British productive machine. What was the nature of defence by productive industry in the first five decades of this century? Short-term solutions by 'practical' businessmen and down-to-earth politicians abounded, but their successes were not manifest. Both the fault and hence the remedy lay elsewhere. In the final reconciliation, the economic and industrial impoverishment of Britain was and remained attributable to a lack of intellectual—in this instance more scientific—understanding of the needs of trade and industry and, simultaneously, to the businessmen's tendency to shy away from encouraging intellectual participation. If this assumption is not wildly incorrect, the economic and industrial renewal of trade and industry could have been better achieved by a new synthesis between practical and intellectual thinking. Such an exercise would have realized that habits of thought and ways of looking at business must be changed, and that short-term expedients for circumventing the ills of industry and trade offer no durable solutions.

Businessmen's myopia

Businessmen's lack of intellectuality and articulation of their problems have resulted in little discernible intellectual support from their trade and industry associations. These association's concern (with exceptions of course) is pedestrian; often they remained insufficiently informed about the state of business in their trade, about the likely effects of impending (i.e. lobbying) or recently passed legislation, and they rarely offered a lead in support or in opposition to ideas advanced by government about, for example, foreign competitors or the trade unions. While the role of these associations should not be dismissed, many have not been very active or meaningful in guiding their particular segment of industry or trade through their problems of change and readjustment; they, too, have largely failed to anticipate what is likely to happen which may affect their member's business, and hence warn or advise them accordingly. Nor is there much evidence of trade associations endeavouring to make useful suggestions to their members about management innovations or practices in other lands or to present a global view of their trade, or help their members on how to demonstrate their business activity to the best advantage and thereby try to heighten the social, economic, or political esteem of their part of trade or industry. Perhaps the only activity which they performed with assiduous care was their role in restrictive practices—not an endeavour to inject entrepreneurial adrenalin into the directorial boards of their member companies. No—the institutional representation of many branches of British business has long been and probably still is 'severely practical', but this time from the trade association side. Industrial or commercial associations have not, for example, taken as part of their brief, the need for careful scrutinization of the entrails of political manifestos which might lead them to a better understanding of what lies ahead in the economic sector, and, hence, lead their industry segment to formulate in advance the necessary defensive or offensive measures to be taken. Associations of businessmen in general have, similarly, achieved little in educating their members to appreciate the need to think in abstractions as well as in practicalities. In this respect, trade associations and trade unions share strange similarities. And last, but not least, they have conspicuously failed to mount a sustained effort to instruct the non-business public about the need for an efficient and profitable industry. The pedestrian profile of businessmen's associations again reflects the long-established wish and tradition of the businessman to be severely 'practical'.

Is it surprising that few trade associations, institutes of learning, or groups of businessmen are concerned continuously about the future of business as a vital activity or, indeed, as an exercise in survival? Britain is probably the only mature industrialized country without a high calibre intellectual pressure group of successful and articulate businessmen. It may also be the only country not to have a (recognized?) private platform where businessmen discuss informally their own and each other's problems with non-businessmen, academics, military men, bishops, trade unionists, members of government, opposition, etc. The propensity for the businessman to stay in his ghetto and study the contents of his in-tray is overwhelming. His alibi for such irrationalism is being busy, terribly busy; in fact, he is simply badly organized. Attitudes such as these are not a sure fire recipe for profitable survival—much less a prescription for success.

What then is the background to the still largely pragmatic preoccupation of the businessman and his organizations with the immediacies of his company in such an imaginative adventure as business? This question deserves close scrunity.

a. Unpreparedness

Businessmen, just as much as their trade associations, are over-preoccupied with the present. Yet, they must look ahead to ensure customer satisfaction and that competitors do not steal a march on them. Forward looking in taking care of the ABCs of business is not extended to the XYZs—a host of problems not immediately concerned with the practicalities of running the firm. Yet the outlook for business in Britain today is not unclouded, as staying in business becomes more complicated. For this, if for no other reason, businessmen and their associations need to understand and envisage the consequences of the forces shaping business enterprise in the world today; general observations and elegant summaries are inadequate, it is necessary to focus on the specifics of how a particular business or industry will be affected—and cerebate in abstract terms. Couched in such terms, business problems will be more comprehensible to the policy makers, the opinion-makers and the man on the Clapham omnibus—who could be a trade unionist. But, taking a narrower view, where are the businesmen and their associations grappling with clearly stated major issues of the day, offering position papers, understood by government, by the unions and the universities? There are, of course, not a few individual, forward-thinking businessmen in Britain; curiously, most of them tend to be in banking, investment and allied services rather than in manufacturing industry. There is little doubt that the financial community has better contingency plans for the eventuality of the new Left's translation to power than the business community or their trade associations.

b. Obscurantism

In broad terms, the British business community is relatively less well prepared and hence is less successful in the pursuit of its chosen objective than its foreign competitors. Such inadequacies extend to technical and commercial realities,to general and university education, to public esteem, and to the ability to influence central and local government by means of dialogues. These shortcomings may in the past have influenced the growth of an anti-industrial tradition; but the financial and banking communities are successful in bending the ear of successive governments and of the other estates of the realm. Their standing in the hierarchy of occupations is much higher in the public esteem and their successes are widely heralded and acclaimed. The invisible export statistics reveal their splendid performance at every opportunity. Perhaps the financial and especially, the merchant banking community, has always been able to intellectualize its policies and its views. Or, perhaps, one might speculate and suggest that Britain boasts of an anti-industry rather than an anti-capitalist tradition?

One might attribute the relatively uncombative stance of businesmen to the belief that business still does not rank high in social esteem. Such a realization one may argue (or use as an alibi) cannot bring out the best in its devotees. Furthermore, it is sometimes put forward that an element of amateurism continues to survive in the conduct of many businesses. A wider acceptance that such amateurism exists could in part explain a popular misconception that business is easy, that there is little skill in its pursuit. Only on the basis of such a misunderstanding can one comprehend an amusing story reported about a college at one of the ancient universities extending its students' quarters and employing a builder who was about to go insolvent; as the college financed the builder they assumed the right to appoint a new managing director to carry on the firm and, at least, complete the work for new dormitories. Who should the college appoint as managing director of the building firm—but its chaplain! The notion that business activity must be carried out competently and not by amateurs has not yet reached their quadrangle. Perhaps this particular college runs too many courses in economics!

c. Organizing industry

A more intellectual approach to industrial organization could have foreseen the demise of certain firms or the rising number of unemployed over the years in the manufacturing industry. A similar approach would not have supported dying industries but encouraged new ones. Lack of public comprehension why so many firms are unprofitable or go bankrupt leaves too many with the false belief that politicians and capitalists between them want to cause unemployment and dispense hardship for their own, unspecified, evil purposes. Belief that Britain is the unwilling victim of certain governmental economic doctrines or of industrial conspiracies leading to unemployment because of hatred for union labour continues to linger. It would be salutary to explain to uncommitted minds that in recent years Britain has merely come up against those economic forces which Canute governments, businessmen and trade unionists have for so long attempted to defy. Many of the firms gone out of business were on their last legs, even before the inflationary crises of the mid and late 1970s; important decisions essential in the running of firms must be explained in comprehensible terms—are we back to intellectuality again?—by the business community to the non-business world. Perhaps in no other country is the gap between the leaders of trade and industry and the other elites so great as in Britain. The industrial and commercial illiteracy of the British people outside business—and of not a few inside business—is simply stunning.

d. On profits

Nothing embitters more the poorly paid, the unemployed, the business illiterate, the anti-business league or the deliberately destructive with his polarized -ism than the spectacle of firms reporting tens and sometimes hundreds of millions of pounds of profits, particularly in hard times. The embers of such envy are fanned by the media, because they offer a refracted view, hence they rarely offer informed comment, as well as by the politically motivat d in sensitive positions where they manufacture opportunities to pontificate. Confusion about company profits is undesirable in itself, but is made more bizarre by the anaemic attempts of businessmen or their associations to explain the nature of profit, the way firms earn it, the many different formulae for its distribution, and the taxes paid by the corporation and shareholders on this profit. Or, take another example, it is all very well for a major British company to officially disclaim innuendoes that by under-recording its profits it has short-changed the Revenue on taxes. A company disclaimer will achieve little in the public mind. A specially prepared accountancy statement verified by independent auditors and a strongly worded denial by the head of the company must back up any repudiation to be effective. Revelations by the press travel fast and far; their correction must be manifestly forceful to cover the same mileage, and more. Again, company announcements are all very well, and, indeed, any company so mentioned may be as pure as the driven snow, but it is vital that its counter-thrust be well supported by independent opinion and easily understood and widely disseminated. The worst disservice the businessman can do to himself and his firm is to believe that he is being victimized and considers himself to be too grand to defend himself: he must learn a trick or two about the need for a good public profile. In Britain, profits quite often seem to cause envy, incite the uninformed and innumerate, and sometimes make headlines. When one of the largest UK companies announces earning hundreds of millions of pounds before tax and the news item is blandly reported on newspaper front pages without much explanation of what, in the end, this means to the shareholders, the vision of immense amounts of monies distributed to the gentrified *rentier* stands out in isolation. The sad reality about money is that few understand, say, a million pounds and everybody understands fifty quid. Thus, company finances must be, intellectually, brought down to the fifty quid level for their adequate understanding by all—including most shareholders.

Presentation of corporate financial information can 'suffer' great improvements; the spending of money and the ways of earning it by the firm should be put into an understandable perspective. The constant pressure by company and other laws for more disclosure has not made company accounts more comprehensible to the laity. Even the 'simplified', 'condescending' accounts issued by companies for internal use for their employees stubbornly refuse to yield the kind of information that work and office people want to read and understand. Simplicity and clarity should be the guiding lights. Why should the report of the chairman and the annual accounts of a company be more difficult to understand than a football pool blank?

e. Influencing education

More 'informed' energy should be spent by businessmen to influence the type and quality of education. Companies are the passive recipients of candidates churned out by the academic machine—from the middle and higher reaches of education. Business must influence the educational system positively by helping to introduce new courses. The remoteness of most businesses from schools and universities excepting the large companies should not be allowed to continue. Would the universities have been such eager protagonists of the explosion of social science faculties since the 1960s if they had had a better grasp of the higher educational requirements of industry?

One of the keys to build a better industrial machine in Britain is the general extension of refresher courses. Key persons should be sent back to courses at intervals to learn about the latest techniques, developments, and their applications. The acquisition of new competence and an awareness of new ideas is difficult while at work, just by reading professional literature or by drifting along to occasional lectures. The suggestion of a wider extension of refreshers has ramifications outside business—in all the professions and, most of all, in teaching. Nor should the idea of sabbaticals be confined to graduate employees in industry, scientists in research establishments, or high-level administrators in government or secretaries in trade unions or indeed members of the armed forces. Business skills, too, are a wasting asset—new skills can be learnt by the successful entrepreneur, for instance, whose firm's success has grown beyond his business competence. Unless the entrepreneur is also prepared to learn new tricks, his firm's progress will slow down and he may prematurely have to be acquired as he is unable to organize and control his firm beyond a certain critical size— he is simply devoid of the necessary abstract skills; a little more intellectuality perhaps?

Up-to-date technical learning must be accompanied by a better understanding of business principles—as opposed to economics. However, it promises to be difficult to cut down on unhelpful courses in economics, particularly in mathematical and statistical economics, and to introduce useful courses about the organization of the firm, the way to negotiate with unions, customers or suppliers, the nature of foreign competition, etc. Perhaps the study of psychology, in conjunction with economics might help in an understanding of markets. The separation of economics from trade and industry at university level has turned out graduates who will exercise judgement about business issues in irrelevant economic terms. Such an approach can derail the small firm where sophistication is most needed. This approach also explains why 'economic planning' in Britain has suffered such setbacks, while in France, where economists' understanding of business is ensured by their training, it has not been unsuccessful. Doubtless, French—not to mention North American—economic graduates keep their noses closer to the 'industrial ground' than their less well-instructed British counterparts who, rightly, claim only an abstract understanding of commercial life! The strictly limited utility of economics to business is the real reason why market research, economic research, and corporate planning in corporations are often decorative supplements without much authority and, equally, without much propensity for contribution to profits. That is why their relevance to the firm is often ephemeral, despite being placed so near the power base—the office of the chairman of the board.

Their undoubted intellectual energies have not been focused on the profitable survival of the firm. And the result of the small contribution of these sheltered centres of activity in the firm has been a notable reduction in numbers during the more competitive years of the 1980s. No alibi for cutting down in these spheres was required in industry! An alibi for demonstrative sophistication in the company was needed to build them up!

Another little exploited opportunity of further education in Britain is placing people 'on exchange' for a limited but worthwhile period: exchanges of employees between government departments and universities has long been extant, as it has been more recently between government and business, though, in the case of the latter, nothing like on the scale needed. No iconoclasm is inherent in the suggestion that sales managers should be seconded to the diplomatic service as commercial attaches and *vice versa*; more university teachers might consider temporary work in institutions, foundations and business, to explore how the other worlds work and away from their routine employ. Potentially, the most important educational exchange which needs to take place is between middle and top management in businesses and principals and assistant secretaries in the civil service; as well as between company executives and the shop or area organizers and assistant secretaries or general secretaries of trade unions. Such temporary job exchanges would bring significant mutual benefit not only to the organizations involved but to the national scene. The realization of such novel exchanges promises to improve labour/employer peace and help industry/government dialogue. Officials in institutionalized agencies responsible for policy recommendations would gain greater awareness of the forces shaping business and the need to meet competition, and equally business executives devoted to earning profits could be made more aware of the political and economic problems of government and of the unions. There is no valid, pragmatic reason why trade unions, government departments, and trading and industrial firms should not succeed in effecting such exchanges: after all, they are all deeply concerned with and interested in growing prosperity—all fruits of collaboration. Alibis of ignorance will thus be gradually removed.

f. On and off the media

Many a businessman's self-imposed strait-jacket, as a 'practical man' influences his dealings with the media. Articulacy, the ability to think on one's feet and quick-witted repartee are neglected arts, luxuries rarely displayed by the businessman when exposed to press, radio or television, or a public platform. Those less keen of being thought of as merely 'practical', and endowed with more resolution to display their intellectual propensities, come off better when in touch with public affairs. One need not be an intellectual to make a statement which arouses interest—after all much depends on the content, but, equally, much hinges on the way a statement is put. What is implied here is that an intellectual way of thinking, i.e. an ability to express one's thoughts, feelings and prejudices in a clear, organized fashion, is important. Because few industrialists' encounters with the media are wildly successful, received wisdom informs that the less a businessman is exposed to the media the better. This is sheer fallacy: pressmen, television interviewers, radio reporters, all like talking to the boss and not to those shielding him from exposure. If businessmen are reluctant to face the media, will they ever learn to cope with public affairs? But beyond the mechanics of exposure businessmen must understand that they have a message to convey to several constituencies with conviction; and this is where the rub comes. Still too many businessmen have not rationalized the intellectual kernel of their raison d'être—so how can they really be confident in replying to intellectually searching questions? Media shyness of business is just another species of the hopefully passing British business disease—which takes pride in not explaining. Businessmen of other nations seem a little better at it, better on the whole, and that is what counts at the margin. How can this inevitable and necessary exposure to the media be turned to advantage?

The chairman of a major bank—seeking advice on how to put the City of London in a better light—was told that to publish yet another book about the Stock Exchange, would be otiose; friends of the free market would praise the book unread, and friends of central planning would condemn it unread. It was suggested that a better investment for the future would be to try and influence favourably two fledgling intellectuals of the day, tomorrow's opinion-makers; it was further put to him that if knowledgeable or 'even' interesting information were disseminated in institutions of higher learning about activities in the City in English literature classes and not only in post-graduate programmes on banking, the likelihood of a more favourable understanding of City activities might be formed with greater certainity over a wide area but over a longer period. Towards such ends, it was put to him that to lunch at the bank the current-day equivalents of F. R. Leavis or Rebecca West, and explain to them a wrinkle or two about City business, could not easily be bettered. More understanding by the literati about money and business would shine through their writings or lecturing, and influence those who set the climate of opinion. This approach 'my' friendly, neighbourhood banker could not comprehend. The reason why such and similar 'oblique' suggestions meet with resistance is due to a lack of intellectual understanding of the immense influence of contemporary literature. The distorting influence on business of the early nineteenth-century women novelists, of mid-century Charles Dickens and later William Morris, in labelling the entrepreneur as anti-social and business as a detestable occupation, continues to linger.

Indeed the incomplete mental picture of trade and industry held by the multitude and by many of the elite has to be rectified if general notions about business and the businessman are to change for the better. Anti-business sentiment is not confined to Britain, though it has been more widely shared here than elsewhere. The Media Institute in Washington revealed that half the businessmen portrayed in American films were shown to engage in illegal activities—from tax evasion, to protection rackets and murder. On celluloid , at least, they were shown to be utterly ruthless. Yet, if there is one characteristic atypical of the majority of British businessmen, it is ruthlessness; some of them could be labled as ostentatious because they are insecure—a trait which is more of a social gaffe over here than anywhere else. At all events, the British businessman in general does not seem to exude that degree of competence or confidence which his contemporary professionals radiate in the civil service, the medical, scientific, legal or trade union worlds. What are the reasons for this?

Too many businessmen mistakenly believe, or perhaps wish to believe, they have no need to create and radiate public confidence by emphasizing the positive, constructive aspect of their activities. But will the continuing crescendo of censure on business, big and not so big alike, revise their attitudes? How can the businessman cope with such new demands? First, he must realize that the public want to know from him—the head of the firm—details about his business in comprehensible but easily digestible form. With exceptions, a remarkable degree of illiteracy about business still abounds. This lack of knowledge about business must be changed by offering information i.e. education. The first business-man—manufacturer or retailer—who is prepared to buy a three or four minute slot on commercial television 'at peak viewing times' and explain the contents of his annual report or give an account of his company's business in simple terms and with easy illustrations, could become a minor public personality for his lifetime. Moreover he is in a position to explain to the widest audience the workings of capitalism and the free market. Such a television commercial can reveal how money is earned and distributed in wages, in purchases, in investment, and in tax, and how a small residue fully taxed is paid out in dividends. Such a company chairman will receive wide acclaim for his courage and will forge a more loyal workforce as well as help materially increase the demand for his products or services. Public interest and enlightened self-interest do converge. Explaining them bestows on business a human face.

Intellectual rigours for businessmen

The forces hostile to business will, eventually, force businessmen to take counter-measures by partaking in a species of show-bizz, in a form specially suited to their vocation and temperament. In this 'game' of image-creation for the public, the founders, the entrepreneurs of modern businesses (they are mostly but need not be the founders) may come off less well than their more institutionalized and invariably better educated contemporaries in the more formally structured and longer established businesses. The young chairman of Britain's largest computer maker when interviewed was not at a loss for words about justifying his high salary or his company-aided house buying. That he had to indulge in such explanations tells us a good deal about the critical, not to say envious way many look upon businessmen. The fact that all foreign diplomats and many foreign businessmen in Britain live rent-free or enjoy heavily subsidized rents does not seem to have occurred to complaining shareholders or indignant press reporters.

For the modern businessman to make a favourable impact on his surroundings, his brief must include thinking and talking intellectually about politics. Yet it is remarkable how many business-men proudly proclaim to be non-political, as though politics was an avoidable disease, and not contributing to the coffers of a political party—i.e. by standing aloof—conferred on them a species of sainthood. One wonders whether meanness, overt cowardice, fear of guilt by association, lack of political conviction or fear of possible political backlash may account for this curious form of political sterility. Or is it an alibi for ostensible virtue? While the simile is not fully comparable, trade unions contribute diligently to their political party and in former times it demanded an active, conscious decision not to pay—i.e. to 'contract out'. Here then is an interesting difference in attitude, not reflecting too well on the businessman. But perhaps times are changing; the board of a well-known and respected investment trust has decided and publicly announced it will consider sympathetically the possibility of providing support to the Social Democratic Party and Liberal Party if they become a 'viable' force in British politics. This undertaking came in the face of shareholder criticism of this firm's contribution to the coffers of the Conservative party at the annual general meeting. At least, members of this board stood up to be counted. They were prepared to discuss and fight off shareholders' political or emotional objections. The chairman explained the donation to the Conservatives very simply—the Conservative government had helped the investment trust movement. Another director emphasized that they would look favourably also on a rival party to the Conservatives, clearly in support of capitalism and private enterprise. What—no alibis?

Businessmen's collective complacency about the unfamiliar must also be relegated to history. Responsible business must enlist, nurture and support a group or several groups of youngish businessmen to meet regularly and discuss the future of business. This would include thinking about and discussing likely 'happenings' some time ahead; happenings, which might change the structure of industry, the volume of trade, the level of profits or employment opportunities. Such groups might also contemplate what defensive stance to assume now to ward off vulnerability arising from political changes tomorrow. Such groups would be businessmen groups, focusing on generalities on a wide canvas as well as concentrating on narrow specifics. Their individual tasks would include the present while thinking of the future, personally cultivating all shades of political opinion, getting to know trade unionists, university teachers, journalists, lobbyists, politicians in and out of office, i.e. all those in public affairs whose work impinges on business—and establish informal contacts of confidence and credibility. If industry needs an 'old boy's network' then this is it. It is insufficient to leave politics to trade or industry associations. The trouble is that specialized industry organizations rarely have the talent for giving comprehensive guidance to their members, while the national bodies embrace too many—sometimes conflicting interests—to be specifically, as against generally, useful.

Finally, back to the businessman and his ideas about himself! Apart from being successful in his business, he must also openly show that he enjoys his work, that business is not a burden; that his labours serve their appointed useful purposes and that his company is progressive and aims at excellence. The image of businessman as the strong silent type, the epitome of understatement, must not endure. I have long suspected that understatement is often the refuge of the undertalented—an alibi ennobled by Victorian mores as a hallmark of gentility. The need for more willingness and greater cogency to explain business must go hand in hand with combativeness and clear thinking. Businessmen in general have been complacent, myopic and often ignorant about the forces unsympathetic to them. The desire to sit tight and do little for fear to rock the boat, and a wish to be thought of as a 'nice guy' by saying little that could be offensive has resulted in businessmen often being thought of as pushovers, or as pliable toys for politically inspired experiments. This view of the businessman as docile is often revealed by industrialists believing themselves to be part of the 'establishment', or by those who would like to indulge in the fantasy of belonging to it. Not for them to take too many risks and exploit opportunities—rather wait until someone else's venture is successful and then buy it up expensively! After all, by not investing in grass roots ventures it cannot involve them in failure—the spectre of potential failure has made industrialists rigidly cautious. Yet occasional failures are an element in risk-taking and to paraphrase Oscar Wilde, 'a man who has had no failures has nothing!' These are the same timid businessmen who will not willingly come into the open and condemn disruptive trade union practices or inadequate support by the financial sector—particularly when not personally involved.

The reasons for the businessmen's timidity are understandable in the short term. By practising complacencey they do not appear to endanger their power, prestige, emoluments, and, most important, their pensions. Their self-assured and vivacious pronouncements in annual reports, in businessmen's clubs and elsewhere ooze discreet suggestions but rarely any thoughtful or purposefully addressed words on the nitty-gritty. If it were suggested to them at their endless series of uninspired board luncheons that foolish government measures or recalcitrant trade union conduct could be better mitigated by businessmen physically lobbying Parliament or they might consider personally intervening about a dispute on the factory floor and explain their ideas and beliefs, they would be hurt and staggered that such suggestions could even be put to them!

It has never been adequate for the businessman to act in the role of the non-interventionist, the tribal chief of his industrial or trading company, enjoying the simple trust placed in him; this must be particularly so when the calibre of his competitors, and the quality of his union negotiators has risen rapidly; he must, in person, be present himself at the place of trouble, and intervene with courage and knowledge. There is no room for contracting out any longer. And it is on such occasions when friction is generated and must be resolved that the successful businessman will apply intellectuality to convince his workers or shareholders or customers or suppliers or trade unions or government departments—all of whom want convincing—with well thought-out arguments and not with ageing platitudes and primitive bluffing in this increasingly open industrial society of Britain.

ON PROFESSIONALS
AND INTELLECTUALS

Sequels to a Victorian heritage

The Renaissance concept of high culture, symbolized and extolled by an enlightened elite in eighteenth-century England, was gradually relegated to limbo in the century following; cultural unity gave way to diversity with its inevitable concomitant of fragmentation. Cultural changes can be a force for social cohesion, economic improvement, dynamism and growth, or a damper on innovation and enterprise and a source of social divisiveness. In supporting England's industrial strength and continuing prosperity, nineteenth-century cultural developments were not always propitious; the spiritual beliefs, social standards and the fragile self-esteem of the industrial classes were infected with uncertainties and doubts by the arbiters of culture; this tended to puncture their confidence and discourage their ambition. The confidence of the 'industrial primitive' in his mission of progress and wealth creation had begun to abate.

Cultural changes in Victorian England developed hostility to industry and to capitalism, to the notion of enterprise and to the market place; hence, for well over a century, from about the 1850s onward, industry and trade were diverted from the mainstream of national culture—where they properly belong—and remained in that catastrophic position until the third quarter of the twentieth century. The social acceptability and utility of business, and the dedication of the middle classes to the pursuit of trade and industry were exposed to the multi-warhead attacks of an intelligentsia—the dons, the professionals and the men of letters and by a genteel, professional and aspiring middle class afraid of the business class attaining parity of esteem with them. The esteem previously accorded to business and the rising bourgeoisie managing it—in a country of traders, first to develop an industrial muscle—were twin supports of national sobriety. The decline of industrial England from her position of primacy was a direct result of the denigration of the spirit of business—of the market place in which it operated; and the shrinkage of England's political influence followed her economic misfortunes after a respectable delay. The muscularity of the English industrial thrust in the 1850s was still powerful enough to resist its decline for over half a century. Not until the post-First World War economic plagues hit the world did Britain reveal how feeble her industry had become. Economic sobriety and the exercise of political will are inseparable from industrial and commercial success—an axiom not properly understood by the moral and cultural leaders of mid-nineteenth-century England. Their denigration of business and its culture left Britain with a heritage of social deformities, economic vicissitudes, lost educational opportunities and diminishing political impact on world affairs, from which recovery has only just begun.

The seeds of decline during Victoria's reign were not sown deliberately to weaken or destroy the pre-eminent position of Britain in the comity of nations. Indeed, it might be argued that it was the high noon of the country's standing and its long enjoyed prosperity which made possible the appearance of such a variety of influential social critics of her industrial culture. Perhaps the 'surplus product', agonized over by Marx, became too freely available, helping to foster counter-cultures and the evolution of destructive anti-enterprise, anti-industrial movements; such were the problems of success of mid-nineteenth-century industry. It is wrong to assume that it was stupidity or mere destructiveness which helped to undermine the high and prosperous industrial culture of nineteenth-century England; rather it was compounded of a search for a display of virtue, coupled with unawareness of possible consequences. On that reading, it is difficult to decide if stupidity or unawareness is the greater of the deadly sins! The mid- and late-Victorian cognoscenti who played with fire did not really know what fire was. A comparison with twentieth-century English elites reveal a similar naivety—on this occasion in the political sphere with the inevitable accompaniment of skewed-up thinking about economics—hence weakening industry and trade.

The reality of an industrial culture in England—which like all cultures needs to be nurtured to survive and to enrich its catchment area—has until more recently been very imperfectly perceived among the opinion-forming elite. T. S. Eliot, observed:

In an illuminating supplement to the *Christian News-Letter* of July 24, 1946, Miss Marjorie Reeves has a very suggestive paragraph on 'The Culture of an Industry'. If she somewhat enlarged her meaning, what she says would fit in with my own way of using the word 'culture'. She says, of the culture of an industry, which she believes quite rightly should be presented to the young worker; 'it includes the geography of its raw materials and final markets, its historical evolution, inventions and scientific background, its economics, and so forth'. It includes all this, certainly; but an industry, if it is to engage the interest of more than the conscious mind of the worker, should also have a way of life somewhat peculiar to its initiates, with its own forms of festivity and observances. I mention this interesting reminder of the culture of industry, however, as evidence that I am aware of other nuclei of culture than those discussed in this book. (*Notes Towards the Definition of Culture*, Faber & Faber, London 1948, p.16)

These sentiments were expressed by Eliot in 1948; the type of awareness of industry—alas a little condescending—which Eliot adumbrates was scarcely perceived by the elites for another thirty years; a succession of labour-socialist and conservative-socialist governments, whose understanding of the country's industrial culture must, at best, have been incomplete, cannot escape a share of the responsibility for the decline of industrial power. They have ruled post-Second World War Britain largely from their inter-war memories of what a once prosperous country could accomplish—but their policies and political ambitions were not geared to the power of a debilitated economic machine. The realization of folk-memories became a major exercise—the flavour of past greatness a policy objective. Not until the arrival of radical conservative governments in the 1980s did a new reconciliation begin between political frailty and industrial and economic stagnation. The new entrepreneurial spirit unleashed on Britain in the 1980s does not yet command overwhelming assent, but enjoys sufficient consensus to make it workable. For the first time in a century, or longer, a stream of new ideas and impulses is building up towards a renewal of a healthy industrial culture where incentives are revived and achievement recognized and incompetence punished. It has taken the emergence of three million and more unemployed to force a change in the industrial culture, to focus again on the importance of nurturing enterprise and innovation and to endow successful businessmen with the esteem enjoyed by other successful elites.

Contributing to the protracted economic stagnation of Britain were the twin nineteenth-century cultural and occupational developments—the rise of the forces of intellectualism and professionalism: the moral of history seems to declare that Victorian Britain had taken her 'professionals' too seriously and her 'intellectuals' not seriously enough. While the advice of the professional was largely unquestioned, the criticism of the intellectual was largely unheeded.

Rise of the professional

It is difficult to determine whether the rise of professionalism or of intellectualism proved the more hazardous for the unfettered progress of a healthy industrial culture of Victorian Britain; on balance, I think, the harmful spirit of restrictionist professionalism was more retarding. After all, there was then, as there are now, many more professional workers than self-professed, identifiable practising intellectuals. And while intellectuals criticize and debate, they sometimes give wings to ideas which, if tenable, may after a time be translated into action; professionals are in constant touch with individuals and industry and their advice has *gravitas* and imme- diacy; professionals are working members of the community with specific skills, with whom people and firms consult. Few consult intellectuals—their cerebrations are revealed, their texts disseminated but only a few take note of them. The nexus between professionals and the public is closer than between intellectuals and the people. Some professionals have intellectual propensities but this does not turn them into intellectuals—or vice versa.

Professionals wish to identify themselves socially, with the 'upper crust', and associate their social ambition for the professional man with their ideals of the gentleman. When several new professional cadres emerged around the 1830s, they wished to be considered, like the members of the older established professions, a 'cut above' the so-called new middle class whose rise from nowhere crystallized the success of the industrial primitive. The professional rejected middle-class commercial values, since such values stood for entrepreneurial action, the market place, hence for competition. Successful manufacturers and traders in the Victorian era reached for and assumed middle-class values effortlessly and proudly spent their 'new money' lavishly. Those who resented their successes affected to respect 'old money' more highly than 'new money' and distanced themselves from these 'manufacturing savages'—as Mrs Trollope called them, and as other novelists of the nineteenth century described them. I ascribe one of the reasons for the rise of an anti-commercial culture to fear of social relegation by 'new money'. After all, the social position of the earlier professionals—lawyers, doctors, clergymen—remained precarious as they were not automatically recognized by the gentry as equals; however they considered themselves above the bourgeoisie and their alibi for a parity with the gentry was to dispatch the rising industrial classes to a social Hades. Social insecurity is a powerful motor and, in this instance, it offered a convenient incentive to disdain the energy, look down on the achievements, and sneer at the wealth of the up-and-coming bourgeois, the entrepreneurial class.

The newer disciplines' desire for professionalization as they emerged during the Victorian era greatly influenced cultural developments. T. W. Heyck[1] suggests that the impact of science in England from the 1830s onwards was the core of this development. Science dominated the thinking of progressive people. Huxley and his contemporaries helped introduce it into the universities. Science was universally acclaimed in Victorian Britain—there was plenty of it around. The reason why this outburst of science failed to benefit English industry in full and in the longer term, quite as fully as it did the industries of other countries, may be attributed to science and scientific research becoming university-bound. The evidence is strong to support this contention.

Science, then, was the rage of Victorian England; science prevailed when confronted by religion; science was 'the new calling to be pursued—and the aspiring scientist was recruited to the cause from the industrial and commercial as well as other classes, that is largely from among middle-class people and artisans. Scientists at mid-nineteenth century shared the middle-class values of upward

[1] T. W. Heyck, *The Transformation of Intellectual Life in Victorian England*, Croom Helm, London 1983.

social mobility and achievement and wished to reach the upper-class echelons by emulating the manners and affectation of the old type professional. These efforts towards identity and professional status combined to affect profoundly the institutional claims and achievements of science in Britain. It was declared that scientists distinguished themselves as a community apart from the rest of society—a community thought of as necessary but not accountable to the nation.'[2] From adopting this posture the idea developed that scientists working from a university would enjoy higher social esteem by making their knowledge available to everyone, rather than by working for industry using their skills only for furthering the prosperity of a client in business. The next step was finding a paymaster for science. Support for science—proclaimed the leading scientists from the 1840s onwards—should be provided by the nation, even if science did not lend itself to instant use, i.e. earning profits by application of useful ends. Scientists succeeded in making their home in the universities and were supported by university stipends and funds for research. Scientific research was equated with profound scholarship, endowing it with great *gravitas* which smacks of German thinking; scientists championed that the endowments of colleges and universities should be used for this specific purpose. Those suggesting the endowment type support for scientific research 'recognised that the principle . . . represented a break with the market place. Research should be endowed precisely because the market place failed to provide for it; but teaching (science) should be thrown upon some kind of fee system, because the market place reflected a demand for it . . . the nation would be richer by its research even though that research was not marketable.'[3] It is not for the first time in the history of ideas that a new development is stunted by arguments unconnected with its essence. How many educational or business decisions are taken for non-educational or non-business reasons? Not a few I would assume.

Science in Victorian England, then, was taken over by the universities and by taking this step it endowed the work and its practitioners with respectability; this takeover deflected the use of science from trade and industry towards the pursuit of dispassionate research—i.e. pure science—the socially more dignified objective of

[2] Ibid., p. 88.
[3] Ibid., pp. 180–1.

professional scientists. University-based research became predominant, outside research in industry remained unimpressive. This had tragic effects on British industry as the endowment of research (in the universities) helped drive a barrier between science and industrial application—i.e. between pure and applied research. Because nineteenth-century scientific research was university-based and college-endowed and its *raison d'être* was not conceived as a commercial utility, research was not integrated into the industrial process; research in universities became science for science's sake just as art was pursued for art's sake—a stance emulated by literature a little later in the last century. British scientists desired to avoid the taint of applied research which German scientists always embraced; thus the decline in British industry coincided with the rise of German industry. Unregenerate nineteenth-century Oxbridge ideas shaped scientists' approach to their work and thus did English science become detached from English industrial culture. It was said that the universities 'sponsored freedom from commitment to the issues of real life.'[4] This spirit became a focal part of the professional tradition of scientists; and the Victorian attitude to the profession of the scientist coloured the cultural-industrial development of other disciplines in the newer professions of engineers, accountants, architects, solicitors, civil servants, and even insurance brokers and stockbrokers (who until recently passed no tests to obtain professional qualifications). A latter-day residue of the early scientists' desire for professional identity and for self-defined professional values has, in turn, sanctified further developments along similar lines.

No personal involvement (i.e. initiative) but, on the record, proferring (usually) excellent (professional) advice; such a consciously mannerized approach of the professional to involvement with clients in commerce and industry may appear a little antiquated so late in the twentieth century; the historical, customary, specialist professional advice by now is a little narrow. Professionals are beginning to think more like businessmen in attacking a problem; a welcome change. However, this very aloofness of the English professional has endowed him and his work with a high standing of probity, honesty, and independence of judgement which is such a source of envy in many other countries. At the end of the day, the

---

[4] Ibid., p. 185.

none-too-rare custom for instance of some American lawyers participating in the damages awarded in court with their clients is not a preferable way of professional conduct—even if it is more profitable! But there is a dividing line between supporting a client and becoming his partner.

The position of the professional accountant is particularly illuminating of his nineteenth-century heritage though he is, invariably, engaged at the 'business end' of firms and individuals. Differences in esteem and status between accountants working in professional practice—i.e. as members of a professional firm—and accountants working in industry remained noticeable until quite recently. The two parallel streams continue to this day—but this artificial gap will be closed sooner or later. Such social differentials are less valid or vivid today than thirty years ago when I scrutinized the social and economic history of the profession in England.[5] While the English talent for fragmentation is thus revealed, this compartmentalization of skills seems not to have benefited overmuch the profession or the public. Artificial exclusivities have locked accountants into specialist roles and have prevented unification of the profession; thus, accountancy remains a fragmented (today less so) profession—with one of the bodies still adhering strictly to the mediaeval guild principle of apprenticeship for its students, while others renounced apprenticeship and widened their doors for admission. Needless to say, the accounting institute perpetuating mediaeval practices of apprenticeship towers above all others in social esteem!

The professionalization of natural science converted other spheres of intellectual activity into professional disciplines, and 'as workers in the crystallized disciplines came to define their activities as *scientific*, they developed new ideas of their proper cultural functions and new relations with society at large.'[6] In the snobbish drive for social esteem, in the anti-industrial culture of elitist Victorian Britain the identification of science with professionalism caused remarkable distortions. Devotees of emerging disciplines emulated the institutional organisation of the scientist and used emblematically the word 'scientific' as a prefix for their activities. In this trend, Germans led the way with their devotion to the 'wissenschaftlich'.

---

[5] *English Accountancy 1800–1954, A Study in Social and Economic History*, Gee & Co, London 1954.
[6] Heyck, op. cit., p. 120.

Philology, sociology, anthropology, economics, politics, and psychology emerged as sciences to which education, literary study, history and theology were added. History as a discipline offered 'the most dramatic example of the formation and professionalization of disciplines along scientific lines'; history was changed 'from literature to science' since the idea was 'to discover the general laws of historical process—i.e. think of history as a science.'[7] This possibility was suggested 'because the rise and fall of nations went through the same pattern/cycle—infancy, transition, maturity; the cyclical character of historical progress gave it scientific basis.'[8]

On reflection, practitioners of the new disciplines were not over circumspect in associating the word 'science' with their pursuits. The question of supporting a scientific basis for history or literature, economics or psychology is not without its difficulties when considering that the inflexible certainties of say the physical sciences cannot easily operate in an area of free will. This preoccupation with the scientific tag, just like the reorganization of the English universities in the 1850s and the 1860s, had once again much to thank German influence. The word *Wissenschaft* (i.e. science) was widely used in Germany as a prefix to disciplines. Affiliation with science has helped emergent causes; it gave prestige, perhaps legitimacy, to political creeds,—socialism and communism are good examples. Imagining the tenets of Marx or the political outpourings of Ruskin or Harold Laski as scientific, conjures up faith in their immortality.

Another development arising from the high esteem of science has been the endowment of research as such with a cachet. Research has become occupationally and socially OK, because of its—not always obvious—association with science. Hence professional and other, allied, workers found that, providing their labours are oriented towards research, taking a job in industry no longer confers on them that lingering lack of prestige still sometimes conferred on business. Market research, statistical research, economic research, advertising research, social or political research, educational or library research—the list is endless—at once became desirable fields for toil as they emerged from the shadows.

A profession can be defined as the pursuit of a vocation which involves learning or training with a certificate of competence at the

[7] Ibid., p.128.
[8] Ibid., p.129.

end; but professionalism in Britain and elsewhere acquired another, singular, definition—the removal of one's labours from competition, from the market place. Being a professional worker, then, implies that one is employed because of competence but not on account of any competitive or dynamic propensities. The professional does not compete or at least gives the appearance of not competing for business in the market place with other professionals; he is entrusted with work at the onset at least because his brass plate indicates he is qualified and he is available; it is only later that he may be engaged on account of his excellent reputation for professional work. More often than not there are standard sets of professional charges to clients which commands general adherence—or it did until recently. An adaptation of this professional attitude outside the professions into trade and industry led to the invention of resale price maintenance—forcing retail outlets to sell merchandise at the manufacturers' fixed, uniform prices. This practice eliminated price competition between retail outlets and efficient retailers were constrained not to sell cheaper than inefficient ones—if they did they were penalized. Hence, the inefficient retailers by eliminating price competition were kept in business as they were assured of margins ensuring a profit. Here was an interesting example of infecting industry with the germ of restrictive practices of the professions. Happily, resale pice maintenance was virtually repealed in 1972, helping manufacturers, retailers and consumers alike.

This cultivated posture of constricting the operations of the market and relegating it to minimal importance was interestingly mirrored in an oblique way by a public school headmaster's comments during the First World War. He suggested that 'English businessmen might not be the equal of the Japanese and Germans in effort, ingenuity and advertising' but the lesson of fair play in sport 'guaranteed trustworthy manufacture even if the products were obsolete.'[9] Here, then, is a schoolmaster's understanding of how industry might be managed by the best type of businessman! Here, then, is a fountain of trustworthy information about the world of industry, written in the middle of the First World War. Quite a bit of this gospel, and of similar gospels survived in the minds of men destined to take responsible positions in business in the '20s and '30s. Did 'playing the game' and pursuing the professional ideal in business contribute to the decline of

[9] J. C. Weldon, *Recollection and Reflections*, London 1915, quoted in J. A. Managan, *Athleticism in the Victorian and Edwardian Public School*, Cambridge University Press 1981, p. 202.

Britain's industrial culture? Not immediately perhaps in the context of mid-nineteenth-century competition from other countries, but more specifically in the changed industrial milieu after the turn of the century when strong, new competitive forces impinged on industrial England.

Rise of the Intellectual

The genesis of the 'professional' during the 1850s as an esteemed specialist pursuit was followed by the 'intellectual' as a new recognized pursuit some thirty years later; some of their *coterie* made a durable—if not unalloyed—contribution to the decline of English industrial culture. There is a traceable conjugation between two social types—professionals may and some do assume an intellectual stance, but intellectuals need not be professionals, though some, in fact, are. Intellectual propensities can be acquired with or without the benefits of formal higher education or training for a profession—and this was particularly valid in the 1880s. Intellectuality can be of advantage in approaching ideas or dissecting problems. However, an early warning is in order; an intellectual approach to 'thinking to some purpose' is not axiomatically cloning an intellectual. Intellectuality is a valuable ingredient in the thinking process and in passing judgements; but it may be useful to emphasize the difference in the definition of the intellectual—which is a critical way of life—from that of intellectuality, which is a less critical and more constructive way of looking at issues. However, these concepts must not be too strictly separated in the 'occupational' compartment.

Intellectuals can become a concentrated form of irritant, a role to which many aspire; equally, some can contribute significantly as critics of life and times. However, a constructive propensity in intellectual cerebration should not be unequivocally assumed. Intellectuals since the nineteenth century and some in previous times invariably assumed censorious (sometimes revolutionary) roles and have been particularly critical of industrial society—its politics, manners, social relations, past performance and future expectations, indeed, of its *raison d'être*, production and profit; the modern intellectual has been hostile to industrial culture and to its progenitor, the bourgeois, yet without them he would not exist as a widely recognizable cadre.

Intellectuals, intriguingly, are an ancient formulation—at home in the monasteries in the middle ages, discovered among humanists towards the end of the Renaissance, and revealed among the eighteenth-century illuminati in France and England and elsewhere. Their rise, as a definable genre, and influence in Britain is barely a century old. The emergence of the intellectual and of the professional as separate, individual pursuits was an unforseen residue of the nineteenth-century fragmentation of high culture. Changes in the attitude to the arts, the heady pursuit of philistinism, the triviality of mass media catering for a semi-literate working-class readership, the decline in religion, the rise of athleticism, the prominence of the *nouveau riche* and a new emphasis on class exclusivities—all these nineteenth-century attributes contributed to the emergence of the intellectual as a social critic. The dissent over the break-up of a homogeneous high culture in England was articulated by the intellectual; his often censorious stance accelerated and widened the process of rejection of the nation's industrial heritage, already assaulted by novelists earlier in the century.

The intellectual's social and economic cradle was late nineteenth-century capitalism; his survival then as now is ensured by the libertarian attitude and proven tolerance of the capitalist engine—the bourgeois. Bourgeois tolerance to hostile forces arises from their respect for economic, political and individual freedom; this self-delighting virtue of the widest tolerance is sound policy since a threat to the intellectual as a critic could subsequently also truncate bourgeois freedoms.[10] To the bourgeois belief in freedom must be added another important component in toleration, their respect for learning—and for two reasons: first, middle-class social amelioration hinged, partly, on the aquisition of more culture, particularly for their offspring; and second, learning for its own sake reflected the mid-nineteenth-century beliefs in art for art's sake and science for science's sake. Progressive societies learn to live with their intellectuals, and receive active encouragement from some of them. Because intellectuals are free in bourgeois societies they can develop into pace-makers, a good reason why their constructive censure of capitalism should not abate. In authoritarian countries the position is invariably unfavourable for intellectuals; they forfeit their orotund

[10] Joseph A. Schumpeter, *Capitalism, Socialism and Democracy*, Harper & Brothers, New York 1947, pp. 145–55.

magisterial role. Under national socialism, fascism or communism intellectuals always had to toe the (party) line. Ironically, few practising intellectuals in free bourgeois societies have been anti-authoritarian—perhaps from a mixture of faith and fear or from respect for force. How else could their customary, collective docility in dictatorial lands be explained? A contemporary example is their manifestly subordinate role in Solidarity, the Polish free trade union movement. It would be revealing to learn how many of Solidarity's martyrs have been card-carrying intellectuals. My gut feeling is not very many. Writing speeches can be useful, and ideas can grow legs, but active resistance going beyond the use of typewriting muscles is the ultimate arbiter of success in dissent. Perhaps society needs more intellectuals manning the barricades!

'The more complex a society, the greater the need for intellectuals' inveighed a leading American practitioner.[11] This observation probably accords with the numbers game — but it is difficult to test. Society almost everywhere is continuously growing in size and complexity, and society's intellectuals too must have multiplied in this process; who would dare to guess in which stages of a country's economic, social and political development intellectuals will wax fastest? At any rate, intellectuals have not made a noticeable contribution to solving the growing complexities of industrial societies, despite being their most powerful critics. With notable exceptions, their problem-solving capabilities for 'improving' Britain's industrial culture have not been particularly prominent: wishing to change policies, issue manifestos, sign and publish statements, are not enough in themselves; a contribution must also be made to coping with the day-to-day nitty-gritty. Intellectuals' hard knowledge of business is parochial; their views and attitudes to industry are often filtered through utopian political beliefs. Hence, is it surprising, in the circumstances, that the exigencies and enhancements of industrial societies are being attended to not by intellectuals but by 'professionals' with minimum political bias, offering dispassionate up-to-date knowledge and practical experience? Intellectuals pursue general principles and, occasionally, new ideas, while professionals are masters of detail and specialized knowledge. Intellectuals must first learn the iconography of business

---

[11] Edward Shils, in Heyck, op. cit., p.14.

before they can be safely let loose to write the prescriptions for its ills. One may dissent, therefore, from the 'received' assumption of a more exalted role for the putative, problem-solving capabilities of intellectuals, in this case to improve the working of industrial societies—unless at first they come to terms with it! The nineteenth-century intellectual was largely ignorant of industry and his influence on it baleful; his late twentieth-century descendant may wish to learn about it to improve its performance for his own survival.

The contribution of intellectuals until quite recently to Britain's industrial culture has been mainly their hostility. No wonder, intellectuals proved unimaginably ineffective in their political and social criticism of business or successful in updating the political and social thinking of their party. A small example which has loomed so large in socialist politics gives an insight to their impotence to shift blatantly archaic beliefs. Little, if any, progress has been made by socialist intellectuals in forcing the reformulation or indeed rejection of the archaic Clause 4 of Labour Party lore; or inventing a form of corporate structure better suited to the economic and social needs of people both as workers and consumers. Similarly, conservative intellectuals' contribution has not been notable in pathfinding unemployment remedies, inventing better development patterns for emerging countries or coining better working formulae to combine economic advance with tolerable inflation. While the potential and actual opportunities for intellectual contribution offered by the industrial culture continuously multiply, the intellectuals' propensity for participation shows signs of late development. All the same, they do make a contribution by simply churning out ideas which help keeping issues afloat.

The language of many practising intellectuals reads a little precious and a little dated when criticizing Britain's industrial culture; when applied to a critique of the arts their vocabulary is also precious, if vividly contemporary. British cultural fragmentation has contributed to the proliferation of intellectuals, which in turn has led to fragmentation of their language. The difficulty in understanding the intellectual critic's output has been mounting in the arts as much as elsewhere. The dissemination of their texts to readers for better cultural understanding cannot therefore be the intellectual's primary aim: too many appear to write for their fellow critics, for the cognoscenti in their 'professional' ghetto; such affectations hold the prospects of their continuing, limited influence and recognition. It might also be remembered that a trigger mechanism of cultural fragmentation was, perversely, the phenomenal mid-nineteenth-century rise of science, and of other disciplines, all of them developing a specialst vocabulary. The evolution of professional organizations, in turn, accelerated and broadened the use of such esotericism. Science fragmentated even further into the pure and applied variety, the prima donna role being awarded to the former—thus was (pure) science separated from (industrial) technology. Bernard Shaw hit the nail on the head when he suggested that 'all professions were a conspiracy against the laity.' He might too have looked at intellectuals and the new Babel of tongues!

As a result of successful industrialization, the rise of specialist professions, the broadening and expansion of literary output, rising occupational and social mobility and general material enrichment, (natural) religion became increasingly remote from (natural) science and the new industrial culture. The onslaught of Darwinism and the concomitant change in ethical values weakened the common ground for public discourse and debilitated religion as a guide in the lives of men. The Evangelical movement during the earlier part and the Romantic movement (in the latter part of the nineteenth century) must be seen as counter-attacks on industrial culture gnawing away at traditional values. Yet, the counter-offensive of evangelism and romanticism failed to stem the tide; if anything they contributed to a further decline of high culture by not adjusting themselves to the new industrial age. Evangelism, by its insistence on heightened personal morality, should have helped to revive religious interest, but its revivalist intolerance pushed many towards unbelief; a hoped-for revival of religion among the working-class—largely urbanized by the 1850s—also failed mainly because of the ecclesiastical disregard of the effects of urbanization via industrialization. The Church of England did not provide churches for the Victorian working-class in the towns—a need that was never met. As a mildly radical priest lamented the misdirected efforts of the early Victorian Church by misreading the signs of the times: 'it is over 100 years [actually, 250 years] since the start of the industrial revolution yet the clerical manpower of the Church is still deployed as though England was an agrarian community.'[12] A similar charge could be levelled against the

[12] Nicolas Stacey, *Who Cares?*, Anthony Blond, London 1971, p. 57.

Church in the 1980s when the 1920s and 1930s type of William Temple socialism was being preached in a largely bourgeois Britain.

The Romantics, similarly, failed to preserve high culture; they encouraged cultural fragmentation by asserting the autonomy of art and by suggesting that art too was a moral activity, superior to society and, by implication, to industrial, middle-class society. Thus, Ruskin's teachings echoed a withdrawal of the artist from society into isolation—and Matthew Arnold urged writers to 'alienate' themselves and remain aloof from contemporary values, a practice which successfully turned them and their devotes towards introspection and criticism and away from involvement with needs of an enlarged reading public. Thus has the literary culture of the last century become its own focus. The anti-industrial tone of most of the nineteenth century also affected the visual arts; artists retreated into a 'pre-Raphael' manner of painting, emulating 400-year old styles and sentiments; neo-Gothic architectural revival became popular and a new form of escape into the past. I suspect that the effects of romanticism in Britain would have crystallized in some form of escapism even without anti-industrial posturings. A similar romantic movement—called the Nazarenes—took hold of Germany pre-ceding the pre-Raphaelites by four decades, starting early in 1810 at a time when among the German bourgeois, industrial values had little currency. In religion, the evangelicals too sought spiritual nourishment from the past, in the teachings of patristic Christianity during its early, formative, centuries. Alas, in the 1840s there was no St Augustine to consult on how to deal with modern Manichaeans!

But, there was no limit to hankering after the past; a retreat into history appealed to many of the educated and intellectually alert as a counter-measure to the materialistic wilderness of industrial culture; fantasies about the 'good old days' helped to denigrate the growth of industry and relegated the bourgeoisie, business and the market economy to a necessary aberration. Protest against the evils of industry, which axiomatically belittled its engine-driver, the bourgeoisie, complaining of the artist's loneliness in this new soulless milieu and later the alienation of the intellectual were the recurring, orchestrated, jeremiads of the period. By being aloof, critical, pessimistic and often offensive, intellectuals helped to retard the coalescence of industrial with general culture. Intellectuals may have rejected the world, but they could offer no workable substitute: they failed to establish themselves as credible leaders of any class or ideology. The intellectuals' failure to lead a successful anti-industrial crusade was sharpened by their lack of influence among their peers, among those who operated the traditional levers of power. The cultivated anti-intellectualism of the English upper classes was well known; their disregard for the intellectual could only compound the intellectuals' sense of failure and frustration to influence, and it heightened their collective isolation. The working-class, similarly, had little time for the intellectuals' cultural criticism of society; only intellectuals with a live concern with socialism managed to stay in touch with grass-roots. Having been treated with much nonchalance, the Edwardian intellectual, in particular, developed special forms of social criticism, and sought out 'missions' with which he could identify. Instead of developing into a helpful cultural critic as did his precursor, the man of letters, and still earlier the cleric, the mid and late nineteenth-century intellectual concentrated on attacking capitalism and railing at business; despised the market mechanism and attacked (bourgeois) employers; indentified with the emerging labour movement—which to this day has scant use for him—to become a champion of the under-dog (the poor Richard syndrome survives); supported fringe movements, aired minority grievances and espoused fashionable cults as they succeeded one another. This is how, by the turn of the century, the intellectual became a licensed dealer in counter-culture, beavering away, extending its frontiers. In Britain's open, liberal, bourgeois society, middle-class intellectuals assumed the patrician's largely cast-off mantle in denouncing business, thus legitimizing an anti-industrialist culture at their layer of the social pyramid. Naturally, there were then, as now, intellectuals and other opinion-formers who understood the importance and the difficulties of wealth creation; but it remained unrealized until the fourth quarter of the twentieth century for 'professional intellectuals' to become persuaded of the material and spiritual superiority of a market economy in liberal societies as against a dirigiste economy in authoritarian societies—a model which they admired for so long and in which they had had such an illogical, vested interest. It is not for the first time that a class as a *coterie* have beavered away at self-castration.

The British intellectual's anti-business syndrome has been inseparable from its attested 'alienation' from the mainstream of bourgeois culture. Alienation was 'discovered' by Matthew Arnold, meaning a process of looking critically at the cultural scene—'as an outsider'. But the concept of alienation travelled much further than merely taking a dispassionate, outside, critical, approach; this feeling of alienation has succumbed to open hostility, even revolt against middle-class values. However, it seems implausible that the effects of alienation alone could engender such cataclysmic effects as the total repudiation of the industrial wealth-creating process; I suspect the main agent of aggravation lay elsewhere. A fuzzy form of alienation at times could well have been felt by some nineteenth- and twentieth-century intellectuals, but a feeling of being a total outsider all the time seems too far-fetched. After all, these opinion-formers—before they became a conscious, oppositional cadre—did have an 'entrée' to social, political, and economic power and some of them participated in its operations; there must have been numerous men of letters, teachers, university dons, etc., practising intellectuality who were invariably middle class, with a benign contemporary world view. I can see in the incontrovertible hostility of the latter-day intellectual to business and consumerism his having been influenced by causes other than just materialism and industry.

One of the culprits undoubtedly was the rise of science which fathered the Victorian technical revolution, contributing to this breaking up of cultural homogeneity so much lamented by intellectuals—and at two levels; first, among professionals, the middle- and upper-middle classes, by growing specialization, and second, among the working classes by sharpening the division of labour. Yet, however much intellectuals and (particularly) the 'condition of England' authors and the early Victorian women novelists lamented the onset of the industrial age, it cannot be denied that the twin evils of specialization and labour division and the fragmentation resulting from them contributed significantly to general prosperity; perhaps improvements in living standards and in well-being were paid for by diminished (traditional) cultural cohesion; the core of which in the contemporary language of Eliot is expressed as a 'separation of elites' from each other; Disraeli called it the 'two nations'.

There was yet another culprit, perhaps an even more powerful anti-intellectual and pro cultural-alienating force at work, making nineteenth-century England a home unfit for intellectuals—the rise of the public schools and their worship of athleticism. Bizarre as it may seem, athleticism in English public schools partly sprouted from the Evangelical movement which espoused austerity and self-reliance; athleticism in schools was also said to be cultivated as an antidote to vandalism—an interesting idea for current-day contemplation! It is perversely amusing to realize that the nineteenth-century machine age also built athletic machines and equipment for athleticism—thus further aiding the alienation of the intellectual by emulating the classical Greek and Roman affection for sport. Public schools, many founded by educational entrepreneurs, rapidly multiplied after 1840—the vast majority of public schools are of Victorian vintage. The worship of sport was encouraged, often at the cost of competence in other subjects, a cultural retrogression passed on subsequently to numerous American universities and later to the athletic crammers in socialist countries for their Olympic hopefuls. Sport became the English upper-class rage in Victorian Britain and boys were encouraged to take up games by their parents and pedagogues. The worship of the athlete—usually upper-class or aspiring to it—gradually became a national pursuit in the course of the nineteenth century; during the present century, the worship of sport increasingly devolved on to the working-class. Today's symbolism of sash, cap and flag by working-class football fans is a direct inheritance of upper-class public school athleticism.

The worship of sport in the English public schools and the celebration of the sportsman has also travelled the Atlantic, manifest in the fading but still powerful American deification of the university athlete, the baseball player. But sport—then as now—was also a social ladder for the less-well born, fortunate enough to be in public schools; outstanding sporting performances lifted up such pupils for acclaim—and significantly for social recognition. The fictional Lord Verricker in the mid-1850s advised his son on his first day at school as follows—'you have not got to earn a living you know, so you need not work your eyes out. I'd rather you got into the eleven.'[13] Many of the aspiring and wealthy tradesmen and manufacturers sent their boys to public schools, hence Lord Verricker's advice could not have been confined to the only too common, anti-intellectual upper-class English gentleman. Intellectually minded, serious students also

[13] J. E. C. Weldon, *Eversley's Friendship* in J. A. Managan, op. cit., p. 134.

found a place in the public schools but their number, by contemporary accounts, was small; denominational schools, particularly the Catholic public schools, managed to nurture students with more intellectual curiosity than their Protestant counterparts. Striving for intellectual excellence is not an insignificant scholastic ingredient in schools for minorities.

Perhaps most pupils at public schools preferred ball games and other sports to serious studying, and athleticism to reading and debates. In subtle and in obvious ways the schools, the educational system, reflect the values and expectations of the home and the work place. The ethos of mid-nineteenth-century public schools was a finely calculated development of the times, when England needed incorruptible civil servants, authoritarian viceroys, and confident colonial administrators. The development of these imperial qualities did not demand large doses of intellectual cerebration; they called for action, courage, masculinity, overt Christianity, and blind obedience. These are the necessary qualities in men to aquire and sustain an empire and the public schools supplied them with enthusiasm. No wonder, public school boys often felt 'discomfort in the presence of an intellectual of questionable masculinity'; their education and training imparted a preference for a manly image. The correct English male values were thus expounded to Harold Nicolson's uncle during his Rugby school days: 'It was taught on all sides that manliness and self-control were the highest aims of English boyhood: he was taught that all but the most material forms of intelligence were slightly effeminate: he learnt, as they all learnt, to rely on action rather than ideas.'[14] A more contemporary observer put it differently, but the message was similar: 'Public-school products knew nothing, cared little, exhausted their keenness on games and considered anything but the most perfunctory interest in school work a gross breach of good form.'[15] Thus, Victorian anti-intellectualism in public schools was both a defence mechanism, a retort to the unstoppable scientific development of England's industrial culture, as well as a desired, combative response for training a new breed of courageous, practical men demanded by an expanding empire; it was social engineering at its best! Lack of cultivated intellectuality in nineteenth-century servants of the colonial empire and in employees

[14] Ibid., p. 106.
[15] S. P. B. Mais in J. A. Managan, op. cit., p. 108.

of the great trading companies might well have been appropriate to the needs of the times—a statement difficult to prove one way or another. But, a few decades later, by the 1910s a heightened intellectual approach to colonial administration might have provided a better social cement to cohere an empire in the face of rising nationalism—but all this is speculation.

Remnants of anti-intellectuality in education today are even less endurable than in the nineteenth century. Today's anti-intellectual teachers are still found in public schools as well as in comprehensives and in secondary schools—the work place of too many teachers without the required culture to have respect for teaching or consideration for pupils under their care. Nor are such teachers—some with a privileged education and social background—more acceptable to the working-class pupils for being trendy; such teachers no longer enjoy the meagre sanction of a socially plausible, anti-intellectual *raison d'être* of a previous age which also dismissed business as the nadir of pursuits. It is sobering therefore to recall the arrogant hypocrisy of Cambridge-educated literacy teachers (all professing Labour politics) preaching to their students as they emerged from illiteracy that it was bourgeois to progress then to O-level exams. (How fashionable the cultural revolution and how convenient being able to switch from Stalin to Mao!) One of the Labour movement's least agreeable characteristics has been a propensity, inherited from Beatrice Webb, to instruct the working classes, in humourless educated tones, what is good for them.'[16] Anti-intellectualism is a hardy virus but is no longer living comfortably in contemporary England. That's good news. In the end, the purpose of sensible education must be to harness intellectuality to the development of English industrial culture in harmony with the rising general culture.

New cultural unity

The postures, the language and the affectations of the professional and of the intellectual have endured beyond the second half of the twentieth century but their attitudes are now in a process of change. Political *débâcles* and retrenchments and economic maladies surfacing during the last sixty years have reluctantly induced greater

[16] *New Statesman*, 2 July 1983, p. 16.

malleability to new ideas and experiments; these have brought with them shifts in cultural values in a changed English milieu; intellectuals are increasingly becoming aware that there is more to credibility than just elegant critism without a follow-up; and professionals have realized their expanding opportunities beyond narrow technicalities and dispassionate advising. Nowadays they may even alert their clients to opportunites! The transformation of the public schools, a less reluctant acceptance of cultural diversity, the slow adaptation to neo-conservativism among the new-breed intellectuals, the realization that business is the source of wealth and must earn profits and not only pay wages and taxes—all these revelations have their genesis in the years between the two World Wars, but this pilgrimage of new approaches was not to accelerate until the fourth quarter of the twentieth century. By the 1980s the intelligentsia as well as other elites have positioned themselves towards recognition of the importance of business. At the end of the social educational scene the embourgeoisement of the working class is taking place meanwhile and has induced cultural similarities between the old and the new bourgeoisie.

Fragmentation is a diluting force—the watering down of dogma since the Reformation is witness to the rise of simpler forms of reformed religions. In the professions, fragmentation had surfaced by the 1930s—at one time 38 different professional accounting organizations were extant; eventually only a handful of them survived. New skills too have been grafted on traditional accountancy activities—management consultancy, corporate finance, taxation advice, legal advice, investment advice, all of which have led to some specialization in firms. In the law, fragmentation has also occurred by specialization—specialist firms of marine lawyers, corporation lawyers, trade union lawyers, etc., have sprung up. The same fragmentation applies to the sciences. Any two scientists of the mid-nineteenth century probably enjoyed between them a greater degree of cultural unity than any two sectional presidents of the British Association could claim at any time during the twentieth century! The long, the artificial separation of pure from applied science is similarly no longer guided by non-commercial values. A narrowing of the gap between the professions and the market place has accelerated through the proliferation of contemporary disciplines into new professions. The stockbroker and the insurance broker are among the latest 'disciplines' to become fully recognized professions; admittance is now subject to examinations and their daily operations are guided by continually more detailed regulations–which the Big Bang has only made more contrived. While professional in every respect, insurance brokers, bankers and stockbrokers have never thought of distancing themselves from the market place—they are part of it; fully aware of their professional advisory role, they also endeavour to do their 'best' for their clients. Perhaps the least responsive or sensitive to the idea of the market—i.e. servicing their customers—have been the joint stock banks who for long looked upon their clients as mendicants! At all events the work of professionals is recognizably different today from their nineteenth-century dispassionate precursors. It may well be that a lessening of the social chasm, indeed its virtual disappearance, has helped the British to like each other more and hence to be more helpful to each other. Could pompous professionalism have masqueraded in the past as an alibi for social superiorty?

A significant recent development in the professions is that accountants and lawyers are being allowed certains forms of advertising: by having to compete for business they will now recognize themselves more vividly than as being in the market place and not out of it. The English Institute of Chartered Accountants in favour of advertising, published a guide on 'the marketing and selling of accountancy services'[17] for their members. Here, then, we are observing a change, a highly significant new ethical approach, in manners; chartered accountants are being recommended to enter the market place, a visible severance of previous postures. 'Manners changeth man.' The English legal and accounting professions are following the American practice—and be noted the competence and integrity of American professionals has not noticeably declined by their proximity to the market place. All professions are a form of business—though some of its practioners would have been reluctant to admit this until now—thus sharing many characteristics with the nation's industrial culture. They have become regular business enterprises because, as in the case of accountants, they are facing increasing competition from other professions, bankers and solicitors;

---

[17] Aubrey Wilson, *Marketing Professional Services*, McGraw Hill, Maidenhead 1972.

they must go into the market-place and diversify to drum up work—and to keep their existing clients!

The current day intellectual scene too has changed profoundly; their much vaunted cultural alienation from society seems to have largely vapourized. More than at any time previously their criticism of bourgeois society has diminished since the depression of the 1970s. A likely reason for the intellectuals' better understanding of the economic and industrial machine is their undoubtedly improved education. *Fin de siècle* intellectuals and those who preceded them usually enjoyed limited formal education, while nowadays they pass through the entire gamut of the educational machine. Endowed with academic respectability, enjoying not one but numerous platforms for airing their opinions, practising intellectuals have become more sober, more plausible and more restrained in their criticism of man and matters. Many of them have become specialists, and thus imitate bourgeois ways of earning a living in occupations demanding particular skills in the liberal arts, journalism, etc. They might have also realized the obstacles in the twentieth century in maintaining more than a superficial acquaintance with the wide ramifications of eighteenth-century culture. This is a further reason for their conversion to pay more respect to industrial culture. A growing cadre of intellectuals are embracing neo-conservativism, deserting socialism, utopia and leftism, the traditional oppositional *Standpunkt* of intellectuals . Reposing in conservative values, which can be as radical as any other, the intellectual is now in a position to 'join up' in Britain's industry, and given an opportunity to influence its course.

The prospects, then, of achieving greater cultural unity in the future and greater social cohesion in Britain are favourable. A closer alignment of general culture with industrial culture seems nearer now than at any time since Britain lost her innocence of the pastoral and piscatorial culture to the industrial and the scientific. The process of seamlessly welding together these two cultures is proceeding slowly while the older generation of political, social and economic elites in England with roots and mores formed during the 1940s and 1950s slowly relinquish their leadership roles. Thus a new coalescing of the industrial with the general culture of England must await a more perfect realization by the younger generation of businessmen, professionals, and intellectuals, having assumed leadership. The process has started.

The artificial (social) and real (occupational) differences between the businessman, the professional and the intellectual are beginning to vanish. The healing of Britain's cultural rift is clearly met by another important departure—a rising social esteem for the entrepreneur. The moment cannot be too far away when in business, unorthodox success will *not* be rated equal to orthodox failure!

Yet it must not be assumed that the British elites ever disliked capitalism; their hostility centred not on capitalism but on industry; only the intellectual, subsequently arriving on the scene, luxuriated in a missionary dislike of business and with it the bourgeoisie who stood for capitalism. The anti-bourgeois postures of socialists are based on anti-capitalism—thus the dislike of an economic system has become a source of hostility to a substantial and growing part of the population. Insanity knows no bounds!

ON COWARDICE

Introduction

Heroism has many adherents and even more numerous admirers—cowardice none or perhaps just a few, yet during a lifetime many more examples and varieties of cowardice than of heroism will have been experienced or observed. If economics were to invade morality at this point and pass value judgement, it could be safely assumed that the reason for putting a higher value on bravery as against cowardice is on account of its 'greater scarcity'. Almost all heroism is extolled as a virtue to be emulated, and is considered a courageous and selfless act; cowardice is condemned as a weakness or, at best, as a sin to be shunned. The literature of heroism, real and imaginary, the songs, sagas, and ballads extolling it may be traced back into obscurity and remain with us to this day; the literature of cowardice, not all that extensive, does not extol any of its varieties but acknowledges and condemns it; 'celebrating' cowardice as an inevitable human attribute splinters it into a number of specific forms, many of which have been in vogue for a very long time.

An important type of cowardice is that of the anti-hero. He includes the unsuccessful little man who runs away, often entertaining in his pathos, as well as the romantic, as well as the tilter at windmills escaping real engagement; the about to become ascetic, the professional 'who contracts out', the anchorite withdrawing from the world, to mention just some of the many varieties. Conventional wisdom would not consider those voluntarily renouncing a gift or privilege or those not pressing a just point or not opposing evil in its many forms in any way cowardly; none the less, it is difficult to escape the suspicion that there is a degree of cowardice lurking in their soul, immobilizing their energies—yet such conduct, almost by conspiracy, is rarely verbalized and even more rarely judged. Cowardice, then, is considered unsavoury in polite society and, as it is for the greater part inadmissible, this important human condition has remained largely undiscussed in personal terms, though frequently referred in the collective. Yet cowardice exists, is thriving and living with each of us, everywhere. Everbody lives through moments or periods of cowardice as well as of bravery. What is clearly apparent by the limited literature discussing the subject, is that humanity has found it difficult to come to terms with cowardice in everyday life—though it is aired from time to time under special conditions such as courts martial, or psychiatry. Hence, the almost universal need to invent suitable anodynes, excuses and apologies and well thought out and plausible alibis to cover up. There is nothing wrong with such strenuous endeavours; to sugar the pill which we know to be bitter is to make fallibility and imperfection more immediately acceptable and tolerable. The imaginative use of linguistics, too, is a vehicle of accommodation.

Cowardice has many forms. The physical aspect comes to mind most readily when contemplating its nature or manifestations. It needs to be emphasized that there are varieties of cowardice other than physical—moral and metaphysical—though certain forms of moral cowardice can result in physical action and will involve material consequences. Forming malign, evil, underground, secret societies, for example, whose membership is based upon adherence to some perverted intolerable belief and who are sitting in judgement upon their victims or opponents, resulting in physical action against them or the practice of kidnapping, are some of its current sinister forms, but there are others. Such dualities combining the moral and physical varieties of cowardice recur with some frequency. Physical cowardice alone, however, has only a single object in view, the avoidance of pain or injury or discomfort to any part of one's body, or, if a special relationship exists, to someone else's body; the psychological type of cowardice can induce a whole keyboard of differing emotional reactions—from feeling an outcast to being non-clubbable or just mildly embarrassed—the intensity depending to some degree upon the person's threshold of conscious shame or grief, or perceived degree of deviation from conformist morality or 'received' values. Feeling uncomfortable may or may not have been resolved into any form of moral compromise but being uncomfortable can and sometimes does, if pushed, degenerate into cowardice, or on rare occasions translates into courage.

Acts of cowardice may be committed under a multitude of impulses but they fall into four conceptual categories; one or two of these categories may be combined at the time a cowardly act is being committed. For the purpose of analysis, these four conceptual categories are grouped into intentional and unintentional, and rational and irrational. The borderline between them is often blurred, because cowardice is not a straightforward matter.

Intentional cowardice is premeditated, such as a determination not to fight, or simply succumbing to flight, or deciding to run away from the scene of action—these are all variations on the same theme. To avoid making a telephone call to give or receive bad news, or not turning up to a confrontational meeting are further variations on this theme. Running away from home or not turning up for an interview at a selection committee are both intentional—voluntary—forms of cowardice, with the former being active (running away), and the latter passive (not walking to the appointment, failing to turn up). Oscar Wilde suggests that 'each man kills the thing he loves' which must be a form of voluntarism, an unintended act, because to kill what one cherishes is unreasonable—except for the deranged or the perverse. This then takes the categorization of cowardice a stage further, into the rational and irrational. While the coward plays out his destructive impulse 'with a kiss' and 'the brave man with a sword', Wilde has succeeded in combining the unintentional with the irrational—indeed, irrespective of whether the cowardly or the brave are put in focus. Rational cowardice—that is, finding a logical alibi for indulging in it—combined with intentional efforts to avoid facing consequences can also become joint products. Thus, one or more of these four quasi-ethical characteristics of cowardice singly or in combination is likely to colour any actual cowardly act.

Physical cowardice

Physical cowardice has always been well documented. This is because the physical variety can be most easily observed in human conduct from its early years; some children and some adults fight, others run away. History books and imaginative literature are full of heroes fighting at the head of their troops and of others who lead armies from the rear and are the first to turn their backs on the enemy when the going gets tough. Most forms of physical cowardice are observable, hence this type constitutes the most relevant and direct experience of mankind. However, this direct genre of physical cowardice—the passive and intentional variety, best expressed as the 'avoidance principle'—is only one among many, not all of which are thought of, or would at first blush appear, as distinct forms of cowardice. In the genre of physical cowardice, pride of place must be given to the rational and intentional type, brilliantly articulated in a dialogue by the murderers in *Richard III* (Act I, Scene IV):

Second murderer:	What, shall we stab him when he sleeps?
First murderer:	No; then he will say twas done cowardly when he wakes . . .
	How does thou feel thyself now?
Second murderer:	Faith, some certain dregs of conscience are yet within me.

Shaw's soldier in *Major Barbara*—a typical GBS character —admits 'Cowardice, it is as universal as seasickness, and matters just as little'. This then is an admission everybody understands and sometimes condones; the alibi for keeping a semblance of respectability despite indulging in cowardice can be expressed in a hopeful way by suggesting that such a soldier will 'live to fight another day'! While, usually, no sympathy would be evoked by a man beating up a woman, how many would call such a man a coward—though he undoubtedly is on a physical basis, justified though he may think he is on psychological or moral grounds. The eighteenth-century poet, John Tobin, is credited with having written: 'the man that lays his hands upon a woman, save in the way of kindness, is a wretch, whom 'twere gross flattery to name a coward.' So that's that!

Not all physical cowardice, however, is quite as easy to indentify and to categorize. When the impetus of organized, intentional cowardice links up with the irrational variety then anarchy of one sort or another raises its head. Politically motivated assassinations rightly belong to this category. Examples of the the Red Brigade, the IRA or Baader Meinhof are pointers here. When a gang of people, determined through ideology, kidnap and kill their victim whatever the motivation or however strong the impulse to impose their ideologies on others, this is nothing short of cowardice of the first degree. But then, slaves of ideologies live vicariously—renouncing reason—only the dogma matters. Kidnapping, capturing and eventually maiming or executing a defenceless captive are ideas and actions which are borne in the minds of both physical and intellectual cowards; such actions are the property of those not prepared—because they are afraid—to put themselves or their ideas to the test of public acceptability through peaceful logic and persuasion. If terror by a group is visited upon a single victim, the latter having no chance to fight back, no chance of escape and no chance of argument or opposition, such a person is a total captive. The deliberate, loud trumpeting of the violent, cowardly acts committed by such groups with their ideas of (nationalistic/ political/proletarian?) justice is again not surprising, as cowardice can be, as in other situations, combined with the wish for exposure (a little narcissism), the need for publicity and a need for an alibi. Information about the kidnap victim is disseminated stealthily, put in dustbins or phone kiosks; the pronouncements are designed to keep everyone in suspense or terror and all statements are uttered anonymously, from safe houses at safe distances in the name of an abstract reality. The last thing such intentional, irrational pseudo-intellectual cowards would wish for is a debate, an argument, or indeed a shoot-out; the consequences of their actions frighten them, so their cowardly lives continue to fester below the surface, enjoying the infantile game of their importance by being secret and conspiratorial; yet from time to time receiving public attention by gangsterism and not by meritorious acts.

Political assassination is a stereotype of cowardice, as is the liquidation of political adversaries by those having gained power. The dictator desires to eliminate opposition to his ideology and threat to his person, not only at home but also abroad. Such a genre of cowardice does not often enjoy publicity because the dictator-aggressor possesses the panoply of power and successfully defeats attributions of murder; but the underground assassin has no name, no power or status, except in isolated moments of consummation, hence his need for publicity to show his effectiveness. The Russians have one great illustration to offer in this category, the liquidation of Trotsky; the Libyans or Bulgarians can account for the liquidation of several minor characters—and icepicks have changed to umbrellas; however, technological revolutions have not bypassed the cowardly assassination business—car bombs, limpet mines, trip wires, time bombs have reinforced the coward's infracted cowardice as new techniques allow destruction of civilized life by remote control. The essence is stealth—the secret attack, the surprise, the scheming to attack the unsuspecting. To catch an enemy unaware during periods of declared hostilities is legitimized in warfare by convention—a form of manners? Such a foray would not be unexpected and an adversary would not be unarmed: but without the preconditions of war, without awareness of such hostile intention and the chance of deflecting it, assassination within a peaceful society becomes cowardly butchery. The physical cowardice which accompanies the attack on the unsuspecting is also compounded by an intellectual cowardice invoking a perverse alibi, justifying the act by declaring that kidnap and murder are in fact a declaration of war on the representatives of an existing, 'hated' system. So conventional are such cowards, they have to justify their outrageous work by conventional bourgeois maxims. But then, most of the primitive revolutionaries enjoy a bourgeois background.

Libido-led craving for personal or political recognition by underground revolutionaries, or revenge killings by political thugs are also different from gang warfare. In the latter, the stakes are directly for material riches and only indirectly for the paraphernalia of power (rarely political), beliefs or influence. By comparison with Ghadafi or Red Brigade members, the Mafia seems to conduct its business in a much more straightforward and, if such a thing is conceivable, in a more sober and predictable manner. This is not to praise the Mafia, just to distance its revealed methods of operation from mere political thuggery. Threats of physical coercion are a common form of extortion, and protection money is levied and paid to avoid injury. It is an open secret who is behind the Mafia rackets; the leaders are often widely known, and feared by their actual and potential victims as much as by their henchmen—hence the surprisingly durable immunity of gang leaders. Could then one assume that making an illicit living by gangsterism is a less soiled type of cowardice than threats, maiming, and assassinations for political ends? Each Mafia family enjoys its pickings from designated territory; when members of one 'family' encroach on the territory of others or when several families vie for supremacy of the same territory or racket, gang battles ensue and people are killed. There is no secret about who killed whom—nothing unexpected—and the revenge killing is expected from a known quarter. It would be ridiculous not to designate the St Valentine's Day Massacre an act of cowardice because it was a secret attack if not entirely unexpected—but even if there is no doubt about the genre, there is a difference in its degree from the strictly political. It was not a gang confronting just one person, although this does also happen—but one armed gang trapping another gang in a garage and killing them. Such Mafia type of cowardice would fall into the intentional-rational category, while the aforementioned political executions bear the distinct mark of irrationality.

Numbers game

The coercive impact of crowds is largely physical and often significant, hence it deserves analysis in the cowardice stakes, Crowds possess variable sets of characteristics—they can form quickly or slowly, they can celebrate or jeer according to their psychological juxtaposition or temporary conditioning and they are subject to quick change of mood; but, most important, if crowds commit acts of cowardice by attacking individuals this may or may not be premeditated. Of course, exceptions abound: crowds in Northern Ireland, or in Poland, would specifically wish to express a (religious) sentiment or a (political) grievance; when the racists attack the blacks or the anti-semites the Jews, these are blatant acts of cowardice as they deliberately set out on a course of action harmful to a minority group or more likely its individual members; the nuclear disarmament devotees express their brand of concern not always peacefully; a demonstration by a crowd of unemployed would rarely end in scuffles in Britain, and even less so when this social evil is endemic.

Crowds are either formed voluntarily or deliberately to perform a certain role or function, such as watching the State Opening of Parliament or to cheer the home team to victory on the football field; crowds can gather spontaneously in response to certain happenings, such as to cheer a brave act of a fireman rescuing children from a blazing inferno, or on recognizing a pop star on leaving his hotel. These occasions show the benign face of crowds. Mussolini's or Hitler's crowds were organized on a combative, destructive basis—their task was to be hostile to all non-fascists and in over whelming numbers they (bravely?) attacked the few and destroyed their property. The cowardice of a fascist crowd in this instance is further underscored by the added advantage of the wrong-doers' impunity from the law; however, crowds may not, as a rule, be singled out for manifest acts of deliberate cowardice, unless they were specifically stage-managed to become destructive. Gangs and mobs may be described as the cadet branch of crowds, sharing numerical similarities in a minor key. Mobs are hostile by linguistic definition; they can and are formed deliberately when the necessary conditions exist; when sufficiently incited they cause physical intimidation, injury and violence. When one mob meets another, perhaps each seeking out the other, the nature of combat involves no overt expression of cowardice on either side, as both sides have prepared for confrontation; when the mob (the people?), however, attack an individual or his property—as in the celebrated case of Joseph Priestly, a revered scientist and a man of letters whose house, which held possibly the best equipped chemical laboratory in England in 1791, was burned down—then such an act of the mob whatever the springs of action—is calculated cowardice. No wonder Priestly escaped to America, never to return. Mr Pickwick had a commendable understanding of mobs; he suggested that 'it's best to do [on these occasions] what the mob do'. 'But', Mr Snodgrass inquired, 'what if there are two mobs?' 'Shout with the largest,' replied Mr Pickwick! If Mr Pickwick was not a coward he was certainly no hero. But is being Pickwickian enough?

The OED has widely differing definitions for 'mobs' and 'gangs' but the underlying impression in both cases is that, potentially at least, they are up to no good and upright citizens should keep away, Though no numerical precision is attempted, one is persuaded that in such bifurcation of assembled talents a gang is made up of fewer souls than a mob. Al Capone led a gang, Priestly's house was burnt down by a mob. If the general supposition is allowed to stand, that gangs are collections of men with a defined common purpose visiting in packs and acting in unison then their action against external phenomena may be defensive or offensive. If their enemies are other gangs or mobs and combat is expected and carried out in the open, no overt act of cowardice has been committed; this would not apply in this or in any other case when the many in the gang—stealthily or even openly—attack one person or just a few. The extent of inferiority in numbers of the attacked plays a crucial role in determining degrees of cowardice. The range of possibilities and the scope for judgement here are diverse.

One form of cowardice, then, can be expressed as the actions of the many prevailing over the one or the few; and such cowardice can be physical or, less likely, moral—and when the attack is, as it is mostly, committed in stealth. Another form, already touched on, is when one person attacks another, again stealthily and often equipped for the attack, for gain or advantage. Casual judgement on the demerits of one-to-one attacks is usually less censorious than when a gang attacks an individual. It is submitted that such a more benign diagnosis on one-to-one attacks is misguided because the degree of cowardice by the attacker can be and in some cases is great. The attack by youths, singly or in groups, on old age pensioners, on the aged and the sick in their council dwellings or on the young or the lame in a deserted alley, to rob them of their scanty possessions, often beating them up and even murdering them—these are acts of the greatest imaginable cowardice.

The reason why immobile, sick and old citizens are attacked are two-fold; they are bound to have some ready money, however little, and they are almost totally defenceless. Thus, when the young lout attacks the defenceless old person the classic formula for cowardice is played out. Here again, two important forms of cowardice have surfaced in the mind of the attacker; first, the knowledge that the old are easy victims, as they can hardly put up a reasonable defence, and it is traditional for physical cowards (i.e. bullies) to attack the weak; and, second, the moral cowardice of the attacker is axiomatic, since the act of stealing or robbing implies an inability to acquire (i.e. earn) money by purposeful, sustained effort or in the usual way of working for it. Cowardice is socially despised, but when such a robber or killer is brought before the courts the law does not judge him with additional severity just because he is a coward. This is because few would consider robbery with or without violence as a species of overt cowardice in a 'permissive' society at peace. The general public might consider it beastly, horrid, or inhuman, but rarely cowardly. Under different circumstances such overt acts of cowardice are grossly punished—in war, for instance the coward could pay for his sins with his life, *pour encourager les autres*. But the soldier who has run away, indulging in an act of rational and intentional type of cowardice, has not killed anyone (and, of course, he wants to avoid being killed); in fact he has made a point of not wanting to do so by running away. Had this same soldier conquered his cowardice he might have killed many enemy soldiers. Had the teenage hooligan conquered his cowardice in facing the world he would have gone out into the world and earned a living instead of killing defenceless old people. The value judgements society puts on different types of cowardice are fragile for their inconsistency. The best alibis are those sanctified by society—i.e. by the State.

The 'fighting soldier' has no valid excuse for cowardice, after all his task is to be the opposite of a coward, to be brave and fight and conquer the enemy. That is why conventional wisdom condemns the cowardly soldier, courts sentence him and social esteem deserts him—if not for good, certainly for a very long time. The case is entirely different when judging the conduct of 'would-be soldiers'. Here a good case can be made for suggesting that unwillingness to serve, under certain circumstances, earns not the stigma of cowardice but the merit of praise; this is because a stance of non-performance has been engendered by moral beliefs or intellectual reasoning. Thus, the phenomenon of Quakers or Pacifists not wanting to exercise the martial arts, but being quite willing to serve in wars as non-combatants has long been accepted without any stigma of cowardice. Their open refusal over many years, supported by religious beliefs (in a quasi-non religious age?), has converted other people's rational judgement of their non-combatant attitudes to something other than cowardice—to something which they are prepared to condone, perhaps even praise. A judgement of cowardice would not be absent, one might assume, if moral—i.e. religious—sanctions were withdrawn from conscientious objections.

What, then, is one to make of the young American draft-dodgers of the 1960s? To burn draft cards—call-up papers—while illegal, became an act of daring among the college intelligentsia during the Vietnam war, and was executed with bravado, often in public, and little punished. Would it be realistic to contemplate that a genuine, protest movement against a war—an unpopular war at that as in the case of Vietnam—could be largely confined to undergraduate and graduate students, for the greater part from the better universities? For certainly the range of the protest movement in the States at that time enjoyed a narrow scatter. No other organized section of

American national life repudiated with violence their allegiance to fighting the war except a special bevy of students. A plausible explanation might be that the students' latent cowardice was—in their own eyes at least—vindicated by their excessive and conveniently cultivated hothouse moral values. This excessive personal concern—special pleading perhaps—with moral values, in relation to national issues did not appear to engulf too many others quite as actively outside the American student community.. There was vocal opposition to the war in the States as there is to all wars in a democracy, but such opposition is healthy and is peacefully resolved by the common will.

Much the same innuendo can justifiably be made about a similar but perhaps more veiled cowardice by some American students during the Vietnam years—as well as before and after the war—who elected to indulge in more and more education, piling degree upon degree, by continuing their studies, so as to avoid call-up. It was not only the the call up they wished to circumvent—they were actively afraid to step into a real life, after their student college years! In this case, then, added to the well-known propensity of many young Americans to become eternal students (another well recognized species of cowardice—this time not physical but moral and examined in more detail under another heading) was the opportunity to escape the unpronounced terror of going to war by staying 'at school'. As those pursuing studies for a higher degree are often drawn from the middle and upper-middle ranks of society, it seemed such students wished to continue their protected and privileged lives to a large extent at other people's expense. It would be difficult to accept their views uncritically; such action must have a nexus with cowardice. While indulging in varieties of concealed cowardice—burning draft cards and postponing departure from the campus—students did not flock to underground societies or secret societies or open anti-war societies in great numbers: some obviously did, most did not. Thus, their anti-war feelings were intentional and rational but in a very low key—it was intentional and rational to stay out of the affray; not forceful enough to be vehemently against the war on the basis of principles deeply held; passivity and a good alibi proved sufficient for this particular occasion.

Wars, then, probably account for the bulk of examples of manifest courage and cowardice. In fact, in a shooting war, acts of overt

cowardice are few, or at least few are reported. Courage in war is
extolled and well publicized. Both examples are sometimes magnified
to show up their stark differences. In the annals of cowardice, few have
been able to convert this all-embracing feeling of fear to prove the
reversable impulse, courage. To dredge courage out of fear and to
manifest this courage is, in a sense, an act of redemption. Such
successful opportunities do not abound and are not offered to many;
but such an opportunity did present itself to a Jewish youth from
Poland, when he attempted but did not succeed in crossing the
Channel at Boulogne, during the Second World War. One of the two
lorries in the convoy in which he cadged a lift was shot at by a German
sniper, badly wounding one of the crew. The boy decided he must go to
his aid, jumped down from his lorry, and with hands in trouser pockets
walked up to the badly wounded soldier in the other lorry. 'My heart',
he said, 'jumped wildly', but nothing happened, the sniper desisted.
The boy rescued the soldier and took him to hospital. This is how he
described the incident later in his autobiography: 'I had thought of all
the doubts I had about Jewish physical courage in general, and my
own in particular. I thought of all the jeers, accusations of cowardice
and cheap sarcasm I had to suffer from Poles as a child and as a boy.
The chance had come my way and I have taken it.' In the crucible of
war, and under attack, assumed or real cowardice may and can turn
into physical courage of great personal fortitude.

For cowardice, as for other recognizable human frailties and
characteristics, pigeon-holing and classifying are common pursuits,
because these allow avoidance of having to judge each situation, as it
arises, on its merits. Classification leads to stereotypes, to lumping
together people, particularly concerning national characteristics.
Italians are a good example; they are frequently accused of cowardice
because they have not been a marked martial success in modern
European history. Such a classification does not reflect reality but is
nevertheless real in the public mind. To some Europeans, Italians
appear to be cowards; but the reason for this apparent cowardice is not
because they lack courage. It must be understood clearly that, despite
the Risorgimento of 1856, Italy is not a united, homogeneous nation,
like the British, the Americans, or the French. Italians remain the
children of their province or of their town—and not of Italy: they have
not developed a taste for fighting for the greater glory of Italy. This is
as good an explanation as any as to why Mussolini's military stance

always bordered on the comic. Let it never be forgotten, however, that the Italians are good fighters, as their partisans have shown; but they do not cherish fighting for other Italians. They are a good example of apparent physical cowardice which is unconnected to their true physical and spiritual disposition of courage!

Application of self-therapy for physical cowardice takes much more skill than the ability to describe it; it is an admirable achievement, little emulated. Indeed, self-conquest is difficult and rare, inner power overcoming inner fears. But what about external power or persuasion overcoming internal cowardice? Montaigne in his *Essays* quotes a situation of particular relevance; he observed that the Athenians before the law-giver Charondas 'were wont to punish those with death who for fear did run away from Battell; where hee only ordained that for three days together, clad in women's attire, they should be made to sit in the market place; hoping yet to have some service at their hands, and by means of this reproach they might recover their courage again'. This, then was an unorthodox remedy for cowardice, rationally administered, to inculcate courage in place of fear by ridicule. Who knows, perhaps it worked. The line between deliberately eschewing facing reality and acts of overt cowardice is very finely and indistinctly drawn. In the real physical world, an act of cowardice is easily manifest, the sources of action not being particularly relevant except to psychiatrists and certainly not to the commonality who pass simple judgement like 'white hats, good man, black hats, bad man'. The issues surrounding non-physical cowardice are more difficult to discern, or to judge, but its victims are just as real none the less. Moral cowardice extends into all departments of human endeavour. While conscience will tell an individual whether he acted justly, wisely, generously, badly, heroically, or cowardly—providing he admits it to himself—for the outsider it is perhaps more difficult to judge such non-physical types of cowardice. Some or many of the judgements about cowardice may be assumed as borderline cases, vacillating between irresolution, tergiversation, caprice, weakness, submissiveness, or servility, and its obverse, derring-do, resoluteness, Dutch courage, rashness, pluckiness, dashing, of steadfast morals or fearlessness. Alas, only manifest cowardice and its related sentiments are a matter for concern here, though it should be emphasized again how our own disposition and value judgements affect the adjectives assigned to such deeds.

Non-physical cowards

All cowards, other than physical, are types of moral cowards of widely different kinds and degree. As already suggested, it is more difficult to pronounce on moral cowardice as it is not indentifiable as simply as physical cowardice. In the world of tentative reality, cowardice is perhaps capable of interpretation and explanation by reference to a psychic state or, for instance, a reflex condition as a result of the education of the person concerned. Thus, psychology can and often does offer plausible explanations, especially for moral types of cowardice. The psychological escape clause—the exploitation of the subconscious as an alibi, a material factor in the more recent rise of moral cowardice—is a matter of some note and must remain a concern for study. The range of 'metaphysical' cowardice is immense and not capable of being easily catalogued, but a few examples will offer a glimpse of the more common types of this genre.

   Social situations, attributes and taboos can give rise to cowardly conduct on a grand scale. There are many such equations—they can arise in isolation such as the individual's self-oppressions or hatred of his class, or in tandem with other situations, such as his occupation, education, childhood friends, religion, or the social position of parents. Social-moral cowardice does not fall into neat categories; social aspects almost invariably have a part to play in all non-physical cowardice, but some cowardice is more social than others. Some affect society, while others impact largely on individuals. Matrimonial cowardice has a minimum of two, but may claim three or more *dramatis personae*; cowardice arising from family problems can involve a whole tightly-knit community, while the cowardice of a prince can affect an entire country. A bizarre society divorce can shake up an exclusive *coterie* while the divorce of a monarch will scandalize an entire nation. However, one should remember that certain acts, such as an incompatible couple staying together for fear of scandal, would nowadays be considered as social cowardice because separation and divorce are being committed too frequently to elicit the censure they might or might not deserve, or should deserve, or used to deserve; smoking pot, and more recently even rape, are looked upon more lightly as is failure in business; cruelty to and abuse of children and drunkenness while driving, and not stopping after a car accident are acts of cowardice being perhaps taken more seriously. How the social mores change!

a. In the family

An evergreen variety of cowardly conduct, nowadays much discussed and often fobbed off as permissiveness, occurs in the parent-child relationship. How often will a parent, out of cowardice, be reluctant to face a confrontation with the child and will capitulate before his tantrums? The answer is more often than one would like to think. How often will parents cave in because they believe—rightly or mistakenly, who knows?—that determined parental opposition, manifest as discipline, will probably erode the child's affection for them? The growing tyranny of children over parents is a more recent manifestation of parental moral cowardice, largely unknown in previous ages. The cowardly surrender of parents in enforcing the required discipline is a form of bribery, hoping it will yield continuing affection from the child; in sum, it is a species of protection money paid as a result of cowardice.

Another not uncommon example of collective family cowardice in the upbringing of children is the impulse to explain away certain unfortunate or disagreeable happenings or an inelegant background history to members of the family. Such efforts can also lead to mouthing false values and posturings. A good example here is a possible attitude by the successful son of an immigrant family. Such a son, first-generation, native born, still remembers the hardships endured by his parents and the sacrifices imposed on themselves to educate him. Now here he is, well-educated and well-to-do as a result of his parents' sacrifices; he will always remember his parents' tough times and will perhaps feel a little guilty that he is having such a rich, full life, while his parents who stinted themselves to give him a good start are still living modestly. Meanwhile, he will be indulging *his* children's whim as only a first generation native born *nouveau riche* can; to compensate for his material indulgences, about which he feels guilty, he will preach to his children a confused kind of liberation theology or even a mild Marxist credo. These acts can be marshalled as alibis; such a father can not easily endure—because he does not have the courage to acknowledge—the social, occupational, and financial apotheosis of his own family, without such spurious socio-political justification, while freely enjoying its fruits; it is a form of cowardice mouthing revolutionary egalitarianism to his children while consciously striving to belong to an elite and to consume conspicuously. Such a father will fail by having espoused false values, and he will be found out by his progeny. He lacks the courage not to feel guilty and to enjoy his just deserts and good luck. In the end, his cowardice may also unhinge his children's values—they may come to believe that good living at home is totally compatible with the practice of radical chic politics and socialist morality outside the home—hence, the student unrest at Nanterre, or the Strawberry Revolution at Columbia University in 1968. The parents' act of moral cowardice has misled their children who will spend a lifetime endeavouring to reconcile wealth privately enjoyed with wealth to be denied or talked about publicly. Schizophrenia has many parents.

This propensity of some parents to embrace wealth and simultaneously preach the merits of revolutionary egalitarianism to their children has many elements of moral and intellectual dishonesty. Instead of employing money sensibly, or enjoying their own family's march to riches, or admiring the financial advance of other people and still passing on an element of prudence about spending money wisely, they keep harping on about its evil nature. It is sobering to realize that all such chicanery about money in the family has its counterpart in politics. Such cowardice can turn rich men into radical socialists, and what is manifest in the political sphere also has its counterpart in the religious—but that comes later. A dedicated socialist, communist or fascist stance by the wealthy is a particularly unattractive form of moral cowardice—because it is often little else but a type of insurance cover for when the day of reckoning arrives ('come the revolution') signalling the demise of the wealthy. Many such examples abound in Europe. Some wealthy people are secret supporters of extreme-left doctrines, others have been know to offer money and safe houses to revolutionaries, and yet others play a crypto role in revolutionary activities. Such wealthy supporters of hard-left socialist parties—or indeed hard-right fascist parties—are all the greater cowards, the greater the secret of their involvement. A little reflection on the history of revolutions and the fate of many of their initiators, financiers and supporters should give the misguided rich even less reason to believe in their assumed immunity from persecution. From the French Revolution to the October Revolution, cautionary tales are legion about the fatuousness of adopting a false credo from cowardice.

The variety of social cowardice in families is considerable, especially when focused on money. As indicated, a well-heeled, first-generation immigrant might be sufficiently cowardly to feel the need for absolution, for a guilt-laden explanation to his children about his bourgeois life-style. But, then, there is the other extreme of similar cowardly conduct when the family clings to an aura of wealth which it once possessed, or pretended to possess, but no longer has. A familiar example is the burden of private schooling on fixed-income families, particularly in inflationary times, when they are no longer capable to afford school fees without self-impoverishment. The act of removing their children from private schools and transferring them into state-aided schools, however, cannot be an easy step because it will appear as a social defeat, not to mention their awareness of the likelihood of inferior teaching in the latter. But the social stigma of having to take a child out of a 'public school'—however minor—is an act so momentous that most families are too cowardly to countenance it—short of disaster—resulting in untold hardships on the family which of course are eventually visited on the child. Keeping up the façade of gentility, and simulating financial ease is almost as strong in some families as is the impulse to explain it away in others. Social guilt of either type, of not owning up to realities, will drive families to invent alibis for committing acts of cowardice which will prove to be damaging.

b. In marriage

Much emphasis nowadays is put on the prevalence of the nuclear family and on occupational, social and geographical mobility as major causes for the break-up of marriages and the undesirable consequences for the participants, their respective families and dependents. Another school of thought would contend that many marriage breakdowns are caused by the expanding lifespan of men and women and the increasingly long time they now have to spend together. Two hundred years ago, the average life-span was probably half what it is today. Ten to fifteen years' marriage was probably the norm in the sixteenth century; today half a century of married bliss is not uncommon. Alas, few couples and families are facing up to the extended lifespan they can now enjoy, and to their changed and improved material circumstances: few analyse the manifold impact of these circumstances on their own marriage and give proper care and attention to these changes. The result is a growing divorce rate and, the higher the living standards, the higher that rate. But there are other, equally significant, reasons for the rise in divorces and some of these may found be in the new financial equality of women with men. The moral cowardice lies in not attributing the financial calculus as a significant cause in the growing divorce rate; the reality is that when women can and do earn as much and more than men, they tend to behave as men—i.e. with independence, which can be a plausible reason for incompatibility. Many such women—not all, of course—tend to assume an increasingly authoritarian stance, coupled with an increasing sense of their self-importance to the world, including to their husbands. This is neither a good thing nor a bad thing, it is simply a fact. The cowardly stance is to attribute reasons for estrangement to other, more 'socially acceptable' reasons. It is more acceptable for a woman to suggest a trendy or a convential cause for a break-up—anything from her husband's male menopause to the typist turning his head. Or, where the man has been deserted, this may be attributed to the wifes' love of money, vaulting social ambition, financial independence turning her head, or just to her adulterous disposition. But the real reason, for men and women, might have been the desire for new challenges or a different life, translated into reality with—or without—another partner. A man's cowardice is well illuminated by overlooking his own obvious inadequacies as a husband, companion, lover, or breadwinner, and excusing his own frailties which led to a break-up by referring to his wife's social ambitions, or lack of intellectual progression; there are a host of personal reasons which can be dregged up and forged into excuses.

Cowardice can affect the life of families for generations; nor is cowardice in such circumstances clearly apparent; it is often disguised under the banner of honour, or mistaken honour. What is one to think of the, allegedly allegoric, fate of a Central European nobleman who, having gambled and lost his mansion and his riches, chose to pick only a single rose from his garden and walked off unconcerned with a smile when the winner offered him the opportunity of taking any object he desired as a memento! In this context, it is the simulated death-wish that is cowardly. When the son of a well-to-do family incurs a gambling debt—another example of the same theme—and the father or the mother pays up to save his son's honour, mistakenly construed as the honour of the family, a cowardly act is committed on two accounts: first, the son escapes deserved punishment—no social odium will stick to him for non-payment of debt, and the wrath of the family is of little account to the son as the kind of indulgent parents who pay up are of a mould likely to offer quick forgiveness; and, second, by paying the son's debt the parents may have disinherited other members of the family by short-changing them. This type of cowardice by the family which elects to pay, is compounded by the child who runs up gambling debts time and time again. In a celebrated family situation, the son, a hardened gambler, stopped gambling at once after the suicide of the father who was no longer able to pay his son's debts. To boot, the gambling son is also a coward—he stops playing after the death of his paymaster, his father, since henceforth he is responsible for his own debts!

The conduct of 'princes' concerns everyone; that is why their overt acts of cowardice in family matters are such durable fare for public consumption. Refusal to marry a commoner may be construed as loyalty to the family, but such filial pieties can also be seen in a different light. Using the family as a shield implies either that the love relationship was not of sufficient strength to endure the fixative of marriage or that personal cowardice, not wanting to face the resulting withdrawal of privilege or loss of status, was the more powerful influence. However, while such many-faceted decisions are personal matters in the families of princes, they are also of public concern. No special value judgement is relevant here on account of the exposed position of the participants—only a suggestion that cowardice can play a major, but certainly not the only, part in delicate family decisions.

c. In education

Cowardice in tyros is a common quality, starting with the first shattering experience at social integration outside the family—the first day at school. The cowardice of pupils arising from this overture to school life will quickly abate, so much is vouchsafed; but, equally, other forms of cowardice will probably take their place during scholastic life. Teachers, while spending some of their time allaying the fears of the taught, themselves are assailed by cowardice when, for instance, failing to resist attempts at indiscipline in class and to censure and punish offensive conduct. Teacher cowardice is clearly manifest when not standing up to pupils, to their parents, or even to the school managers, or local authorities, thereby failing to support the school's or their own ideas or beliefs, known to be generally to the advantage of the pupils. Equally, certain kinds of teacher cowardice may at times be wise; a good example is when an individual teacher, unsupported by his colleagues, refuses to assail his local education authority or the ministry which 'deals' in education; such confrontations with powerful institutions are better carried out by the teachers collectively or the teachers' representative associations.

In secondary schools, the teacher-parent relationship is important in this context. The most common forms of cowardice at this level of relationship are two. First, when the parent attacks the teacher for subjecting the child to discipline. Whether by words or action, the teacher has disciplined the child who wishes to protect himself from further punishment—an intentional and rational form of cowardice—by telling his parents about it; in effect the child is asking for protection because he is afraid. The child's cowardice can, in turn, be aided or discouraged by his parents. The second type of cowardice arises from the first; it is indulged in by the parent who is not supporting the teacher's justified stand—i.e. by repudiating the virtuous values the teacher wishes to inculcate in the pupil. The cowardice of the parent is manifest in preventing to enforce the discipline of the school which endeavours to shape the pupil into a diligent student and good citizen; such a stance reflects the ignorance of parents who fail to understand that certain values imparted to their child but unfamiliar to them may be good values—even if they differ from their own mores. The greater the insecurity of parents about their own values, the stronger their stand about them and the more strenuous their resistance to new ideas. This form of emotional cowardice, i.e. rejection, will tend to grow with the exposure to a longer educational process in a greater number of children—particularly when teaching working-class children other than working-class values.

A teacher's declared objective is to care for his pupils. But such care should not be excessive or (translated) 'disabling'; that is, instead of assisting a person's ability to learn, to grow and to better face the world, it could become counter-productive. Care for students must not be equated with overdue compassion for their wayward conduct or overlooking indifferent educational performance. A misguided attempt to be soft on examinations because some may excel and others fail—pursued in the cause of a righteous notion of equality where everyone is as good as everyone else—must result in a reduction in educational standards; the eventual effect on pupils is undermining their own goals and fulfilment, and on the community an enforced backwardness in the name of phoney equality. Such notions of unthinking egalitarianism must prove anti-social in the end. As the human desire for improvement is one of the few in-built cherished atavisms, the refusal to test such attempts at betterment—i.e. learning or greater competence—are an act of teacher cowardice. Such teacher cowardice may rebound on pupils in later life because the teacher has failed to test their educational competence and cultural heritage—both transmitted at school. There is also a plausible interpretation of such cowardice to the effect that a 'levelling down' teacher, refusing to mark papers or judge performance is a sign of the teacher's own political alignment, cherishing anti-competitiveness—having its roots in lack of courage or even competence. Let it not be forgotten that excessive and perhaps mistaken egalitarianism is tantamount to a form of self-protectionism. If performance standards for pupils are abolished, teachers' own performance cannot easily be judged by the knowledge and competence imparted to their pupils in the absence of examination; thus, refusal to be tested where this is necessary is a form of cowardice—whatever received wisdoms of permissiveness may be advanced as plausible reasons.

The commonest form of pupil cowardice may be found at the start and at the finish of the educational process; the first is at the outset of a pupil's career, when the child does not want to leave home and parents and attend school, but as already examined this reluctance is quickly overcome. The second is at the end of the educational process, when the student has been through school and university but this time, clinging to the same syndrome in a reverse fashion—he is irrationally afraid of leaving the safe scholastic embrace. When such cowardice is crystallized, the 'eternal student' is born. This genre of cowardice has been masked for some time by the growing wealth of industrial countries and their ability to provide enlarged (further) educational opportunities for an almost indefinite time and inexhaustible volume. The postponement of adult responsibilities can be achieved by more adult education —by remaining a student. The eternal student syndrome luxuriates at university level, and the name of the often unnecessary scholastic game is working for a 'post-graduate degree', or constant attendance at workshops, seminars and lectures. Much of this participation is passive, hence its yield is derisory; such further education is being used simply as a sequence of rearguard actions, a process to delay leaving the academic womb. This is a form of cowardice in which it is relatively easy to indulge without detection, since it is not easily identifiable. Would it be over-harsh to suggest that 'eternal students' are more likely to be found among devotees of the liberal arts than among science students?

The characteristic rightly ascribed to some eternal students is their desire to escape from the hurly-burly of real life. An educated parent is likely to be sceptical of an over-long incubation period of his child at a university—and will encourage an early start in business or profession. A largely uneducated, but successful self-made businessman as a parent is not quite in a position to judge the worthwhileness of yet another academic gong for his intellectually oriented offspring. On the contrary, being an unreserved admirer of education on account of his lack of it, he may well think another degree is not only a necessity, but a positive achievement, a social embellishment no less. Happy the eternal student who can boast of under-matriculated parents! Both the eternal student and his parents will have plausible alibis for continuing this educational carousel!

Now, about the content of education which, in a roundabout way, is also a victim of cowardice. A remarkable feature of secondary and higher education in Britain has been the reluctance of the teaching profession, compounded by educational administrators, from educating students in an elementary understanding of business and the use and abuse of money. An interesting study awaits to be written on why the dispensers of culture and education eschew to teach students at school about industry and commerce when most of their pupils will earn their living by beavering away in some kind of business for thirty years and more. Such a situation has not come about by accident; it is the result of muddled and prejudiced thinking about the vital role of Britain's industrial culture—still largely ignored, but perhaps less than before, in today's socio-occupational climate. However, let us not pillory the teachers alone for their oft out-dated but I believe slowly eroding prejudices about business, commerce and money. If modern schoolmen still hold the view that any fool can get into business because business is easy, then the business community shoulders considerable responsibility for insufficiently voicing their grievances about the skills needed for business but not taught in schools. There is a large element of cowardice in half-hearted fighting for recognition of needs—and then complaining about not receiving them. Are we back to the businessman's inferiority feelings about complaining to the educational gurus?

d. In working

Gainful employment offers its share of moral and psychological cowardice, and these are grouped around the concept of job responsibility and accountability—about being held responsible for the consequences and quality of one's work. The most direct judgement about success or failure in a job is usually found in trade and industry. The reason for this is simple: judgement is not made on the basis of some abstract values but on the easily measurable basis of money. If a business is profitable and progressive it is successful, and is there for all to see; if a business stands still and loses money, everybody can see that it is unsuccessful, even if only temporarily. To start a new business, to run a successful business or to rescue a business from the slaughter-house of liquidators calls for courage; it is a test of the qualities of a manager. The cowardice in an individual's job selection may lie in endeavouring to avoid responsibility for making or losing money, by pursuing work where accountability is not required or cannot be clearly delineated. The coward's fear of failure is greater than his avarice for money to crown his success. There are, of course, a range of occupations where achievements other than earning money visibly register performance—and by which the incumbent is judged—and these are occupations as demanding as money-making in business. Those with cowardly dispositions will also avoid such non-business occupations. The distinction, therefore, must be drawn between competitive and non-competitive occupations. An individual's disposition towards courage or cowardice will determine his choice.

There is no stigma attached to preferring occupations where the competitive element is minimal or virtually absent. This implies employment away from commercial or industrial activities—though there are competitive touchstones in every occupation. In non-business occupations, competition takes different forms—usually only remotely concerned with earning money for the organization, i.e. the employer. Good performance through extra effort is rewarded differently from the way a business would compensate such effort. It must not, therefore, come as a surprise that there are highly competitive, even entrepreneurial, civil servants and combative university teachers in the same way as, unsurprisingly, there are non-competitive industrial managers and unaggressive managing directors of companies.

This analysis about employment selection need not be pressed further, except to say that conventional social mores still linger, decreeing that non-business, non-money-making occupations rank higher in the established order of values—snob values at that. Such conspicuous irrelevances can, however, injure the industrial culture. Such vestigial 'social compulsives' may have made it desirable for many to settle for a non-competitive but lower paid, relatively secure job, as against adventure in a better paid but not so secure job. It takes a brave man to buck a comfortable status quo in job selection. Dynamic occupations are still often considered an insufficient incentive to be exchanged for a comfortable occupation. This is the only sensible explanation for the declared or undeclared cowardice of so many educated and talented men—one can not of course generalize—who have given a career in business a wide berth.

The successful businessman's residual memories of his socio-occupational position—at the outset—could offer hostages to cowardice in the course of his later business career. The entrepreneur's potential cowardice, especially before he has finally made good, is reflected in the social and educational: an appropriate example is when such a self-made man confronts a first division civil servant, an articulate politician, a glib financial journalist or a curator of an important art collection. The entrepreneur will not shun such confrontation but is timid in their presence because of his lack of formal education—or shall we call it cultural heritage?

e. In politics

Occupations offer ready-made opportunities for courage as well as cowardice—characteristics more easily observed than defined. In numerous pursuits, and education is one of them, neither courage nor cowardice shine through unequivocally, since education is a relatively private, largely unobserved activity where judgements about competence or incompetence will take time to discern.

Education is compartmentalized, confined to a limited number in a classroom or lecture room and in tutorials often on a one-to-one basis. The businessman and his conduct of business come into a clearer public focus—hence the way he performs can be judged relatively quickly. In one sphere, however, courage or cowardice is immediately apparent—in politics; because in politics there is a considerable element of 'showbiz', its participants are constantly on parade. Moreover, because those involved in politics sometimes hold and certainly often express their views forcefully, politicians' value judgements, comments and conduct are constantly under the microscope. Moreover, individuals and institutions all have an interest in politics, hence the constant monitoring of and judgement on politicians' performances—how far they compromise or stand fast on their beliefs and allegiances.

The error must not be made in thinking that political cowardice is the sole province of politicians; it is also indulged in by those choosing politicians or their programmes—namely the electorate, or power groups representing (alas often misrepresenting) selected members of the electorate. An interesting up-to-date form of political cowardice is being played out both in the Conservative and Labour Parties. Mrs Thatcher, the Conservative prime minister dedicated to extirpating inflation has had to administer heavy doses of deflation during her first two administrations, with resultant disagreeable economic consequences. Mrs Thatcher is a politician of principle, an accolade she must receive irrespective of political allegiances, and is more or less determinedly clinging to the deflationary measures she and her colleagues introduced, believing, sincerely, these will eventually bring Britain back to prosperity. The electorate decided thrice to choose Mrs Thatcher's, fully documented, electoral manifesto as a recipe for recovery, after three languishing decades during which many disastrous political and economic choices have been made, resulting in a maladjusted and 'overheated' Britain, visibly undermined. Where political cowardice could manifest is not in Mrs Thatcher sticking to her policies, but in the reasons offered by the strident voices opposing her measures inside and outside her Cabinet. Many of those visibly nervous and audibly vocal about Mrs Thatcher's economic policies are, one assumes, motivated by honest sentiment; some may have ulterior motives; some do not understand the changes required in approach to solve old problems; attitudes such as these have major implications for political honesty. What are the primary duties of politicians—party loyalty or national interest? When does opportunism become cowardice?

To suggest that politicians are sensitive to public clamour is an understatement; they have an in-built Geiger counter, particularly at a time when the changes affecting the people of Britain and their governments have been profound, disturbing to many and painful to some. This stigma applies to both parties. Politicians are usually aware of the country's needs in terms of realities; but they are also motivated by another, personal reality, the need to improve their (re-)election chances. It is necessary to underline the propensity for and the speed of politicians in power in shifting gears; and their subsequent manoeuvres to change policy opportunistically may be described as political cowardice—or is it wisdom? It could well be that what, at the time, is pilloried as political cowardice will in the end be seen or resolved as a political triumph—simply by virtue of the fact that the re-election of the party has been successful and this in itself vindicates its policy. However, the successful outcome of any political *volte-face* does not necessarily diminish a deliberate act of political cowardice, which originally fuelled the change. Thus, sometimes, a shift to caution can be described as cowardly, as it gives the impression of wishing to prepare for the next election by jettisoning some aspects of policy judged unpopular, though believed to be imperative for improving the state of the nation.

When contrasting Mrs Thatcher's single-mindness about her political programme—even if it seems to have been compromised here and there—with that of Sir Harold Wilson, the prevalence of political cowardice becomes even more startling. Sir Harold Wilson's policies consisted of trying to accommodate well-nigh everybody's views and wishes within the Labour Party—the 'broad church' alibi to ensure unity however fragile; lack of courage to resist and to grapple with the oft recurring British disease called fragmentation—in business as in politics—has led within a very short time to the electoral defeat and subsequently to the virtual disintegration of the Labour Party. Those on the inside track of Labour politics during Sir Harold's and his successor, Mr Callaghan's premierships will label such actions as the pursuit of compromise policies to keep the Labour Party intact; appeasement

1970s style? All such endeavours failed in the end because the political menu was clearly not acceptable to the electorate. Neither Labour prime ministers insisted on presenting a Labour party shorn of its taboos; it needed three defeats in a row to rejuvenate Labour thinking. The political cowardice of a later leader, Mr Michael Foot, was of a lesser order because he was not judged as much of a politician—though Labour unity came under even greater strain during his period in office which witnessed such a humiliating defeat at the polls. To those in the opposition parties always, and to those outside politics very often, a policy of continuing accommodation looks suspiciously like political cowardice. Sir Harold's apparent cowardice to resist bloodletting prevented the break-up of the Labour Party during his period of office: perhaps Mr Foot may lament that it would have been more prudent to face the music earlier as it must be sooner or later. Much depends on the context in which actions are judged—in politics rarely charitably.

Cowardice in a politician standing at the crossroads at mid-term, wondering what to do before elections, wondering how far he can go in promises and how far he can go back on them, is nothing new. Cowardice in an electorate is equally important, if less frequent, but one particularly glowing example was offered before the 1974 general election. The ministry of Mr Edward Heath is the case in point; the miners' recalcitrance led to the three-day week; resulting in an immense amount of inconvenience for industry and people—both in their role as workers and as private citizens—as well as in substantial economic damage to the nation. The strike and its consequences set public opinion firmly against the miners. Mr Heath, then prime minister, had a mandate to govern with a Commons majority of nineteen and over fifteen more months of parliamentary life; however, he chose to hold an early general election, putting forward the miners as the main issue—i.e. who governs Britain?—to have his mandate confirmed. Sir Harold Wilson observed at the time, with the understanding of a savant in such matters, that Mr Heath was 'running for cover' by calling for an election. While Mr Heath stood up to the miners for a time, in the end he exhibited political weakness by refusing to govern without the electorate reconfirming his resolve. In the event, Mr Heath lost the election—and for two equally important reasons: first, the length of time between the dispute and the polling date worked against him—which demonstrates how fickle is public reaction and how quickly people forget or want to forget; and, second, the cowardice of the electorate which would not snub the miners by re-electing Mr Heath at the possible cost of a general strike.—i.e. a little more inconvenience to themselves. The cowardice of the electorate is not in doubt; the question is, did they perceive a degree of insecurity and uncertainty in their Prime Minister at the time which aided and abetted their own cowardice?

Political cowardice is a many-headed hydra; acts played out in the open are public knowledge; but many are played out in private and do not surface or if they do, only after a time in the textbooks of historians or in critical biographies. Was it cowardice for that political entrepreneur *de luxe*, Joseph Chamberlain, not to have grasped the chance of leadership of the Conservative party when he had every opportunity to do so? The same may well be asked of Lord Butler, but here the historical perspective is still partly lacking. None the less it maybe uncharitable but true to assume that someone who practised Butlerism would find it uncomfortable to engage in the tough struggle for leadership. Certainly, Chamberlain could have competed with Balfour for the leadership but his social cowardice prevented him from joining the contest, as he feared a fight with his social superior. Yet, as a Conservative politician, he alone in the country at that time had a widely based popular appeal and considerable success in the ministries he held.

Would it be too far-fetched in any way to suggest that in the case of Joseph Chamberlain's cowardice, the sins of the father had been visited on the son? Neville Chamberlain must be judged as a political coward—he could not have been a political simpleton—in his dealings with Hitler; he did not wish to acknowledge the evil nature of the German leader because he did not want to see Britain dragged into another war. Hitler manufactured suitable alibis for Chamberlain to sustain his stance—mainly in the form of pieces of paper—to keep Britain neutral. For more up-to-date political cowardice the conduct of the Labour Party in the 1980s warrants mentioning. At a time when the dogma of socialism has been largely discredited in its original home in the USSR, as well as in China and largely in Eastern Europe, the Labour Party still adhered to its Clause IV—which desires bringing into national ownership the means of production, distribution and exchange. The cowardice stems from the Labour Party not repudiating this clause for fear of a tug-of-war with its left wingers—yet on sober reflection its leadership must realize that in an economically more liberal society this clause has lead and with other antiquated policies will lead to its demise at the polls.

Nor are the trade unions and many of their leaders exempt from cowardice; the cosy and comfortable stance taken by scores of trade unionists in positions of influence over matters demanding rethinking such as the rationale of unionism in a changed world is a tell-tale sign of psychological cowardice. A new look trade unionism, fit to contribute its share for national prosperity, can no longer tolerate myopic management; it must tackle the issues of the day affecting its members and their conditions of work and not fall back on mouthing rousing slogans.

In the same vein, decades of political timidity in the face of trade union militancy towards industry has enabled the unions to become for a time a significant extra-Parliamentary force. Ministers shied away from taking on the unions for the best part of four decades after the 1939-1945 war. While the trade unions have become an estate of the realm, this did not entitle them to strive for the establishment of a semi-socialist state—which in essence was their stance; a producers' economy taking little notice of the consumer. That's why strikes were settled invariably by the unions gaining the upper hand in negotiations. Politicians showed timidity, shall I say cowardice, in the face of union demands—especially the demands of the big powerful unions. This was graphically illustrated in the coal miners strike in 1974.

A more successful formula for trade-union togetherness has been the politicization of appropriate issues. This has been sparked off by a belief that any continuing material improvements for trade unionists must come from political activism; clearly, some leaders have realized that further financial improvements could only be secured by political action in the absence of any commercial rationale. Added to this is the radical-intellectual upbringing of many younger trade unionists who assume naturally a militant political posture. In the end, this development must lead a number of trade unions into an untenable position because it gives the impression that their leaders—less than their members?—are political partisans first and professional trade union leaders second.

Loyalty to one political party and latent, but constant, hostility to another is, perhaps, one of the more enduring conservative traits of the majority of the 'radical' British labour movement; here again one can observe an element of cowardice—this time by their monopolistic adherence to one school (Labour) of political thought only, instead of fishing around for more up to date political ideas (Liberal/SDP) equally perhaps benefiting their members and the nation. While the collective political loyalty of the trade union movement to one party has long been unquestioned, useful legislative changes affecting unions, and proposed by their favoured political party, have in the past been opposed by them. When it comes to defending the status quo, the archaic conservatism of the unions is to be admired.

Cowardice about openly declaring dissenting views is a retrograde feature of imposed togetherness; is it that trade-union tradition, harking back to an uncritical acceptance of working-class solidarity, makes willing cowards by a deliberate suspension of critical judgements? Does loyalty to a political creed, social class or trade union impose unyielding adherence? Perhaps this situation no longer obtains as the recent expulsion of the Electrical, Electronic, Telecommunication and Plumbing Union from the TUC has shown. Unremarkably, the alibi for the expulsion seems a little shaky.

Miscellaneous explorations

Cowardice in its diverse roles often affects our thinking, impedes our actions and reactions: we all indulge from time to time in its many forms, and often without realizing or indeed understanding it. There are good reasons for this. Some common forms of cowardice hardly deserve the adjective, because the term itself—deeply embedded, particularly in physical fear—has become pejorative, hence offensive. Our feelings about cowardice are atavistic. and their perpetuation offers another hostage to the durability of man's shibboleths.

A mild form of cowardice is commonly called 'white lies'. Uttering such minor untruths either gets one out of an embarrassing situation or, surprisingly, it may confer pleasure on its recipient. A good example of the latter would be the remark 'you are getting slimmer', when in fact the person has put on more weight since the last encounter. This is a form of practised social—note, not anti-social—cowardice to give pleasure, however unreal or ephemeral. This is a desirable type of cowardice insufficiently practised.

Growing older brings with it novel types of cowardice—the desire to cheat nature and to be brushed with immortality. A seasoned sportsman recovering from an illness is a good illustration. His new regimen is less drinking and little exercise; but after overcoming the initial shock and having largely readjusted to his previous life-style, he may start drinking again and increase his sporting activities. Such indulgence is an over-reaction, illustrated by over-performance, to the fear that he is no longer as good as he was before his illness. Cowardice born of temporary infirmity induces in him bravado to demonstrate excessive performance—mainly to himself—a form of auto-suggestion that he is perfectly healthy, unchanged in prowess. In a different but equally mild form, this variety of cowardice is rife among women who have once been very beautiful and knew it, and continue to dress in the fashions of the times when they were young, beautiful and successful. Hoping to hold on tight to the present by recycling a successful past in this way is also a mild, perhaps even attractive, form of cowardice—a desire not to recognize changes in circumstances; it is also a reasonably acceptable alibi. But this is a harmless form of cowardice which only deludes the self. This attitude may be epitomized in the 'I will not allow it to happen to me' syndrome. A sportsman's unreasonable bravado *vis-à-vis* his own health, or a woman's unrealistic reactions to the inevitable effects of age are indulgences of common forms of cowardice, without external social impact.

A much more important decision with external social impact, is a doctor's choice and judgement about saving life—or not saving it. The doctor's dilemma is unavoidable and this open knowledge about alternatives makes his position difficult, as he works under professional and public scrutiny. A recurring issue for a doctor, presenting itself in diverse forms is whether or not life should be preserved in *all* circumstances. The life of the person, his or her probable future as well as the happiness or unhappiness of the parents, relatives or partners are matters of real concern. Should the sick person develop into a total and expensive burden, can the family cope? Cowardice by the doctor in such an instance may allow the person to live—though it might or might not have been better otherwise. Civilized society cherishes all life and no one is allowed to extinguish someone else's. This is an advantage and a burden resulting from mankind's continuous civilizing process. It may well be a cowardly approach, but other solutions would be worse; or would they?

Cowardice plays an important role in the realm of ideas. Because ideas travel easily, often at speed and are difficult to stop except with better ideas, cowardice in coping with them is quickly detected. Authoritarian rule, as we have seen, insecure about critical world opinion, will ban the importation of the printed word, jam radio waves and assume a monopoly in the dissemination of news and thus endeavours to cut off the country as far as possible from 'undesirable' foreign influences. Left-wing and right-wing fascist countries give a good demonstration of this type of cowardice by denying freedom of information. The divine right of dictators to rule nowadays is far more sacred and more widely and firmly established than the divine right of kings and emperors ever was. Technology has been the springboard for the great leap forward in enhancing man's comforts and lifespan; but it has also made possible the more complete sealing off of communities from one another. However, despite the rapid development and wide application in the suppression of information, so extensively practised by many countries, durable success has not crowned their practitioners; the manipulators have not succeeded in shutting out outside ideas and cultural influences. Examples abound of how dictatorial countries of different colourings treat those holding dissenting political or social views from the official doctrine—i.e. those expressing alternative ideas. It will be sufficient to point out that gulags for dissidents are overt signs of ruling-class intellectual cowardice. These are unsubtle and obvious examples of repression born of cowardice based on fear.

However, there are other forms of cowardice, especially in the cultural sphere. In order to stem the intrusion of a dynamic culture into another, official barricades are easily erected, but prove difficult to man. This form of contemporary cultural cowardice has been manifest in many countries—particularly, in France and Russia, including the lands dominated by the latter. While there is nothing new in cultural xenophobia—an overt sign of a national inferiority complex—it is distressing that contemporary France should be one of its victims. But, then, even an ancient culture, such as the Chinese, vacillates between trying to halt the intrusion of the 'West' and trying to encourage it! The authorities have been trying to stop the southern Chinese from watching decadent television shows from Hong Kong. If cultural defence is to stem the ingress of another culture, it needs more than prohibitions—it needs workable alternatives.

The interesting feature of France's *nouvelle vague* cultural protectionism is that it is being assumed by a country that can boast of a long period of cultural hegemony not only during the *grand siècle*, but right up to the end of the First World War. Not only were French manners emulated throughout the civilized world—just as Spanish manners were dominant in Europe while the Habsburgs' star was in the ascendant—but French cultural dominance in the arts, cuisine, and literature enjoyed an influence straddling two centuries. At the Russian foreign ministry, until the Soviets rose to government in 1917, French was the spoken and written language. It was the diplomatic language throughout the nineteenth century, and an indispensable second language among the emancipated and better-off classes throughout Europe until relatively recently, when English replaced French as the leading language throughout the world. Two reasons account for this: first, the language of science and technology is English and, second, the economic and political dominance first of Britain and then of an English-speaking United States.

Having been cultural exporters, the French find it difficult to become cultural importers—and particularly when it affects their language. French cultural xenophobia about language has reached such proportions that the use of certain foreign words has been officially banned. These words and expressions are almost exclusively English, or better, American-English. When American-English words reach Calais, this imported language turns to Franglais; the French cannot resist it, it seems, incorporating the name of France even into the intruding language—or, better, the intruding culture. For the reality is that the language and the cultural values of the most dominant world power at a given time invariably gain wide currency. Dynamism in social and political spheres undoubtedly brings with it a dynamism in expression, in language. While scientific and technological vocabulary has been for a long time largely English, more recently, the language of sport, of management science, of business communication and even fashion too, has become American-English. From 'le weekend' to 'le blue-jeans' to 'le discounted cashflow', there seem to be scarcely any language substitutes which could be equally meaningful. It seems implausible that the verbal invasion of France by American-English will cease with a French-enforced language UDI. Where the French are fearful, of course, is not only because Anglo-American expressions are likely to be increasingly used in discourse and literature—in the spoken and written word—but being a cultivated nation, they realize that in the use of language, perhaps, a time fuse lies buried: for I believe that people acquire the characteristics of the language they speak—and on that assumption it is plain that the French are fearful of an Americanization of their culture. Ukases against its impact are a sign of cultural cowardice. The remedy lies in reinvigorating French cultural influence through achievement and not by unenforceable import controls.

While Franglais impacts on French culture, the Russians have until recently been fearful of artistic imports with an impact—they fear unfavourable—on their hothouse political culture. Communist Russia has not made too many notable cultural contributions to world heritage since its inception in 1917, largely I think because its development as the greatest destructive machine on earth has left too many of its people both drunk and hungry; it could be added that blind political authoritarianism has stultified domestic cultural progress. Art contains the seeds of progress and revolution just as much as literature (particularly, language in the novel) or new approaches to philosophical verities. Music has rarely been classed as truly revolutionary material alongside with inflammatory literature and untraditional art—except perhaps for jazz, and that is a bourgeois preoccupation one has been led to believe. Interestingly, it was the Russians who composed music considered revolutionary at the time—one has to think only of Stravinsky. Now, a few decades later, because of its anticipated political impact, imported pop music in Russia has occasionally run the gauntlet of official opposition. Popular rock groups have been attacked for spreading subversive ideas among Russian youth—and one such attack has been mounted from an unpredictable source, an official youth newspaper.

The communist authorities' attack on pop music in the USSR stems from their fear of a three-pronged effect, two induced by cultural cowardice and one by political cowardice. The first piece of cultural cowardice is the dislike by Soviet officialdom of the lyrics of popular rock groups; apparently, the lyrics 'contradict' official propoganda and thereby 'hinder the furtherance of communist ideas' among the young. One particular group has also been accused of 'sexual ambiguity'—how curious that despots are invariably among the greatest prudes—because, I suppose, these lyrics are not reminiscent of 'traditional bourgeois modesty' so closely embraced by the Soviet state. The lyrics express pessimism, another indictment of the group, because they use words 'I do not believe in promises, and I will not do so in the future'. Apparently, such a text is anti-state because the Soviet authorities want art to imitate not life but their policies and dispositions of the moment. The second cultural cowardice is an admission that pop is a dangerous import—being a Western bourgeois influence—and should be restrained as it encourages further deviation from recognized nostrums. Here again, an intrusion of a dynamic culture from outside is officially constricted, but even the Soviets realize that music recognizes no frontiers. It will be increasingly impossible to keep the lid on the USSR musical ghetto where even the sound of music, not to mention its text, has been subservient to political expediency. The third cowardice is political, because pop, rock, modernity of all sorts, fashionable clothing, and attractive accoutrements to clothing are all Western, mainly American, exports. Now the unforgiveable in the Soviet cultural vocabulary would be 'recognition' that the American or British way of life has anything attractive to offer—hence its contagion. The slightest admission of Anglo-Saxon cultural dominance, particularly on the uncommitted young, would be tantamount to heresy. Totalitarianism must govern all, or it governs nothing; by using force through the authority of the state to influence art it ensures its eventual cultural insignificance and demise. What durable art has the October Revolution produced, except the literature of protest?

Conclusion

Cowardice—just like heroism, bravery or courage—is a corollary of the human condition; carried beyond conventionally recognized tolerances, cowardice attracts penalties while courage earns praise. The allowable tolerances for cowardice vary from one culture, or even sub-culture to another. It would be divine providence if cowardice were always punished, and courage or bravery invariably rewarded. Certain actions, whose springs lie hidden or half-revealed, could be considered as cowardice but if such cowardice happens to be state policy, or committed by a majority, or too mild for serious reaction or reprimand, some or many will prefer not to consider such acts as cowardice. Perhaps, in the circumstances, it will be unsurprising that in the case of physical cowardice, in particular, safety valves are essential. Cowardice can imply actions or an absence of action; moral cowardice perhaps involves absence of action more than active participation.

Cowardice is a pejorative word, associated particularly in male minds with a weakling, timid, non-macho disposition, hence the repugnance, and hence its loaded semantic value. In considering cowardice in its broadest implications, two important characteristics should not be overlooked—though they often are. First, physical cowardice; because it is so obviously manifest, it is easily attributable, it is easy to judge, and those who like to sit in judgement on others find physical cowardice or even its shadow a ready-made vehicle for exercising censure. Punishment of physical cowardice is sometimes justified, sometimes not. Conventional wisdom about this vexed phenomenon should be influenced by human understanding which is possible even without reading much Freud and becomes easier through reading the novel, the literature of the imagination.

Second, moral cowardice; physical cowardice rarely impacts beyond the individual coward—it may affect as a secondary consequence his or her family but the stigma and the penalty are focused on the individual. Individual, moral cowardice, however, can influence the fate of millions; moreover, since moral cowardice can often be concealed under high-falutin' slogans, it frequently remains unnoticed and is sometimes applauded. Britain's last pre-1939 war government is a good example of all these delusive qualities. But, in any case, it is difficult to pinpoint moral cowardice—and for two good reasons; its perpetration is usually not apparent, in fact it is studied deliberate concealment, and, as a result, those at the receiving end may be unaware of it, unaware of other options or in some instances, unwilling to face alternatives. Moral cowardice can become a contagious vogue.

It may well be that cowardice is the mother of cruelty, certainly in the mind of the self-realized coward; and cowardice is usually humiliating to the self even if to no one else. This is why conquering cowardice is such a victory over the self. However, cowardice may also be a form of therapy, in liberating us with little effort from what we find unacceptable. So long as it affects the self alone, cowardice is a strictly limited experience, and not invariable anti-social; the danger lies in a form of cowardice, mostly moral, which contaminates. This is the species against which we must guard.